Advanced Civil Litigation (Professional Negligence) in Practice

Advanced Civil Litigation (Professional Negligence) in Practice

Inns of Court School of Law

Institute of Law, City University, London

OXFORD

UNIVERSITY PRESS

Great Clarendon Street, Oxford OX2 6DP

Oxford University Press is a department of the University of Oxford.
It furthers the University's objective of excellence in research, scholarship,
and education by publishing worldwide in

Oxford New York

Auckland Cape Town Dar es Salaam Hong Kong Karachi
Kuala Lumpur Madrid Melbourne Mexico City Nairobi
New Delhi Shanghai Taipei Toronto

With offices in

Argentina Austria Brazil Chile Czech Republic France Greece
Guatemala Hungary Italy Japan Poland Portugal Singapore
South Korea Switzerland Thailand Turkey Ukraine Vietnam

Oxford is a registered trade mark of Oxford University Press
in the UK and in certain other countries

Published in the United States
by Oxford University Press Inc., New York

British Library Cataloguing in Publication Data
Data available

Library of Congress Cataloging in Publication Data
Data available

Typeset by Newgen Imaging Systems (P) Ltd., Chennai, India
Printed in Great Britain
on acid-free paper by
Antony Rowe Ltd, Chippenham, Wiltshire

ISBN 0–19–928491–1   978–0–19–928491–7

1 3 5 7 9 10 8 6 4 2

FOREWORD

It is a privilege to write this Foreword, following the tradition set by my predecessor, the Hon. Mr Justice Elias.

The Bar Vocational Course (BVC) bridges the gap between completion of a university degree and the start of a professional working life, whether by way of pupillage preliminary to a career at the Bar, or otherwise. These Manuals are geared to the practical and professional approach that is central to the BVC. Updated and revised, the Manuals form an integral part of the student's vocational training; as such, they are an important ingredient in the constant drive to raise standards in the public interest.

The Manuals are written by staff at the Inns of Court School of Law (ICSL). The range and coverage of the Manuals have grown steadily. They are intended to provide a useful resource for all concerned in the training of legal skills, hopefully at whichever validated institution such training takes place.

Legal vocational training does not stand still; the ICSL and authors would welcome feedback from any source, which may assist to improve the Manuals in the future. Any such comments should be addressed to the BVC Course Director at the ICSL.

Finally a word of thanks is appropriate to the publishers for their enthusiasm and efficiency in arranging production and publication of the Manuals.

The Hon. Mr. Justice Gross
Chairman, Advisory Board of the Institute of Law
City University, London
October 2005

Dedicated to the memory of
David Bridgman

OUTLINE CONTENTS

DETAILED CONTENTS

TABLE OF CASES

TABLE OF STATUTES

TABLE OF SECONDARY LEGISLATION

Part I

Introduction and substantive law

Introduction

Almost all barristers at the independent Bar whose practice is not exclusively criminal are involved in a form of civil litigation. The rules governing the processes of civil litigation are considered in detail elsewhere on the course. The purpose of the Advanced Civil Litigation Option is to put the principles governing the civil justice system into an applied context. You will be introduced to the complex legal issues surrounding professional negligence and encouraged to apply those to different factual situations. You will be brought down to ground by a consideration of the available methods of funding such litigation. You will examine the impact of procedural and evidential rules on both the conduct and the outcome of cases. You will begin to develop a confidence to apply the rules tactically. The drafting skills which you have already learned will be built upon in the context of professional negligence claims, demonstrating how a statement of case can be a persuasive tool. Your ability to give accurate and clear advice to a client as to risk in any given context will be tested and improved. The Manual and the course together seek to give you an understanding of how a civil case can be most effectively prepared and presented within the context of both a clinical negligence dispute and a solicitors' negligence dispute.

This Manual concentrates upon those two areas of professional negligence. Clinical negligence raises matters pertinent to all personal injury litigation but also allows for an examination of law and evidence in a more complex area. It was an area singled out by Lord Woolf for special treatment in the radical review of the civil justice system in the late 1990s. Solicitors' negligence is a useful vehicle through which to consider many aspects of the professional's duty of care and the recoverable losses caused by its breach. Each area demands a different evidential approach.

Professional negligence and personal injury work is specialist work. It requires a high level of professional competence in the application of the substantive and constantly developing law of negligence, concurrent duties in contract, statutory duties, regulations and professional guidelines. It requires forensic abilities and experience in the analysis, consideration and testing of expert and other specific types of evidence. Specialist knowledge of separate court procedures, the rules and law of evidence and the customs of assessing quantum is required. Many professional negligence and personal injury cases are settled before trial. The barrister consequently needs very developed skills for pre-trial work: eliciting relevant evidence from professional clients and experts in conference, drafting Statements of Case, making interim applications, drafting written questions to experts, assessing risk, advising as to risk, advising as to payments into court and offers to settle, and in negotiation.

Many of the skills developed in a professional negligence context are transferable to other aspects of civil litigation, particularly those involving negligence and breach of contract. The Manual is therefore aimed at students who intend to practise in civil common law chambers, particularly in the areas of personal injury and professional negligence.

2

Clinical negligence

2.1 Introduction

The purpose of this chapter is to provide you with an overview of the principles and authorities which govern clinical negligence actions. It is intended to be a starting point only and you will need to refer to practitioner texts such as Jackson & Powell, *Professional Negligence* (5th edn, Sweet & Maxwell) and Powers & Harris, *Clinical Negligence* (3rd edn, Butterworths).

2.2 Duty of care to patients

A claimant who wishes to pursue a claim for damages arising out of injuries sustained during the course of medical treatment has two potential causes of action: breach of contract and negligence.

2.2.1 Contractual duties

Where the treatment has been provided by the National Health Service, there is no contract between the doctor and the patient. Accordingly, it will only be possible to base a clinical negligence action on breach of contract if the treatment complained of has been provided on a private, fee-paying basis. In such cases, the starting point is to consider the nature and scope of the medical practitioner's contractual duties which will be defined by both express and implied terms.

The express terms will vary from case to case. They can be both written and oral and, in order to ascertain what they are, you will need to refer to the retainer.

In an action for clinical negligence, the most significant term implied by law is that the medical practitioner will carry out the examination, diagnosis and treatment of the patient with reasonable care and skill (Supply of Goods and Services Act 1982, s 13). It is important to appreciate that this duty is entirely different from an obligation to guarantee that the treatment will be successful. No such term will be implied into a contract between a doctor and his patient. Indeed, a doctor will only be regarded as having guaranteed the success of the treatment if he did so in express and unequivocal terms (*Eyre v Masday* [1986] 1 All ER 488; *Worcester v City and Hackney Health Authority* The Times, 22 June 1987).

2.2.2   Tortious duties

Whether or not a contractual relationship exists, a claim for damages for breach of duty lies in the tort of negligence. In order to succeed a claimant will need to establish that there was a duty of care owed, that it was breached and that damage was suffered as a result:

(a) Duty of care: Immediately a medical practitioner accepts a patient for treatment a doctor/patient relationship arises and the practitioner owes the patient a duty to exercise reasonable care and skill in examining, diagnosing and treating him (*Sidaway v Bethlem Royal Hospital Governors* [1985] 1 All ER 643). This duty arises in all cases where a practitioner assumes responsibility for the treatment and care of a patient, irrespective of whether there is a contract between them.

(b) Breach: A negligent error in carrying out treatment or a negligent omission to provide adequate treatment will amount to a breach of this duty.

(c) Damage: The claimant must show that the breach resulted in damage. Generally speaking, where the alleged damage is either a physical or a psychological injury the patient will almost certainly have a case. The position is less clear where the only damage suffered is pure economic loss. Whether a doctor owes a duty of care in respect of such loss will depend on the particular circumstances of the case. For example, under the principles of *Hedley Byrne & Co Ltd v Heller & Partners Ltd* [1964] AC 465, HL, where a doctor advised a patient and he knew or ought to have known that the patient would rely on his advice, and the patient thereby suffered economic loss, then, assuming of course that the advice was negligent, the doctor will be held liable. Conversely, if a doctor is unaware that a patient intended to rely on his advice or the patient relied on it for an unintended or unexpected purpose then it is unlikely that liability will attach.

2.2.3   Concurrent duties in contract and tort

You will have noted that the duty owed in tort is indistinguishable from that which is implied into a contract between a doctor and his patient by virtue of the Supply of Goods and Services Act 1982, s 13. The practical effect of this is that in cases involving private medicine, the contractual and the tortious duty will be concurrent and the claim should be pleaded in both contract and tort.

2.3   Duties to third parties

A medical practitioner may also owe a duty of care to someone who is not his patient. The circumstances in which such a duty is most likely to arise can be categorised as follows: donor cases, psychiatric injury (nervous shock), injury through contact with a patient, unborn children and economic loss.

2.3.1   Donor cases

In the Canadian case of *Urbanski v Patel* (1978) 84 DLR (3d) 650 the defendant practitioner removed the patient's only kidney, believing it to be a cyst. The patient's father donated one of his kidneys in a vain attempt to save her life. He then successfully sued the doctor for the injury he had suffered as a result of donating the organ.

The English courts have not yet had to consider the point. However, it is submitted that they are likely to adopt the same approach.

2.3.2 Nervous shock

Before embarking on a case which includes a claim for nervous shock, you will need to have a solid understanding of the principles governing liability for negligently caused psychiatric injury.

A detailed analysis of these principles is beyond the scope of this chapter. What appears below is a summary of the fundamental rules and how they are applied in clinical negligence actions.

In all cases where damages are sought for nervous shock, the starting point is to consider whether the claimant is a primary or a secondary victim of the alleged negligence.

Put simply, the claimant will be a primary victim if it was reasonably foreseeable that the defendant's conduct would cause him physical injury. Conversely, the claimant will be a secondary victim if he himself was not physically endangered but he witnessed a shocking event that physically endangered others. The importance of this distinction is set out below.

In order to recover damages for nervous shock a primary victim only has to establish that he was in the range of foreseeable physical or psychiatric injury (*Page v Smith* [1996] AC 155 (HL)).

The test applied to secondary victims is more specific. They have to show that it was reasonably foreseeable that they would suffer psychiatric injury. In order to succeed in this, a number of conditions must be satisfied. These were laid down by the House of Lords in *McLoughlin v O'Brien* [1983] AC 410 and *Alcock v Chief Constable of South Yorkshire* [1992] 1 AC 310 (HL) and can be summarised as follows:

- There must have been a close relationship between the victim and the claimant such that psychiatric injury was foreseeable to the claimant.

- There must have been proximity in time and space between the accident or its immediate aftermath and the claimant's discovery of the victim's injuries.

- The claimant must have discovered the injury directly by sight and sound.

- The discovery of the injury by sight and sound must shock the claimant so as to cause him psychiatric damage.

Third parties are, by definition, secondary victims. In clinical negligence actions, the most difficult obstacle to success for claimants within this class is establishing that the injury was caused by the shock of the sudden appreciation by sight and sound of a horrifying event. Often there is a very fine line between those who satisfy this test and those who do not and much will turn on the facts of the particular case. This point is demonstrated by the different outcomes in *Sion v Hampstead Health Authority* (1994) 5 Med LR 170 and *Tredget v Bexley Health Authority* (1994) 5 Med LR 178.

In *Sion*, the claimant was a father whose adult son was injured in a road traffic accident. He sat at his son's hospital bedside for 14 days and witnessed his decline and death. The claimant alleged that the hospital had been negligent in failing to diagnose the internal bleeding which caused his son to fall into a coma. He sought damages for psychiatric illness which he alleged he had suffered as a result of what he had seen at the hospital. His action was struck out by the Court of Appeal on the basis that his illness had been caused by a combination of grief and the gradual realisation of the seriousness of his son's condition, rather than by a sudden and violent apprehension of events.

In *Tredget*, the claimants were a married couple who suffered psychiatric injury as a result of the defendant's negligence during the birth of their child. Mr Tredget was present throughout the birth and witnessed everything that took place. He saw the chaos in the delivery room and was even requested to actively participate in the efforts to deliver the child by encouraging his wife. Both parents saw their child in intensive care before the life support machine was switched off. They sued the defendants for damages for psychiatric injury. White J found for the claimants on the basis that their injuries had been caused by a sudden and direct appreciation of a horrifying event (p 183):

The actual birth with its 'chaos' and 'pandemonium', the difficulties that the mother had of delivery, the sense in the room that something was wrong and the arrival of the child in a distressed condition requiring immediate resuscitation was, for those immediately and directly involved as each of the parents was, frightening and horrifying.

Tredget can be distinguished from *Sion* on the grounds that in *Tredget* there was a greater degree of involvement in and immediacy to the medical treatment and the negligence complained of. See also the more recent case of *North Glamorgan NHS Trust v Walters* [2003] Lloyd's Rep Med 49 where a mother who suffered psychiatric injury caused by the shock of witnessing the last distressing 36 hours of her baby son's life successfully recovered damages for nervous shock from the hospital authority that negligently misdiagnosed and treated his condition.

You will remember that the *McLoughlin/Alcock* test permits secondary victims to recover for injuries resulting from the shock caused by witnessing the immediate aftermath of the horrifying event. In the context of a clinical negligence claim, however, it is extremely unlikely that a third party will succeed in recovering damages for an injury which has been caused in this way. Again, this is because the necessary element of shock is usually absent. For instance, in *Taylor v Somerset Health Authority* (1993) 4 Med LR 34, the defendant failed to diagnose the claimant's husband's heart condition. He suffered a heart attack at work and died shortly thereafter in hospital. Approximately half an hour later the claimant was informed of his death. She asked to see his body and was permitted to do so. Her claim for damages for psychiatric injury was rejected. It was held that there had not been a traumatic event or sudden event caused by the defendant's negligence. The heart attack was the final result of gradual deterioration which the defendant had failed to stop. Furthermore, even if the heart attack was a qualifying event, the claimant's subsequent visit to the mortuary did not fall within the immediate aftermath requirement. It was not soon enough after the event and the claimant's husband's body did not bear any marks which would have conveyed to her the circumstances of the attack.

There is one final point on third parties and nervous shock in clinical negligence cases: the negligent act/omission itself does not have to be sudden or violent. Rather, it is the impact of the event on the claimant's mind which is relevant.

2.3.3 Injury through contact with patients

A medical practitioner who knows or ought to know that his patient presents a danger to other people may owe a duty of care to those people. The situations which are most likely to give rise to such a duty of care are where the patient is either:

- suffering from an infectious disease which he may pass onto others through sexual contact or otherwise; or
- dangerous by reason of psychiatric illness.

In any event, whatever the particular circumstances of the case might be, recent authorities suggest that a third party will only succeed against the doctor if he can satisfy the three requirements laid down in *Caparo Industries plc v Dickman* [1990] 2 AC 605, namely, foreseeability, proximity of relationship and that the imposition of a duty would be fair, just and reasonable.

For instance, in *Goodwill v Pregnancy Advisory Service* [1996] 2 All ER 161, M underwent a vasectomy operation. The defendants advised him that the operation had been successful and that he would not need to use contraception in the future. Some years later M began an intimate relationship with the claimant. No contraception was used and she became pregnant. She sued the defendants. The Court of Appeal held that the defendants did not owe a duty of care to the claimant in advising M. At the time the advice was given she was one of an indeterminately large class of women who might be a future sexual partner of M. In these circumstances, there was an insufficient proximity of relationship between the parties to justify the imposition of a duty.

In *Palmer v Tees Health Authority* [1999] Lloyd's Rep Med 351, A abducted, sexually assaulted and murdered R, a four-year-old girl. At the time of this incident, A was under the care of the defendants as a psychiatric patient. R's mother brought an action in negligence against the defendants on her own behalf and also on behalf of R's estate. She alleged that the defendants failed to diagnose that there was a real risk of A committing any sexual offences against children and of causing serious bodily injury to any child victims. She also alleged that the defendants failed to provide any adequate treatment for A to reduce the risk of him committing such offences. Dismissing the claimant's claim, the Court of Appeal held that in order to establish proximity, it was a minimum requirement that the victim be identifiable. Here the identity of the victim was unknown so that the defendants were unable to issue any warning. Accordingly, there was no proximity between the parties.

2.3.4 Unborn children

Where a medical practitioner is treating a patient who he knows, or ought to know, is pregnant he owes a duty of care to the unborn child, *Burton v Islington Health Authority & De Martell v Merton & Sutton Health Authority* [1993] QB 204, CA. A claim can be brought for injuries sustained prior to birth which cause disabilities under the Congenital Disabilities (Civil Liability) Act 1976. The Human Fertilisation and Embryology Act 1990 s 44 extends the effect of the Congenital Disabilities Act to provide a cause of action to those disabled as a result of the damage to the egg, sperm or embryo during the course of infertility treatment.

2.3.5 Economic loss

A doctor who is requested by his patient to provide a medical report to a third party may owe a duty of care to the third party to prepare the report carefully so that the third party does not suffer financial loss as a result of it. For example, if the doctor knows who the recipient of the report will be, the purpose for which it will be used and that the third party intends to rely on it, he will be deemed to have undertaken a responsibility to the third party such that he owes it a duty to exercise reasonable skill and care when preparing the report (*Hedley Byrne and Co Ltd v Heller and Partners Ltd* [1964] AC 465).

The recoverability of damages for pure economic (ie, not consequent on personal injury) is yet to be decided. It would of course depend on the facts of the claim, and an application of the principles of (in particular) *Caparo Industries plc v Dickman* [1990] 2 AC 605 and *South Australia Asset Management Corp v York Montague Ltd* [1997] AC 191.

2.4   Standard of care

It has already been said that the medical practitioner is not obliged to achieve success. Rather, his duty is to exercise reasonable care and skill. This begs the question: What is the standard of care that is required before a doctor will be found to have discharged his duty?

2.4.1   The *Bolam* test

The two leading authorities on the standard of care required of a doctor are *Bolam v Friern Hospital Management Committee* [1957] 1 WLR 582 and *Sidaway v Governors of the Bethlem Royal Hospital* [1985] AC 871.

In *Bolam*, the claimant was a voluntary patient being treated for depression in the defendant's hospital. He was given electro-convulsive therapy (ECT) which was known to cause violent compulsive movements. These could be almost completely eliminated by the use of a relaxant drug. The treating doctor did not administer the drug or apply any manual restraints. Neither did he warn the claimant about the risks involved in the procedure. During the ECT the claimant sustained fractures to his pelvis. He brought an action in negligence for the doctor's failure to administer the drug, to apply restraints and to warn him about the risks. It was common ground that there was a firm body of medical opinion opposed to the use of the drug because of the risks associated with it. It was also common ground that there were a number of competent and respected practitioners who considered that the less manual restraint there was, the less was the risk of injury to the patient. McNair J gave the following direction to the jury which subsequently found for the defendant:

The test is the standard of the ordinary skilled man exercising and professing to have that special skill. A man need not possess the highest expert skill; it is well established law that it is sufficient if he exercises the ordinary skill of an ordinary competent man exercising that particular art.

This test is most commonly known as '*Bolam* test'. It was reformulated by Lord Scarman in his judgment in *Sidaway:*

A doctor is not negligent if he acts in accordance with a practice accepted as proper by a responsible body of medical opinion even though other doctors adopt a different practice.

Also in *Sidaway*, the House of Lords held that the *Bolam* test applies to all aspects of a medical practitioner's work. Lord Diplock stated at p 893H–894A:

My Lords no convincing reason has in my view been advanced before your Lordships that would justify treating the Bolam test as doing anything less than laying down a principle of English law that is comprehensive as applicable to every aspect of the duty of care owed by a doctor to his patient in the exercise of his healing functions in respect of that patient.

In any given case, when considering whether or not the medical practitioner has satisfied the *Bolam* test, you will need to have reference to the following factors: the current state of medical knowledge, the specialisation of the practitioner and the status of the practitioner.

2.4.2   Current state of knowledge

The relevant state of knowledge is the knowledge of the profession at the time of the act or omission complained of. Accordingly, you must ignore any medical advances made between the date of the alleged negligence and the trial of the action (*Roe v Minister of Health* [1954] 2 QB 66).

Perhaps not surprisingly, it is frequently the case that the main issue at a clinical negli-gence trial is what the state of knowledge was at the relevant time. In order to resolve this issue, the court will need to rely on both the expert evidence and on the literature which was available at the date in question. In respect of the latter, you should note that whilst a doctor is under an obligation to keep himself informed he is not expected to read every publication (*Gascoigne v Ian Sheridan & Co* (1994) 5 Med LR 437).

One further point which you should be aware of is that the defendant's conduct will be judged by reference to the prevailing British standard. It is unlikely that evidence of the state of knowledge of practitioners in other countries will be relevant to determining the state of knowledge in this country.

2.4.3 Area of practice

A practitioner who specialises in a particular area of medicine must be judged by the stand-ard of skill and care of that speciality (*Whitehouse v Jordan* [1981] 1 WLR 246; *Maynard v West Midlands Regional Health Authority* [1984] 1 WLR 634; *Poynter v Hillingdon Health Authority* (1997) 37 BMLR 192). Again, the standard required is that of the ordinary doctor practising within that particular specialisation. The defendant does not have to be of the same standard of the most qualified or experienced specialists.

2.4.4 Status of the practitioner

When considering the standard by which a practitioner should be judged, reference must be made to the post he occupied at the time of the alleged negligence, rather than his own individual experience. This principle was laid down by the Court of Appeal in *Wilsher v Essex Area Health Authority* [1987] QB 730 and was followed in *Djemal v Bexley Health Authority* (1995) 6 Med LR 269.

In *Wilsher*, the claimant was born prematurely and was treated in a specialist baby unit. The unit was staffed by two consultants, a senior registrar and a number of junior doctors. One of the issues before the court concerned the standard of care to be expected of the junior doctors. The Court of Appeal held by a majority of two to one that the duty of care should be defined by reference not to the individual doctor but rather to the post held by the individual. Mustill LJ stated:

The standard is not just that of the averagely competent and well-informed junior houseman (or whatever the position of the doctor) but of such a person who fills a post in a unit offering a highly specialised service.

In *Djemal*, a practitioner with four months' experience as a senior houseman acting as a casualty officer failed to take a proper history from a patient. As a result, he wrongly diag-nosed a throat infection and discharged the patient. Unhappily, the patient was in fact suffering from a condition called epiglottitis. His condition deteriorated and he suffered brain damage. The doctor was found negligent. It was held that the standard of care required in diagnosing a patient attending the accident and emergency department of a hospital was that of a reasonably competent senior houseman acting as a casualty officer, without any reference to the length of his experience.

2.4.5 General and approved practice

You would be forgiven for concluding that, by virtue of the *Bolam* test (see **2.4.1**), a defendant will automatically escape liability if he can show that his conduct was within approved practice according to a responsible body of opinion. This, however, is not the case. In *Bolitho v City & Hackney Health Authority* [1998] AC 232, the House of Lords held that when applying the *Bolam* test, the court must be satisfied that the body of opinion relied on has a logical basis. This principle is clearly stated in the following extract from the judgment of Lord Browne-Wilkinson at pp 778e–778g:

> The use of these adjectives — responsible, reasonable and respectable — all show that the court has to be satisfied that the exponents of the body of opinion relied upon can demonstrate that such opinion has a logical basis. In particular in cases involving, as they so often do, the weighing of risks against benefits, the judge before accepting a body of opinion as being responsible, reasonable or respectable, will need to be satisfied that, in forming their views, the experts have directed their minds to the question of comparative risks and benefits and have reached a defensible conclusion on the matter.

Bolitho is a relatively recent case. However, a similar principle was established in relation to actions for solicitors' negligence as early as 1984. In *Edward Wong Finance Co Ltd v Johnson, Stokes and Master* [1984] AC 296 the solicitors had followed accepted practice but were nevertheless found to be negligent on the basis that the body of professional opinion, although almost universally held, was neither reasonable nor responsible.

Although there is an interesting parallel between *Bolitho* and *Edward Wong Finance*, it is submitted that the rejection by the court of a body of professional opinion as reasonable or responsible is far more likely to occur in cases involving solicitors' negligence than it is in those involving clinical negligence. This is because the courts are more familiar with the solicitors' profession than they are with the medical profession. It follows that in clinical negligence cases they will have to rely heavily on expert evidence and it will be rare that they will be persuaded to reject the view of a distinguished expert.

The *Bolitho* principle was applied in the claimant's favour in the recent *Organ Retention Litigation* [2005] 2 WLR 358. There had been a universally adopted practice by doctors of not informing parents that organs might be retained from their children at post-mortem. It was held that the practice was not acceptable and that a duty of care did exist which required clinicians to inform parents about the purpose of the post-mortem and what it involved.

It should be noted that *Bolitho* was concerned with conventional medicine. The position is not necessarily the same where the court is concerned with the standards adopted by a practitioner of alternative medicine. For example in *Shakoor v Situ* [2001] 1 WLR 410, it was held that when a court had to consider the standard of care given by a practitioner of alternative medicine it would, contrary to *Bolitho*, often not be enough to judge him by the standards of an ordinary practitioner skilled in that particular art. Rather, it would often be necessary: (a) to have regard to the fact that the practitioner was practising his alternative medicine alongside conventional medicine and (b) for the court to consider whether the standards adopted by the alternative practitioner had taken account of the implications of that fact.

2.5 Specific breaches of duty in clinical negligence

When considering whether a defendant has breached his duty of care in any given set of circumstances, you need to apply the *Bolam* test (as modified by *Bolitho*). You ask yourself the question: Did this clinician act in accordance with a practice which was accepted as proper by a responsible, reasonable and respectable body of medical opinion? You ultimately answer the question by reference to expert evidence. It can however be helpful, when preparing the case and particularly when working out questions to ask the expert to address, to consider a court's application of the *Bolam* test in a similar situation. Of course, medical practice is constantly changing and each factual scenario is different and so other cases are of limited use. Nevertheless, there are certain categories of case which frequently arise and where a body of case law has developed which is of assistance and of which you should be aware. It is not proposed to provide a comprehensive summary here; reference can usefully be made to *Jackson & Powell, Profesional Negligence*, chapter 6, and to other specialist texts.

Discussed below are some of the most common types of breach of duty in clinical negligence.

2.5.1 Failing to attend/examine patient

Falling into this category are the following types of case:

(a) A general practitioner fails to visit a patient after a call (eg, *Stockdale v Nicholls* (1993) 4 Med LR 191 — GP not negligent for sending practice nurse to visit a reportedly unwell baby).

(b) A failure to examine a patient thoroughly (eg, *Barnett v Chelsea and Kensington Hospital Management Committee* [1969] 1 QB 428 — negligent failure by the casualty officer to examine new arrivals, although this case failed on causation).

(c) An insufficient history has been elicited from the patient. Taking a proper history is a part of the skilled work of a doctor, it is not enough merely to accept at face value the patient's explanations (see *Djemal v Bexley Health Authority* (1995) 6 Med LR 269).

2.5.2 Wrong diagnosis

Many clinical negligence cases turn on an allegation of misdiagnosis. Specific cases are of little assistance to the practitioner because medical knowledge and diagnostic tools are constantly evolving. In order to assist you, and ultimately the court, in applying the *Bolam* test, you will need evidence as to at least the following circumstances existing at the time of the diagnosis:

- The patient's medical history in fact and as taken by the clinician.
- The presenting symptoms.
- The 'usual' history and symptoms in a case of the actual injury/illness.
- The available investigative tools.
- The specialism of the proposed defendant clinician and the available referral clinicians.
- The actual examination and investigations carried out or referrals made.
- The type of examinations/investigations/referrals which would be expected in these circumstances.
- The conclusions drawn from those examinations/investigations.
- The conclusions which ought to have been drawn.
- What other clinicians connected with the patient thought, eg, did many doctors make the same misdiagnosis?
- The state of medical knowledge amongst the relevant class of professionals at the date of diagnosis.

- Any relevant system, guidance or protocols which the clinician ought to have been following (eg, accident and emergency departments have protocols).

- The importance of getting the diagnosis correct at the relevant stage.

The error will not be negligent if, on the material that was available to the defendant, a reasonably competent medical practitioner would have made the same mistake. See, in particular, *Maynard v West Midlands Regional Health Authority* [1984] 1 WLR 634.

The missing of a common and obvious condition will support a finding of negligence.

Negligence can consist in failing to obtain sufficient material in order to make a full diagnosis (see, in particular, *Djemal v Bexley Health Authority* (1995) 6 Med LR 269), where a failure to elicit a full history of the patient's symptoms was negligent, and *Langley v Campbell* The Times, 6 November 1975, where a failure to refer or consult a specialist on a tropical disease was held negligent).

An initial misdiagnosis may not be negligent in itself, but a doctor is under a continuing duty to revisit the diagnosis if there is any room for its being wrong. Where treatment is given and no improvement is made, the doctor should reassess the diagnosis. See, for example, *Bova v Spring* (1994) 5 Med LR 120, where the GP failed to recognise that his initial diagnosis was incorrect and so failed to prescribe follow-up treatment which would have later revealed the correct diagnosis (pneumonia).

2.5.3 Breakdown of communications

It is not only when exercising clinical expertise, that errors occur. A failure to ensure proper communication between different hospitals and medical practitioners can cause real harm and may amount to negligence.

The breakdown can be in a specific area or there can be a more general failure such as a failure to devise and maintain an adequate system for communication in a hospital. For example, in *Bull v Devon Health Authority* (1993) 4 Med LR 117, CA, a child was born with brain damage as a result of a failure by the hospital to find an obstetrician to get to the difficult birth sufficiently quickly. The failure to have a system to prevent this was found to be negligent.

When considering a case, remember to investigate lines of communication, for example:

- (Where appropriate) what systems had the hospital devised to ensure adequate communication

- Was a proper history given by the ambulance crew/the doctor/the nurse to the treating doctor?

- What happenned to the notes/X-rays etc?

- When a test was requested by a doctor was the right one carried out?

- When was the result known?

- Was the result communicated to the appropriate person and was it done so timeously?

- Was the follow-up care properly set up?

- Were appropriate letters written from the hospital to the GP and vice versa?

Once you understand what happened you will be in a position to ask the expert the right questions to assist in the application of the *Bolam* test. Of course, not all breakdowns in communication will result in a finding of negligence. For example, in *Chapman v Rix* (1959) 5 Med LR 238, the patient suffered a wound to the abdomen, the defendant examined him and (without negligence) concluded that the wound had not penetrated the peritoneum. Advice was given that he should attend his own doctor, this he did, but the patient wrongly reported that the hospital had told him the wound was superficial. A second wrong diagnosis was made. The House of Lords considered that although it would have been better for the defendant to send a letter, not doing so was not negligent.

2.5.4   Consent to treatment: the duty to explain treatment or give warnings

A doctor has no legal right to treat a patient unless he has their consent (there are exceptions in relation to minors and mentally-ill patients). Must that consent be informed consent? In other words, must the patient be informed of all possible risks involved in the treatment before a doctor can properly say that the patient consented? It is now settled law in this jurisdiction that there is no absolute obligation to inform the patient of all possible risks. The doctrine of informed consent is not recognised by the law in this country in this respect. The question of whether sufficient risks have been disclosed to the patient will be considered in the light of current standards of professional care (ie, in the light of the *Bolam* test). The decision as to the degree of disclosure is recognised to be a matter primarily for clinical judgment (*Sidaway v Governors of the Bethlem Royal Hospital* [1985] AC 871).

Parties in clinical negligence cases involving issues of consent/failure to warn will therefore depend upon expert evidence as to the appropriate degree of disclosure in the current climate. For an application of *Sidaway* in the light of *Bolitho* see *Pearce v United Bristol Healthcare NHS Trust* [1999] PIQR P53. The claimant complained that she had not been advised of the risks of stillbirth in proceeding to have a normal birth without intervention when her baby was already 14 days beyond term. The court scrutinised but accepted the medical opinion that it was not reasonable to advise of this risk, because it was not a 'significant risk'.

In other jurisdictions, a stricter obligation to disclose risks has evolved. It can seem unfair to apply the *Bolam* test in these cases when faced with a claimant who genuinely insists that, had she been given full disclosure, she would not have undergone the relevant treatment. However, the *Bolam* test has the advantage of keeping up-to-date with modern clinical practice and so as social pressure dictates that doctors give more information to their patients so the courts begin to find a failure to do so negligent. For example, in the case of *Gold v Haringey Health Authority* [1988] QB 481, a woman underwent a sterilisation operation but later became pregnant. The operation itself was not carried out negligently. The claimant brought her action on the basis that the failure to warn her of the risk that the operation would not work and that, without the use of contraception, she might become pregnant again, was negligent. The operation had been carried out in 1979 and there was at that time a substantial body of doctors who would have given the same advice and consequently the claim failed. However, medical practice has now changed so that patients are warned of the risks of failure inherent in sterilisation operations. Consequently, a failure to warn is likely to be found to be negligent (see, eg, *Lybert v Warrington Health Authority* (1996) 7 Med LR 71).

When a patient asks questions, the doctor is under a duty to answer truthfully even if that means disclosing a risk which he would not otherwise have disclosed. See further *Pearce* cited above.

In *Chester v Afshar* [2004] 1 AC 134, the House of Lords considered the issue of causation in the context of a failure by a surgeon to warn the claimant of a risk of paralysis involved in her back operation. This is discussed in more detail in **2.6.1.5**. However, it should be noted here that the House of Lords emphasised the importance of the patient's right to be informed of risks involved in any treatment and indicated that such a right was central to a patient's ability to make an informed choice and necessary to protect the patient's dignity and autonomy.

2.5.5   Psychiatric cases

Cases involving a breach of the duty owed by a clinician to a psychiatric patient can arise in many circumstances, for example:

(a) Failure to protect the patient from self harm by failing to give sufficient treatment or sufficient supervision. In relation to a failure to prevent suicide, see the important House of Lords' decision in *Reeves v Commissioner of Police of the Metropolis* [2000] 1 AC 360 — this case in fact concerns the duties of police custodians, but is of general application. Note, in particular, the relevance of contributory negligence.

(b) Failure to protect the patient from harming others and so exposing himself to criminal sanctions and worsening mental illness.

(c) Negligently certifying a patient under the Mental Health Acts and so falsely detaining him. The written recommendation of two medical practitioners is required under Part II of the Mental Health Act for compulsory admission of a psychiatric patient. It has been long established (see *Hall v Semple* (1862) 3 F & F 337, *Everett v Griffiths* [1920] 3 KB 163, CA, and *Harnett v Fisher* [1927] AC 573) that reasonable care must be exercised in certifying, or else the negligently certified person will in principle have a claim. This is not affected by the statutory restriction of proceedings contained in the Mental Health Act 1983, s 139(1).

(d) It is now extremely doubtful whether a medical practitioner owes any duty to members of the public injured by a person who is negligently not certified for admission. See, in particular, *Palmer v Tees Health Authority* [1999] Lloyd's Rep Med 351.

2.5.6   Errors or accidents which are not negligent

It is important to remember that even if there is a mistake in the course of treatment this may or may not be negligent. Mistakes can occur despite the exercise of reasonable care. Mistakes without negligence are more likely to happen where the operation or treatment is complex or unusual, or performed in haste (where such expedition was itself reasonably necessary).

See, in particular *Whitehouse v Jordan* [1981] 1 WLR 246, where, on appeal, alleged excessive pulling during a forceps delivery was found not to be negligent.

In *White v Board of Governors of Westminster Hospital* The Times, 26 October 1961, the surgeon was operating on tiny nerves around the eye when he accidentally cut the retina which resulted in the eye having to be removed. This was held to be a non-negligent accident.

When considering each case, remember to bear in mind:

• the nature of the treatment;

• the surrounding circumstances (eg, urgency);

• what safeguards the clinician ought to have employed to avoid this type of error.

Where appropriate, ask the expert whether the error could be considered to be a non-negligent accident.

2.5.7   *Res ipsa loquitur*

Although the use of Latin tags has been deprecated by the Court of Appeal (see per May LJ in *Fryer v Pearson* The Times, 4 April 2000), this does not alter the fact that certain happenings, such as the leaving of a swab in a patient's body, are (without explanation) more consistent with negligence, than proper treatment. So, although the phrase *res ipsa loquitur* should not be used, where the very fact of the injury is relied upon as evidence of negligence this should be expressly stated.

It is open to the defendant to seek to rebut this inference by showing that reasonable care was exercised or that there is an alternative, non-negligent, explanation for the claimant's misfortune. See, for example, *Roe v Minister of Health* [1954] 2 QB 66.

In the case of *Ratcliffe v Plymouth & Torbay Health Authority* [1998] Lloyd's Rep Med 162, Brooke LJ discussed the applicability of res ipsa loquitur to clinical negligence actions. Whilst he accepted that in some cases the maxim would apply (eg, surgeon cuts off the wrong foot, leaves a swab in the body after an operation or the patient wakes up during an operation), this type of case would be very unusual. Rarely in a clinical negligence case would a judge be prepared to draw an inference of negligence purely because something had gone wrong in the course of treatment. Expert evidence will almost always be required in practice to establish negligence to the judge's satisfaction, which means that the judge is 'deciding the case on inferences he [is] entitled to draw from the whole of the evidence (including the expert evidence) and not on the application of the maxim in its purest form'.

2.6   Causation and remoteness

For a claimant to recover damages in a negligence claim, it is not enough that there is a proven breach of duty by the defendant, and that the claimant has suffered injury. It is necessary to establish a causal connection between the two. The claimant must show:

- the injury was caused by the breach of duty — causation; and
- the injury was reasonably foreseeable and the loss is recoverable in law — remoteness.

2.6.1   Causation

The claimant must usually establish that the negligence has in fact caused or contributed to his injuries. This requires a comparison between:

- what in fact happened (factual); and
- what would have happened if the negligence had not occurred (hypothetical).

Broadly speaking, if, on the balance of probabilities, the adverse outcome would not have happened but for the negligence, that negligence is a cause. If it would have happened anyway, the negligence is not a cause. This is of course the familiar 'but for test'.

The test sounds easy to apply but all too often it creates difficulties. You should remember that 'the function of the test is merely to act as preliminary filter and eliminate the irrelevant rather than to allocate legal responsibility' (*Winfield & Jolowicz on Tort*). The 'but for' test is only one aspect of factual causation. The test of factual causation is material contribution to the injury and this depends upon questions of both common sense and policy. Many happenings satisfy the 'but for' test but the application of common sense or policy might mean that some such happenings would not be held to be a cause of injury. Conversely, the courts have not treated the 'but for' test as a necessary condition of liability where that would produce an unjust result. This chapter considers factual causation in some simple as well as difficult circumstances.

2.6.1.1   Application of the 'but for' test

This can be fairly straightforward to apply in clinical negligence cases. For example, a claim will fail if the ultimate injury would have occurred anyway despite competent treatment. In *Barnett v Chelsea & Kensington Hosptial Management Committee* [1969] 1 QB 428, three nightwatchmen were presented at casualty at night vomiting after drinking tea. The casualty officer and nurse sent them home with instructions to visit the doctor in the morning. The claimant's husband died of arsenic poisoning that night. Had he been examined and the diagnosis been made correctly, he would have been admitted for treatment. The failure to examine, admit and treat him was in breach of the duty owed to him. However, he would still have died as treatment would not have saved him in any event. The claim was therefore dismissed despite a finding of negligence, because the claim could not establish causation.

2.6.1.2   Competing causes in clinical negligence

Factual causation is much more difficult to determine where there are competing causes of an injury. This is rarely the case in simple personal injury cases (eg, a road traffic accident or accident at work) but is very frequent in clinical negligence cases (eg, the underlying medical problem, side effects of treatment and the negligent act or omission). This explains why many of the leading cases in relation to causation are clinical negligence cases.

In *Wilsher v Essex Area Health Authority* [1988] 1 AC 1074, the claimant was born prematurely; he succumbed to retrolental fibroplasia (RLF), a condition of the retina resulting in severely impaired vision. In the House of Lords, it was accepted that there had been negligence in permitting excess oxygen to be administered to the baby. There were, however, at least five possible causes of RLF of which excess oxygen was but one. The negligence had certainly increased the risk of the RLF occurring but it was not established that it had in fact been a contributing cause in this case. The trial judge found the defendants liable since they had failed to prove that the condition was not caused by the negligent act. The House of Lords considered that this was, in effect, a reversal of the burden of proof and held that it was not enough for the claimant to show that the excess oxygen increased the risk of RLF, it had to be shown that it actually caused or contributed to the RLF. In view of the other possible causes this could not be presumed.

In *McGhee v National Coal Board* [1973] 1 WLR 1, there was more than one possible cause of the pursuer's dermatitis. The question arose as to whether the pursuer had proved that the negligence of his employers was in fact materially causative of the injury or whether it had merely increased the risk of injury. The House of Lords held the employer liable because it had increased the risk of injury.

In *Fairchild v Glenhaven Funeral Services Ltd* [2002] UKHL 22, [2003] 1 AC 32, the claimants had been exposed to asbestos during periods of employment with more than one employer. They contracted mesothelioma, a malignant tumour which is invariably fatal. The condition is extremely rare except in cases of asbestos exposure. Medical opinion was uncertain of the precise mechanism, though it was accepted that the risk of contracting mesothelioma increases in proportion to the quantity of asbestos fibres inhaled, yet the condition could be caused by a single fibre. There was no way of proving the source of the fibre or fibres which initiated the genetic process which culminated in the malignant tumour. In finding for the claimants the House of Lords applied *McGhee*: the employers were liable because they had increased the risk of mesothelioma.

There is an obvious tension between the decision in *McGhee* and the decision in *Wilsher; Fairchild* attempts, but does not quite achieve, a principled reconciliation. The speeches are different in emphasis and approach, and it is difficult to extract the *ratio*. It is probably the case that *McGhee* applies where it is inherently impossible or almost impossible for the claimant to prove the cause of the condition. It will be unusual for this principle to be applicable in cases of clinical negligence, so that the courts will probably continue to apply *Wilsher*.

In *Hotson v East Berkshire Area Health Authority* [1987] AC 750, the claimant fell from a tree fracturing his hip. The defendant failed to diagnose this correctly and treat the fracture for some five days. Avascular necrosis developed. The trial judge found that if the diagnosis had been made timeously, the claimant would still have been likely to develop avascular necrosis (75% chance) but that the delay in diagnosis made the development of the necrosis inevitable. He awarded the claimant 25% of his claim for damages to reflect the loss of the chance of a good recovery. The Court of Appeal affirmed the decision. The House of Lords allowed the defendant's appeal. In order to establish causation the claimant must prove that the negligent act of the defendant (late diagnosis) was in fact a material cause of the claimant's injury (avascular necrosis). The claimant does so on the balance of probabilities. On the judge's own findings, the injury was probably (75% likely) caused by the fall alone. It followed that the claimant failed on causation and the issue of quantification by the judge should never have arisen. Questions concerning the loss of chance could not arise where there had been a finding that the damage complained of had been sustained (or become inevitable) before the duty of care was owed by the defendant. In other words, at the time of the negligence there was no chance of recovery (on the balance of probabilities) which could have been affected by the failure to diagnose or treat.

2.6.1.3 Loss of a chance

Hotson (see **2.6.1.2**) is interesting because the trial judge and the Court of Appeal treated it as though it were a claim for the loss of a chance of recovery and the claimant asked the House of Lords to decide it on that basis. The House of Lords refused to do so, saying that this case failed on causation and so the question of the loss of a chance in the measure of damages did not arise. The case has been applied in practice so as to exclude claims in clinical negligence for the loss of a chance of recovery. However, Lord Mackay said in *Hotson* that it would be unwise in the present case to lay it down as a rule that a claimant could never succeed by proving a loss of chance in a medical negligence case.

The analogy was drawn to solicitors' negligence cases such as *Kitchen v Royal Air Force Association* [1958] 1 WLR 563, where the negligence was in failing to commence proceedings. Here the loss is characterised as a loss of a chance to bring proceedings. In order to prove some actionable damage, the claimant need only show that the proceedings had some real prospect of success (even where this is less than 50%). So there is a lower threshold of proof of actionable damage, once this is surmounted, then the prospects of success in the primary claim are considered, but this is part of the assessment of damages rather than a necessary condition of actionable damage.

Whilst it is difficult on the face of it to reconcile *Hotson* and *Kitchen*, some further consideration demonstrates a rationale behind the two approaches. In a solicitor's negligence case, if the primary claim would probably have failed (eg, 40% chance of success) it still has a value as the original parties might well have compromised the action at, say 40%, of the value of the claim. The claimant therefore had something of value (a chose in action) which was lost by the solicitor's negligence. Equally, if the primary claim would probably have succeeded (say 80% chance), nonetheless a discount is made to reflect the possible chance of failure. This is an important difference in practical approach.

At the beginning of 2005 the House of Lords gave its eagerly awaited judgment in the case of *Gregg v Scott* [2005] 2 WLR 268 finally giving binding authority to the effect that damages are not recoverable for the loss of a chance of a cure/improvement in clinical negligence cases. The claimant's cancer was diagnosed nine months later than it should have been as a result of the negligence of his general practitioner. Because of this, his chances of a cure were reduced from 42 to 25%. The majority of the House of Lords held that the normal 'but for' causation test should apply and on that basis the claim must fail as the claimant was unable to prove on the balance of probabilities that in the absence of negligence he would have survived. The policy reason behind the judgment was in part to keep the law 'practicable': Baroness Hale explained that allowing this claim would lead to the widespread incorporation of chances in awards, reducing the award made for all outcomes that are probable but less than certain, where on the current law, the proof of a probable event results in full recovery. There were powerful dissenting judgments from Lord Nicholls and Lord Hope who found it unjust that the law would fail to compensate the loss of a chance of a recovery when the duty of the doctor was not to prevent death but to increase the chance of recovery. They considered that courts are well used to dealing with reductions to reflect uncertainties in future awards and that, in any event, the difficulties of assessment should not preclude a claim in principle. The law now appears settled, if somewhat disappointing, on this issue.

When considering causation in clinical negligence cases it helps to remember the following points:

(a) The onus of proof falls squarely on the claimant throughout.

(b) The negligence must be a material cause of the injury.

(c) Unless the case is within the *McGhee* principle it is not enough to show that the risk of injury has been increased, the claimant must satisfy the court that the negligence actually did cause or materially contribute to his condition. The standard of proof is of course the balance of probabilities, but to this extent a definite link must be shown.

(d) Once it has been established that the negligence was a material cause of the injury then there is an evidential burden on the defendant to plead and to prove that it is not responsible for the whole of the loss.

2.6.1.4 Hypothetical acts by the defendant doctors: the decision in *Bolitho*

If the negligent act consists of an omission, such as a failure to attend the patient, before he can establish a causal link, the claimant must show that if the medical practitioner had attended the patient, this would have led to the prevention of the injury.

In *Bolitho v City and Hackney Health Authority* [1998] AC 232, a doctor negligently failed to attend a child patient despite the child's respiratory difficulties being twice reported by a nurse. Causation was not however proven because even if the doctor had attended (as she should have done), no treatment would in fact have been given, nor, according to a reasonable body of medical opinion, should it have been.

The particular importance of this decision is that it makes clear that the defendant cannot escape liability by contending that if the negligent failure to attend had not taken place, the practitioner would have gone on to make a further negligent decision not to treat the patient. So in predicting the hypothetical course of treatment, the defendant cannot rely on an apprehended course of treatment which would have fallen below a reasonable standard. In determining what would have been a reasonable standard, the House of Lords applied the *Bolam* test.

2.6.1.5 Failure to warn and causation

The normal application of the rules of causation demand that where the negligence is a failure to warn of risks of treatment, the claimant must demonstrate that had he been properly advised, he would not have undergone the treatment and would therefore not have suffered the injury. This is not an easy evidential burden to discharge as most defendants are able to say that, when the warning is appropriately given it never/hardly ever deters the patient from accepting the treatment and judges are conscious that the claimant's belief is necessarily retrospective and formed after the risk has materialised. The test is a subjective one but the likely actions of a reasonable person are of assistance when determining what the claimant would in fact have done. See *Smith v Barking Havering & Brentwood Health Authority* (1994) 5 Med LR 385; *Smith v Salford Health Authority* (1995) 6 Med LR 321; *Lybert v Warrington Health Authority* (1996) 7 Med LR 71; *Tabir v Haringey Health Authority* [1998] Lloyd's Rep Med 104 and *Poynter v Hillingdon Health Authority* (1997) 37 BMLR 192.

The issue of causation in cases where there has been a failure to warn was fully considered by the House of Lords in the case of *Chester v Afshar* [2004] 1 AC 134. There was a negligent failure by the defendant surgeon to warn the claimant of a small but significant risk (1 to 2%) of the back surgery failing to cure her condition but instead causing cauda equina syndrome and paralysis. The claimant underwent the surgery which was carried out without negligence. The risk materialised and she was left paralysed. The relevant factual findings were that had she been properly warned, the claimant would probably have undertaken further investigations as to appropriate treatment before ultimately undergoing the same surgery at a later date. In other words she could not establish that she would not have undergone the surgery in the absence of the negligent failure to warn and she could not complain that the negligence had caused or even increased the risk of injury.

Nevertheless, the majority of the House of Lords considered that whilst the claimant could not succeed on the 'but for' test she should still succeed in establishing causation and liability. The basis for this reasoning involved an emphasis on the importance of informed consent. It was recognised that the patient's right to be warned of significant risks is an important right which protects the patient's autonomy. Steyn LJ put it in these terms: the 'right of autonomy and dignity [justifies] a narrow and modest departure from traditional causation principles'. The language of the majority judgments suggests an extension of the causation principle which allows a claimant to succeed where the very risk of which he should have been warned but was not materialises, regardless of whether the negligence in fact altered the course of events.

However, it should be noted that the facts of this case arguably required no extension of the usual principles of causation: but for the surgeon's negligent failure to warn, the operation would have taken place *on a different day*. The chance of the injury occurring on a subsequent occasion was very small (1 to 2%) and so, as Steyn LJ recognised: 'It could therefore be said that the breach of the surgeon resulted in the very injury about which the claimant was entitled to be warned'. In other words, the 'but for' test could indeed be satisfied in this case and this was a material factor in the judgement of Steyn LJ. However, this reasoning was not accepted by Walker LJ.

Overall, the judgments indicate a relaxation of the strict principles of causation but the precise test and/or circumstances in which the principles can be relaxed are not clearly set out and many questions remain to be answered in the future application of the authority.

2.6.1.6   Common sense and policy in factual causation

In some cases, satisfying the 'but for' test may not be enough; for the injury may be outside the scope of the defendant's duty, or otherwise insufficiently closely connected with the negligence.

In *South Australia Asset Management Corp v York Montague Ltd* [1997] AC 191 (a valuer's negligence case), Lord Hoffman posits the example of a mountaineer who is negligently informed that his knee is fit, and decides on this information to go on an expedition. He suffers an injury which is the foreseeable consequence of mountaineering but nothing to do with the knee. While it is true that 'but for' the negligence he would not have gone on the expedition, according to Lord Hoffman, the doctor would not be liable as the injury would be outside the scope of his duty of care. In other words, it is not something which the doctor promises to protect the mountaineer from. This example is discussed and distinguished in *Chester v Afshar* (supra).

For an application of this principle, see *R v Croydon Health Authority* [1998] 2 Lloyd's Rep Med 44. Here a radiologist was engaged by an employer to screen prospective employees, she negligently failed to diagnose an abnormality in a woman, who, if the abnormality had been diagnosed, would not have become pregnant. The Court of Appeal considered that the extent of the defendant's duty did not extend to the claimant's private life and her decision to become pregnant.

If some extraneous event occurs between the medical practitioner's negligence and the injury so that the negligence is not an effective cause of the loss, then the negligent practitioner will not be held responsible. Older texts and cases refer to this as a *novus actus interveniens*. (See *Thompson v Schmidt* (1891) 8 TLR 120 — certificate of unsound mind not the cause of the claimant's detention under the Lunacy Act 1890, this was caused by the act of the relieving officer.)

2.6.2   Remoteness

In the medical context, for the purposes of remoteness, claimants will generally rely on the tortious test of reasonable foreseeability, so that in establishing remoteness, nothing Will ordinarily turn on whether or not there was a contract.

For practical purposes the question is whether the claimant's injury was a reasonably foreseeable consequence of the defendant's negligence.

Of course, if negligence and causation can be shown, it is rare that the defendant doctor will be able to successfully contend that the injurious consequences could not have been foreseen, especially as the quality and extent of injury need not be foreseen. See *Smith v Brighton & Lewes Hospital Management Committee* The Times, 2 May 1958; and *Wiszniewski v Central Manchester Health Authority* (1996) 7 Med LR 248.

2.7   Measure of damages

2.7.1   Personal injury

The principal effect of medical negligence is personal injury. The principles of quantification are dealt with in the **Remedies Manual**. However, in a medical negligence context it is always important to identify and distinguish with precision the pain and injury that was caused by the negligence, from the pain and injury that was inevitable or which cannot be attributed to the negligence. In many cases the negligence will have aggravated an existing condition; in which case it is only the consequences of the aggravation that should be quantified.

2.7.2 Unwanted child

Where a medical practitioner negligently performs a sterilisation or abortion then this may cause the arrival of an unplanned baby.

Where the baby is healthy, it is now settled by the authority of *McFarlane v Tayside Health Board* [2000] 2 AC 59 (HL), that the mother is entitled to damages for the pain, suffering and inconvenience of pregnancy and childbirth, and to recover the financial losses such as extra medical expenses, clothing and loss of earnings due to the pregnancy and birth. The costs of raising a healthy child are not however recoverable.

In *Rees v Darlington Memorial NHS Trust*, 31 October 2003, the House of Lords thoroughly reconsidered *McFarlane* and more recent Court of Appeal decisions concerning claims for wrongful birth. The claimant in *Rees* was disabled, and she claimed for the additional costs of bringing up her child consequent upon her disability. All seven judges upheld the *McFarlane* decision as correct. The majority (of four) held that no exception should be made from *McFarlane* in the case of a healthy baby born to a disabled mother. More innovatively, the majority awarded a 'conventional sum' of £15,000 and held that this sum should be awarded in all wrongful birth claims to redress the legal wrong of the negligent medical treatment. The award is to be made in addition to the award for the suffering of pregnancy and childbirth. No distinction is to be drawn between cases where the mother and/or the child is disabled.

Solicitors' negligence

3.1 Duty of care to client

3.1.1 Contractual duties

In almost every case there will be a contract between the solicitor and client. The contract may place detailed express obligations on the solicitor. It may also include a number of implied obligations. In addition to the terms agreed by the parties, the law imposes an obligation on a solicitor to act with reasonable skill and care (Supply of Goods and Services Act 1982, s 13).

3.1.2 Tortious duties

In addition to his contractual duty to act with reasonable skill and care, a solicitor also owes a concurrent duty of care in tort (see *Midland Bank Trust Co Ltd v Hett, Stubbs and Kemp* [1979] Ch 384 and *Henderson v Merrett Syndicates Ltd* [1995] 2 AC 145). The existence of this concurrent duty is of great significance in the context of limitation: whereas the primary time limit for bringing a cause of action in both contract and tort expires six years after the date upon which the cause of action accrued (Limitation Act 1980, ss 2 and 5), the time limit for bringing a claim in tort may be extended by a further three years dependent upon the client's date of knowledge of the material facts (see Limitation Act 1980, s 14A, as inserted by the Latent Damage Act 1986). This extension is not available in respect of a claim based on a breach of contract.

3.1.3 Fiduciary duties

The retainer between a solicitor and his client is one which gives rise to a relationship of trust and confidence. Such a relationship is known as a fiduciary relationship and it gives rise to a number of duties known as fiduciary duties. The fiduciary duties owed by a solicitor include a duty to act in good faith, not to make a secret profit and not to act where his own interests or the interests of someone else whom he represents conflict with those of the client. A detailed consideration of the nature of fiduciary duties is outside the scope of this Manual. Judicial consideration of fiduciary duties and their consequences in a claim against a solicitor can be found in *Bristol & West Building Society v Mothew* [1998] Ch 1; *Bristol and West Building Society v Fancy and Jackson* [1997] 4 All ER 582 and *Nationwide Building Society v Balmer Radmore* [1999] Lloyd's Rep PN 606.

3.2 Duties to third parties

A solicitor may owe duties of care in the tort of negligence to someone other than his client. For example, the House of Lords has held that a solicitor retained by a testator to draw up a will may be liable to pay damages to the intended beneficiary when he negligently fails to perform the task before the testator's death (*White v Jones* [1995] 2 AC 207).

The courts have adopted a number of different approaches for determining whether or not a duty of care exists in a particular factual situation.

One approach has been to apply the principles enunciated by the House of Lords in *Caparo Industries plc v Dickman* [1990] 2 AC 605 (a case which concerned accountants). This involves asking the following questions:

- Was injury to the third party a foreseeable consequence of the solicitor's negligence?
- Is there a sufficiently proximate relationship between the solicitor and third party?
- Is it fair, just and reasonable to impose a duty of care?
- Can an analogy be drawn with any decided cases?

An alternative approach adopted by the courts when determining the existence of a duty of care is to ask: Has there been a voluntary assumption of responsibility to the third party by the defendant? The doctrine of assumption of responsibility was accorded precedence in *Henderson v Merrett Syndicates Ltd* [1995] 2 AC 145, a case which involved claims brought by Lloyd's names against their brokers. It also appears to have been the basis of the decision in *White v Jones* (above).

It has been said by the Court of Appeal that the result should be the same, whichever approach is used to determine whether or not a duty of care is owed (*Bank of Credit and Commerce International (Overseas) Ltd v Price Waterhouse* [1998] BCC 617). This is likely to be true of most cases, although there may be some instances where the different tests will yield different results. For example, in *Gran Gelato Ltd v Richcliff (Group) Ltd* [1992] Ch 560, the court held that it would not be fair, just or reasonable to make a vendor's solicitor liable to a purchaser for giving incorrect answers to pre-contract enquiries. On the other hand, in *First National Bank plc v Loxleys* [1997] PNLR 211, the Court of Appeal refused to strike out an almost identical claim against a vendor's solicitor on the basis that there may have been an assumption of responsibility by the solicitor to the purchaser. The two cases are difficult to reconcile, although the key may lie in the fact that the courts are generally reluctant at present to determine issues as to the existence of duties of care on a strike out application (see *Barrett v Enfield London Borough Council* [2001] 2 AC 550).

In the litigation context, it was held by Gage J in *Abrams v Woodford & Ackroyd* (1996) 4 PN 129 that a solicitor would not have been liable to his client's opponent for a representation that he was holding monies in a client account pending negotiations. The imposition of such a duty would not have been just or reasonable. On the other hand, in *Al-Kandari v J R Brown & Co* [1988] QB 665, a solicitor was found liable to his client's opponent when he agreed to hold his client's passport but failed to do so. The solicitor had assumed a duty to the opponent and so was liable when his own client left the country.

3.3   Standard of care

3.3.1   General approach

In the absence of express agreement to the contrary, a solicitor's conduct is to be judged by reference to that of a hypothetical reasonably competent solicitor. If the solicitor has professed a special expertise, then his conduct will be judged by reference to that of a reasonably competent solicitor who holds such expertise (see *Duchess of Argyll v Beuselinck* [1972] 2 Lloyd's Rep 172). For example, in *Matrix Securities Ltd v Theodore Goddard* [1998] PNLR 290 it was held that the defendant solicitors should be judged by the standard of a reasonably competent firm of solicitors with a specialist tax department. On the other hand, the fact that a solicitor was relatively junior or inexperienced will not result in a court judging him by a lower standard than that of a reasonably competent solicitor. In *Balamoan v Holden and Co* The Independent, 15 June 1999, it was held that a sole practitioner could not expect a lower standard of care to be applied because he had delegated the work to an unqualified (although highly experienced) member of staff.

3.3.2   Effect of the client's experience

The advice which a reasonable competent solicitor might have given may be affected by the experience or sophistication of his client. Thus in *Carradine Properties v D J Freeman* [1999] Lloyd's Rep PN 483, it was held that a solicitor did not owe a duty to advise a director of a property development company that the company might have an insurance policy which covered the losses which it had suffered by reason of negligence on the part of a building contractor. Conversely, the fact that a client is relatively inexperienced may result in a more onerous duty being imposed. In *Crossnan v Ward Bracewell & Co* (1989) 5 PN 103, a solicitor was found negligent when he failed to advise a client who was charged with a road traffic offence that his insurers might pay for his defence. Unaware of this source of funding, the client represented himself and pleaded guilty.

3.3.3   Extent of the duty

A solicitor will normally be expected to advise upon matters which are expressly covered by his instructions. However, he may additionally owe a duty to advise upon matters which are not expressly covered in his instructions but which are closely related to them. For example, a solicitor who is retained by a mortgagee to investigate the title of a property which it is proposing to take as security for a loan may additionally owe an implied duty to report upon any matters he discovers which cast doubt on the value of the property (*Mortgage Express Ltd v Bowerman* [1995] QB 375).

A related issue is the extent to which a solicitor owes a duty to give his client 'commercial' advice when he has not been instructed expressly to give such advice. The question whether or not such a duty is owed is likely to depend on any of a number of factors, including the experience of the client, whether or not the transaction is manifestly imprudent and whether or not there were dangers which should have been apparent to a solicitor but which would not have been apparent to a lay person.

In *Yager v Fishman & Co* [1944] 1 All ER 552, it was held that a solicitor did not owe a businessman a duty to remind him that the date for the exercise of an option was approaching. Similarly, in *Reeves v Thrings & Long* [1996] PNLR 265, the client purchased a property to which the right of access was subject to a licence agreement. The solicitor explained the terms of the licence agreement to the client. It was held that he did not owe a duty to go on to explain the commercial importance of the licence, still less did he owe a duty to advise the client against making the purchase.

County Personnel (Employment Agency) Ltd v Alan R Pulver [1987] 1 WLR 916 is a case which falls on the other side of the line. In that case an underlease which the client was proposing to take contained an unusual rent review clause which linked increases in rent to increases in rent under the headlease. The solicitor was found liable for failing to advise the client of the risks of proceeding with the transaction without ascertaining the market rents which were due under the headlease. The risk was one which arose directly out of the terms of the lease and whilst it should have been apparent to a reasonably competent solicitor it would not necessarily have been apparent to the client.

3.3.4 Relevance of the *Bolam* Test

In the clinical negligence case of *Bolam v Friern Hospital Management Committee* [1957] 1 WLR 582, it was held that a medical practitioner who acted in accordance with a practice accepted at the time as proper by a responsible body of medical opinion skilled in the particular form of treatment in question was not liable in the tort of negligence. This has become known amongst practitioners as 'the *Bolam* test'.

There is no reason in principle why the *Bolam* test should not apply to solicitors and there are a number of examples of its application. In *Simmons v Pennington* [1955] 1 WLR 183, a solicitor acting for the vendor answered a requisition on title in a manner which accorded with the general practice of conveyancers. Unfortunately, this caused the purchaser to withdraw from the transaction. The court dismissed the vendor's claim against his solicitor for damages for negligence. Similarly, where the solicitor has had to exercise a fine judgment the court may be slow to criticise him as having been negligent. For example, in the Scottish case of *Bell v Strathairn and Blair* (1954) 104 LJ 618, the Outer House held that advice given by a solicitor as to the effect of a purported recission of an agreement, whilst wrong, could not be categorised as negligent.

However, notwithstanding such decisions, the scope for the application of the *Bolam* test to solicitors appears to be more limited than with other professionals. This is in part due to the fact that in many cases there will be a definite and ascertainable answer as to whether or not the legal advice given by a solicitor was correct as a matter of law. It is also explicable on the basis that the courts will often see themselves as being uniquely familiar with the areas of work performed by solicitors. For example, in *Bown v Gould & Swayne* [1996] PNLR 130, the Court of Appeal upheld a judge's decision not to admit expert evidence as to the practice adopted by solicitors in establishing a right of way. The basis of the decision was that the deduction of title was a matter of law, not practice.

Further, even when the *Bolam* test does apply, the body of professional opinion relied upon by the defendant must be a reasonable or responsible one. The judge has to be satisfied that the opinion has a logical basis (see the clinical negligence case of *Bolitho v City and Hackney Health Authority* [1998] AC 232). Where a practice adopted by a solicitor carries obvious risks, the court may find it negligent notwithstanding the fact that the practice is widespread. In *Edward Wong Finance Co Ltd v Johnson, Stokes and Master* [1984] AC 296, the defendant solicitors had adopted a form of conveyancing practice, known as 'Hong Kong style' conveyancing which was customary amongst solicitors throughout the colony. The practice involved paying the purchase monies to the vendor's solicitor in return for an undertaking by the vendor's solicitor to forward the duly executed documents of title. In this case, the vendor's solicitor ran off with the money. The Privy Council held that this was a foreseeable risk and the fact that the practice was wide spread did not prevent finding of negligence against the purchaser's solicitor.

3.3.5 Relevance of codes of practice

Whilst compliance with standard practice will not necessarily prevent a finding of negligence if the practice is inherently risky, non-compliance with codes of conduct adopted by the profession may amount to evidence of negligence. In *Johnson v Bingley, Dyson & Furey* [1997] PNLR 392, a solicitor failed, contrary to advice contained in the Law Society Guide which was in force at the time, to verify that he had his client's direct instructions. He relied instead upon instructions given by his client's son, purportedly on her behalf. The court, finding the solicitor negligent, held that whilst breach of a code of practice could not by itself amount to negligence, it was a factor which could be taken into account.

3.3.6 Expert evidence

Notwithstanding the decision of the Court of Appeal in *Bown v Gould & Swayne* [1996] PNLR 130, it is the experience of practitioners that the courts will, in appropriate cases, admit expert evidence as to practice in claims against solicitors (see, for instance, *UCB Bank v David Pinder plc* [1997] EGCS 179). Guidance can be found in the earlier Court of Appeal decision of *Carradine Properties Ltd v D J Freeman and Co* (1989) 5 Const LJ 267, where it was said that whilst evidence which amounts to no more than an expression of opinion by an expert as to what he would have done had he been in the defendant's position is inadmissible, evidence as to the existence of a practice may be admissible in appropriate cases.

3.4 Specific breaches in solicitors' negligence cases

There are many different ways in which a solicitor can be found to have breached his duty and the following headings are provided for illustration only. Further examples can be found in **Chapter 2** and also in *Professional Negligence Cases* by David Pittaway and Alastair Hammerton (1998, Butterworths) and the standard textbooks on professional negligence such as *Jackson & Powell* (5th edn, Sweet & Maxwell).

3.4.1 Wrong advice

If a solicitor gives incorrect advice when the law is clear, then he is likely to be found negligent. For instance, in *Otter v Church Adams Tatham & Co* [1953] Ch 280, a solicitor was found negligent for misreading a trust deed which was in a 'perfectly ordinary form'. In *Cooper v Smith Llewellyn Partnership* [1999] PNLR 576 the defendant solicitors had failed to advise their clients that the relevant limitation period of six years ran from the date of exchange of contracts and not the date of completion. They had failed to distinguish between causes of action in contract, and causes of action in tort. They had also neglected to consult the case law on the matter. They were held to be negligent. Further, if the construction of a document is difficult or if a solicitor is uncertain of the law, he may arguably owe a duty to qualify his advice, or to advise his client that it would be prudent to seek the advice of experienced counsel.

3.4.2   Failure to give advice

There is rarely any dispute where the solicitor has been asked specifically to advise on a point but fails to do so. More difficult is the extent to which a solicitor owes a duty to give advice upon matters he is not expressly asked to consider. Examples can be found at **3.3.3** above.

3.4.3   Misconduct of litigation

Many professional negligence actions against solicitors involve missed time limits. The cases can arise out of errors during the course of litigation, such as a failure to comply with an unless order, or prior to the litigation even commencing, such as where the solicitor misses a limitation period. Unless the delay can be blamed on a client who has been clearly advised of the consequences of missing the time limit, there is rarely any defence to such claims.

A solicitor has been held negligent for delaying in seeking evidence before the trail went cold (*Balamoan v Holden & Co* (1999) 149 NLJ 898).

If, in the course of doing that for which a solicitor has been retained, he or she becomes aware of a risk to a client, it is the solicitor's duty to inform the client of the risk (see *Credit Lyonnais SA v Russell Jones and Walker* [2003] PNLR 2).

A solicitor will also be expected to take reasonable steps to ensure that a judgment is enforceable. For example, in *Martin Boston & Co v Roberts* [1996] PNLR 45, the Court of Appeal held that a solicitor was negligent for failing to register a caution against the house of a company director who had given a personal guarantee to the solicitor's client in a security for costs application. In *Pearson v Sanders Witherspoon* [2000] Lloyd's Rep PN 151 it was held that a solicitor who had notice that a defendant company was at risk of going insolvent had a duty to prosecute his client's action against that company expeditiously.

3.4.4   Acting without authority

A solicitor who purports to act without his client's instructions may find himself in breach of a warranty of authority to third parties. For instance, in *Penn v Bristol & West Building Society* [1997] 1 WLR 1356, the solicitor accepted instructions from a husband on the sale of a property which he jointly owned with his wife. The wife in fact knew nothing of the sale, which was fraudulent. The solicitor was held liable to the mortgagees of the proposed purchaser on the grounds that by purporting to act on the wife's behalf, he warranted that he had her instructions to do so.

3.4.5   Wasted costs

The court has jurisdiction under the Supreme Court Act 1981, s 51(6)(as amended by the Courts and Legal Services Act 1990) to make an order for wasted costs against a solicitor during the course of litigation. Such costs may be awarded against the solicitor where he has been guilty of 'any improper, unreasonable or negligent act or omission'. In *Ridehalgh v Horsefield* [1994] Ch 205, the Court of Appeal held that 'improper' conduct covered any significant breach of a substantial duty imposed by a relevant code of professional conduct and any other conduct which would be regarded as improper according to a consensus of professional, including judicial, opinion. 'Unreasonable' conduct was said to be conduct which did not permit of reasonable explanation. 'Negligent' conduct meant a failure to act with the competence reasonably to be expected of ordinary members of the profession. In *Persaud v Persaud* [2003] EWCA Civ 394, LTL 6/3/2003, the Court of Appeal held that the fact that a legal representative has given negligent advice to his client is not of itself enough to justify the making of a wasted costs order in favour of an opposing party. To establish liability for wasted costs in such circumstances there needs to be a breach of the legal representative's duty to the court which is akin to abuse of the court's process.

The case of *Persaud* has been considered by the Court of Appeal in *Dempsey v Johnstone* [2003] EWCA Civ 1134, LTL 30/7/2003, which is undecided at the time of writing. Further guidance on the subject can also be found in *Medcalf v Mardell* [2002] UKAL 27, [2003] 1 AC 120 — a case where the House of Lords set aside a wasted costs order which had been made against a barrister.

The Court held that wasted costs orders should only be made under s 51 to the extent that the conduct was directly causative of the wasted costs. Further, even in cases where these preconditions were satisfied, the court still had a discretion — to be exercised judicially — as to whether or not it actually made a wasted costs order.

In *Count Tolstoy-Miloslavsky v Lord Aldington* [1996] 2 All ER 556, a solicitor was ordered to pay wasted costs in circumstances where he acted on a conditional fee in proceedings which were, on their face, an abuse of the process. However, generally speaking the courts have been slow to assume that a hopeless case has been litigated on the advice of a legal representative and it has been said that it is not the function of a legal representative to impose a pre-trial screen through which a litigant has to pass (see *Orchard v South Eastern Electricity Board* [1987] 1 All ER 95).

The procedure to be followed on an application for wasted costs is set out in CPR, r 48.7 (see **Civil Litigation Manual**, 36.6). Applicants for wasted costs orders must bear in mind the principle of proportionality. It has been said that it is not proportionate for the court to spend more time on wasted costs proceedings than had been expended on the substantive proceedings (per Lindsay J, *Re Merc Property Ltd* The Times [1999] 2 BCLC 286.

3.5   Specific defences

The following defences may be of particular relevance in a claim against a solicitor.

3.5.1   Advocates' immunity

By the Courts and Legal Services Act 1990, s 62, any person who is not a barrister, but who lawfully provides any legal services in relation to any proceedings, has the same immunity from liability for negligence in respect of his acts or omissions as he would if he were a barrister lawfully providing those services. This section clearly applies to a solicitor who acts as an advocate.

In *Rondel v Worsley* [1969] 1 AC 191, it was held for public policy reasons that a barrister is immune from an action in negligence brought against him by a client in respect of his conduct and management of a case in court. The reasons given for the immunity included the fact that an advocate owed a duty not just to his client but to the court, the undesirability of re-litigation of issues which had already been decided by a court of competent jurisdiction and a desire for finality in litigation. In *Saif Ali v Sydney Mitchell & Co* [1980] AC 198, it was held that the immunity did not extend to the settling of pleadings by counsel. In that case, the House of Lords adopted a test for advocates' immunity which had been applied by McCarthy P in the New Zealand case of *Rees v Sinclair* [1974] 1 NZLR 180, namely was the work 'so intimately connected with the conduct of the cause in court that it can fairly be said to be a preliminary decision affecting the way the cause is to be conducted when it comes to a hearing?' The House of Lords considered that the immunity should not be given any wider application than was absolutely necessary for the administration of justice.

In *Arthur J S Hall and Co v Simons* [2002] 1 AC 615, the House of Lords held unanimously that the doctrine of advocates' immunity no longer applies to civil proceedings and by a majority that it no longer applies to criminal proceedings. Their lordships held that although *Rondel v Worsley* was rightly decided at the time, the immunity could no longer be sustained in the conditions which prevail today. It is not clear from the case whether or not the abolition of the immunity is of prospective effect only. Lord Hope (who dissented on the question of abolishing the immunity in criminal cases) stated that the decision should not have retrospective effect insofar as it abolished advocates' immunity. However, none of the other judges expressly commented on this question. The existence or otherwise of the immunity was not necessary to determine the outcome of the consolidated appeals heard by the House of Lords in *Arthur J S Hall and Co v Simons* as the defendants in that case were solicitors who had not been acting as advocates.

3.5.2 Abuse of process

In *Hunter v Chief Constable of West Midlands* [1982] AC 529, it was held that where a claim involved a collateral attack upon a final decision of a court of competent jurisdiction in earlier proceedings in which the claimant had a full opportunity of being heard his case would, save in exceptional circumstances, be struck out as an abuse of process.

This principle has provided a fruitful defence for solicitors in many cases where their former client has sought to criticise their conduct of litigation. By way of example, in *Smith v Linskills* [1996] 1 WLR 763, the solicitor's former client was convicted of a criminal offence. Upon his release from prison, he sought to bring an action against his solicitors on the grounds that their preparation and conduct of his defence had been negligent. His claim was held to be an abuse of the process because it called into question the correctness of the original criminal conviction and therefore amounted to a 'collateral' attack on that decision.

The principle in the *Hunter* case has recently been considered by the House of Lords in *Arthur J S Hall and Co v Simons* [2002] 1 AC 615. In that case, the House of Lords emphasised that proceedings involving a collateral attack on an earlier decision were not necessarily an abuse of the process, they just might be. Whilst it would ordinarily be an abuse of the process to bring proceedings which involved asking a civil court to decide that a subsisting criminal conviction was wrong, in general it was not an abuse of process for a client to bring a claim against the lawyers who had represented him in civil proceedings on the grounds that the outcome of those proceedings would have been different but for negligence on their part. Something more was required to make the claims relating to such civil proceedings abusive, for example, the fact that a finding against the solicitor would have wider implications for society generally. Lord Hoffmann gave an example of a case which might be abuse: a defendant is sued for a defamation which he unsuccessfully attempts to justify. He then wishes to sue his solicitor on the basis that if the case had been conducted differently, he would have succeeded in proving that the defamatory statement was true. Such proceedings would have an impact on the reputation of the successful claimant in the original action and so might be considered unfair and an abuse of the process.

A further example of conduct which may amount to an abuse of process is litigating a matter which could and should have been litigated in earlier proceedings. This is sometimes called '*res judicata* in the wider sense'. The question whether or not litigating such a matter in a second claim is abusive is to be judged broadly on the merits of the various competing private and public interests which apply in the particular case, the crucial question being whether the claimant is in all the circumstances misusing or abusing the process of the court (see *Johnson v Gore Wood and Co* [2001] 2 AC 1, where the authorities on this type of abuse of process were comprehensively reviewed by the House of Lords).

3.5.3   Acting on counsel's advice

Where a solicitor has acted upon the advice of properly-instructed counsel, this may provide him with a defence to a claim by his former client. It was said by the Court of Appeal in *Locke v Camberwell Health Authority* (1991) 2 Med LR 249 that for a solicitor without specialist experience in a particular field to rely upon counsel's advice is to make normal and proper use of the Bar. Even where a solicitor has specialist experience, he is entitled to rely upon the advice of properly-instructed specialist counsel unless he considers that there is an important point upon which counsel's opinion is seriously wrong (see *Matrix Securities Ltd v Theodore Goddard* [1998] PNLR 290, where it was held that a solicitor's firm with a specialist tax department was entitled to rely upon the advice of a specialist tax Queen's Counsel).

However, a solicitor is not entitled to rely blindly upon counsel's opinion. He must bring his own experience to bear on matters and exercise his own independent judgment. In *Davy-Chiesman v Davy-Chiesman* [1984] Fam 48, the court made a wasted costs order against a solicitor for failing to draw to the attention of the Legal Aid Board the fact that counsel was proposing to present a claim for ancillary relief in a manner he had previously advised would not succeed.

Similarly, a solicitor will not be excused of negligence if he relies upon counsel's negligent advice on matters which ought to be within his own expertise. For example, in *Bond v Livingstone and Co* [2001] PNLR 692 the defence of a personal injury solicitor that he had relied upon counsel's advice as to the applicable limitation period in a personal injuries action was rejected.

3.5.4   Acting on the client's instructions

Provided that a solicitor has warned his client appropriately of the legal consequences and pit-falls of a particular course of action, he can often successfully plead a defence that he acted upon his client's instructions in pursuing a particular course of action. In *Dutfield v Gilbert H Stephens & Sons* [1988] Fam Law 473, a client in ancillary relief proceedings rejected her solicitor's advice that she should not settle her claim against her exhusband without first fully investigating his assets. In her later claim against her solicitors, Anthony Lincoln J held that whilst it was the duty of a solicitor to inform and advise his client and to ensure that such information and advice was understood by her, it was not part of his duty to force such advice on the client.

On the other hand, where it is apparent that the client is under the undue influence of a third party, there may be some cases where the client's proposed course of action is so disastrous that the solicitor ought to refuse to carry out his instructions. An example is provided by *Powell v Powell* [1900] 1 Ch 243, where it was held that a solicitor owed a duty to refuse to act for a client who insisted upon making a manifestly improper gift to her parent.

3.5.5 Contributory negligence

There is no reason in principle why a plea of contributory negligence under the Law Reform (Contributory Negligence) Act 1945 cannot be relied upon by a solicitor where the claim against him is founded upon an alleged breach of the duty to act with reasonable skill and care. In practice, however, the courts are reluctant to make a finding of contributory negligence against an inexperienced rev. client. *Edwards v Lee* (1991) 141 NLJ 1517 provides a rare example of such a finding being made. In that case, a rogue offered to sell the claimants' car. He gave his solicitor's name as a reference. A member of the public, F, telephoned the claimants a few days later saying that the rogue had tried to sell him their car in suspicious circumstances. At this point the claimants phoned the solicitor for a reference but omitted to tell him about their telephone conversation with F. The solicitor negligently represented that the rogue was reliable notwithstanding the fact that he knew that he was on bail for a number of offences of dishonesty. The solicitor was found liable but the claimants' damages were reduced by 50% because of their failure to mention the telephone conversation.

Arguments on contributory negligence do play a significant role in cases brought by more experienced clients against solicitors — for example, in claims brought by institutional lenders where the solicitor has failed to identify a mortgage fraud. It is not uncommon in such cases for the lender's damages to be reduced on the grounds that its own investigations into the ability and willingness of the borrower to repay were inadequate. The decisions of Blackbourne J in the managed litigation brought by the Nationwide Building Society against a number of firms of solicitors provide examples of findings of contributory negligence in this field (see the 1999 volume of Lloyd's Rep PN).

An area of contentious debate has been the extent to which equitable damages for breach of fiduciary duty by a solicitor can be reduced on the ground that the client has contributed towards his own loss. The Law Reform (Contributory Negligence) Act 1945 does not apply to claims in equity, but in some jurisdictions reductions of equitable damages have been made by analogy (see, for instance, *Day v Mead* [1987] 2 NZLR 443 in New Zealand). However, the position in England would appear to be that such a reduction will not be made, at least not where the breach of fiduciary duty has involved a conscious disloyalty (see *Nationwide Building Society v Balmer Radmore and Others (Introductory Sections)* [1999] Lloyd's Rep PN 241).

3.5.6 Limitation

In both contract and tort the primary limitation period is six years from the date on which the cause of action accrued (Limitation Act 1980, ss 2 and 5 respectively). A cause of action accrues in contract on the date of breach. In tort, it accrues on the date when damage is first suffered. Thus the date upon which time starts to run may be later in tort than in contract.

It should be noted that a claim against a solicitor for the lost opportunity of successfully prosecuting personal injury proceedings is a claim for economic loss. The limitation period is thus six years against the solicitor and not three (see, for example, *Hopkins v MacKenzie* [1995] PIQR P43). However, if it is alleged that the solicitor's negligence itself has *caused* a personal injury, then all of the claims made in the proceedings against him will be subject to the three-year time limit under the Limitation Act 1980, s 11(*Bennett v Greenland* [1998] PNLR 458).

The time limit in tort may be extended under the Limitation Act 1980, s 14A, which provides for an extension of three years from the claimant's date of knowledge of the fact material to his cause of actions subject to a 15-year 'longstop'.

Further, where an action is founded upon the fraud of the defendant or where the defendant has deliberately concealed any fact relevant to the claimant's right of action, then the limitation period does not begin to run until the date upon which the claimant discovers the fraud or could with reasonable diligence discover it (Limitation Act 1980, s 32). The deliberate commission of a breach of duty in circumstances where it is unlikely to be discovered for some time amounts to a deliberate concealment of the facts involved in that breach (s 32(2)). The House of Lords has held that in order to establish such a concealment, the claimant must establish some form of impropriety on the part of the defendant (*Cave v Robinson Jarvis and Rolfe* [2002] 2 WLR 1107).

3.6 Causation and remoteness

3.6.1 Introduction

As in any other claim brought in contract or tort, a claimant must establish a factual connection between the breach and loss about which he complains ('factual causation') and also that the loss is not too remote as a matter of law ('legal causation').

3.6.2 Factual causation

If the claim is that the solicitor gave advice which was wrong or incomplete, the claimant will usually only be able to recover damages if he can prove, on a balance of probabilities, that he would have acted differently had correct or complete advice been given. For example, in *Sykes v Midland Bank Executor and Trustee Co Ltd* [1971] 1 QB 113, the defendant solicitor negligently failed to explain the terms of an underlease to his client. However, in evidence, a partner in the claimant firm conceded that he did not know whether the claimant would have entered into the underlease if properly advised. The Court of Appeal held that in these circumstances the claimant had failed to prove causation.

3.6.3 Legal causation

There are many ways in which the law limits the amount of damages which are recoverable from a defendant. For instance, the law may treat the loss as having been caused by the intervening act of a third party (*novus actus interveniens*), or as not having been reasonably foreseeable or as not falling within the scope of the solicitor's duty.

3.6.3.1 Not within scope of duty

In *Banque Bruxelles Lambert SA v Eagle Star Insurance Co Ltd* [1997] AC 191, a case brought by mortgage lenders against valuers in respect of negligent over-valuations, the House of Lords held that a claimant must show that the defendant owed him a duty in respect of the type of loss which he has suffered. If the loss falls outside the scope of the duty, then it is not recoverable. Thus in *Banque Bruxelles* itself, the liability of each valuer was limited to that part of the lender's loss which was caused by the over-valuation.

This has not proved an easy test to apply in relation to claims against solicitors, particularly in claims brought by lenders. Examples are provided by the decisions of Chadwick J in the claims against solicitors heard under the title of *Bristol & West Building Society v Fancy & Jackson* [1997] 4 All ER 582. Thus in one case (the 'Colin Bishop case'), a solicitor failed to report to his lender client the fact that the security property for the mortgage was the subject of a simultaneous 'back to back' sale whereby the price on the second sale was substantially higher than the price on the first. The borrower defaulted on the mortgage. It was held that although the lender would not have entered into the mortgage transaction had it known of the price differential on the 'back to back' sale, the solicitor's liability was limited to that part of the loss which was caused by the fact that the property was worth less than the lender had believed it to be. He was not liable for all the losses suffered by the lender by reason of the fact that it had entered into the transaction. On the other hand, in another case (the 'Steggles Palmer case'), the solicitor failed to report to his lender client a whole series of matters which called into question the *bona fides* of the borrower. The solicitor was held liable for the whole of the loss suffered by the lender by reason of entering into the transaction. This result can be explained on the basis that protecting his client against fraud fell within the scope of the solicitor's duty.

3.6.3.2   Intervening acts of third parties

The ordinary principles of novus actus interveniens apply to solicitors. In each case the scope of the solicitor's duty will need to be carefully scrutinised. For instance, if the loss has been caused by the fraud of a third party, but it was the solicitor's very duty to protect his client against that fraud, then a plea of novus actus interveniens is unlikely to succeed.

3.6.3.3   Breach the occasion of, but not the cause of, the loss

In some cases the solicitor's breach of duty will be treated as amounting to a background factor which gave rise to an opportunity for the loss being suffered, but which was not a cause of it. For example, in *Young v Purdy* [1997] PNLR 130, a solicitor wrongfully terminated a retainer in matrimonial proceedings. Shortly afterwards, his former client lodged a defective claim form for relief against her former husband, which failed to make any claim for financial provision for herself. Before the form could be remedied, she remarried, thus barring herself from making such a claim. The Court of Appeal held that the solicitor's wrongful termination of his contract merely provided his former client with an opportunity to make an error, but was not the cause of that error.

3.6.3.4   Loss not reasonably foreseeable

Questions of reasonable foreseeability arise in both contract and tort. In the former, foreseeability is judged at the time the contract was made. In the latter, foreseeability is judged at the time the breach of duty was committed.

Precisely what was reasonably foreseeable is likely to depend upon the precise terms of the solicitor's instructions and the extent to which he has knowledge of his client's affairs. For instance, in *Dickinson v Jones Alexander & Co* [1993] 2 FLR 521, the solicitor was instructed in connection with matrimonial proceedings. The solicitor negligently failed to obtain an ouster order compelling the client's former husband to leave the matrimonial home. As a result, the client suffered mental distress. It was held that damages for her mental distress were recoverable because the solicitor had been informed by the client's doctor of the fact that she suffered from an anxiety type of illness related to the disharmony in her marriage. Further mental distress was therefore foreseeable.

3.6.4   Causation in equity

A detailed consideration of the questions of causation which may arise against a solicitor in equity is beyond the scope of this Manual. However, it should be noted that in *Target Holdings Ltd v Redferns* [1996] AC 421, the House of Lords held that rules applicable to traditional trusts had no application to bare trusts in commercial situations which are governed by contracts. Thus, on the facts of that case, the court held that where a solicitor acted in breach of trust by paying mortgage monies to borrowers prior to completion of the underlying purchase, the lender still had to prove that it would not have proceeded with the transaction but for the breach of trust. In *Nationwide Building Society v Balmer Radmore and others (Introductory Sections)* [1999] Lloyd's Rep PN 241, Blackburne J considered the question of causation in relation to breach of fiduciary duties. He held that where a solicitor had breached a fiduciary duty deliberately in bad faith it was not necessary for the client to prove that it would have acted differently had the duty not been breached. In cases which fell short of such deliberate conduct, however, there was no reason why equity should shut its eyes to what the beneficiary would have done had there been no misrepresentation or if appropriate disclosure had been made.

3.7   Measure of damages

3.7.1   Introduction

The general principle is that the damages should be compensatory. In tort, this involves putting the claimant into the position he would have been in had the tort not been committed. In contract, the award of damages should put the claimant into the position he would have been in had the contract not been breached. Where the breach relied upon involves a failure to exercise reasonable care and skill there is in practice no difference between the contractual and tortious measures (see *Esso Petroleum Co Ltd v Mardon* [1976] QB 801).

The courts have adopted a flexible approach to damages in claims against solicitors. In *County Personnel (Employment Agency) Ltd v Alan r Purver & Co* [1987] 1 WLR 916, the Court of Appeal emphasised that the fundamental objective of an award of damages was to put the party who had been injured into the same position as he would have been if he had not been wronged. In order to achieve this objective, rules as to the measure of loss should not be applied mechanistically, nor should rules as to the appropriate date of assessment be so applied.

3.7.2   Illustrations

The following headings are intended to provide a guide as to the approach of the courts in common factual situations. For further examples, reference should be made to Pittaway & Hammerton, *Professional Negligence Cases* and to Jackson & Powell, *Professional Negligence*.

3.7.2.1   Diminution in value

Where the client has bought an asset which is worth less than he believed it to be because of a defect which the solicitor failed to discover, the courts will often award as damages the difference between the price which the client paid and the value of the asset in its true condition. For example, in *Pilkington v Wood* [1953] Ch 770, the client paid £6,000 for a house. His conveyancing solicitor failed to discover that the house was subject to a defect in title. As a result of that defect, its true value was £4,000. The court awarded him damages in the sum of £2,000.

Ford v White [1964] 1 WLR 885 provides an example of a case where on an application of this rule no damages were recoverable. The price at which the land had been offered for sale in that case reflected the fact that it was subject to a restrictive covenant. The purchaser's solicitor negligently informed the purchaser that the land was not subject to restrictive conditions. The purchaser failed to recover any damages because he had not made any over-payment.

3.7.2.2   Costs of extrication

In some cases an award based on the 'diminution in value' principle will not adequately compensate the client. This will be the case, for instance, where the asset had no value and the client has had to incur considerable costs in extricating himself from the situation in which the negligence has placed him. In *County Personnel (Employment Agency) Ltd v Alan R Pulver & Co* [1987] 1 WLR 916, the claimant was offered an underlease of commercial premises. The claimant's conveyancing solicitor failed to inform it that the rent review clause contained in the underlease was unusual and potentially disadvantageous and should be investigated further. Had the claimant been properly advised, it would not have taken the underlease. The transaction proved disastrous. The claimant tried to sell the underlease but was unable to find a buyer. As a result, it had to extricate itself from the situation by surrendering the underlease and paying the landlord a premium. The Court of Appeal held that this premium was recoverable from the solicitor.

3.7.2.3   Loss of a chance

Loss of litigation

The solicitor's negligence may result in his client being deprived of an opportunity to obtain a particular result. This is the case where the negligence results in the client losing the opportunity to prosecute litigation to judgment or a settlement. In *Kitchen v Royal Air Force Association* [1958] 1 WLR 563, the solicitor negligently failed to issue a writ within the relevant limitation period. The result was that the client could not bring an action against the original tortfeasor. In the client's action against the solicitor, the Court of Appeal held that damages should be assessed by evaluating the client's prospects of success against the original tortfeasor. On the facts of the case, the client would have had a 50% chance of success against that person. Thus 50% of the value of that claim would be awarded against the solicitor as damages.

The court will normally assess the value of the original action with reference to a notional trial date. In other words, the court will determine the value of the original action as at the date when, on a balance of probabilities, it would have come to trial had the solicitor not been negligent. This can have important consequences insofar as interest is concerned because the value of the client's claim crystallises on the notional trial date and so he is entitled to interest at the full special account rate as from that date. Prior to the notional trial date, he will only have been entitled, as a head of special damage against the solicitor, to the interest which he would have recovered against the original tortfeasor in the original action had that action not been lost. In a claim for general damages for personal injuries that interest may only have been 2%.

The fixing of a notional trial date may also have important consequences so far as supervening events are concerned. For instance, it is possible that at the notional trial date the court would have assessed damages on the basis that it was unlikely that the claimant would ever recover from his injuries and obtain employment again. Suppose that the claimant then miraculously recovers between the notional trial date and the trial of the solicitor's negligence action. Should the court ignore this fact when assessing the damages payable by the solicitor? In *Charles v Hugh James Jones & Jenkins* [2000] 1 All ER 289, the Court of Appeal said that the court should not ignore such intervening events. In that case, the claimant's injury deteriorated between the notional trial date and the trial of the claim against her solicitor. The Court of Appeal held that damages should be assessed taking into account the deterioration. The court indicated, however, that the position might be different if an entirely new condition manifested itself after the notional trial date.

Lost chances in other contexts

The 'loss of a chance' method of assessment will often be appropriate in cases where the answer to the question 'what would have happened if the solicitor had not been negligent?' depends in part on the hypothetical actions of a third party. For example, in *Allied Maples Group Ltd v Simmons & Simmons* [1995] 1 WLR 1602, the purchaser wished to purchase a number of businesses and their premises. During negotiations with the vendor, the purchaser's solicitor failed to inform his client that a draft warranty which would have protected his client against certain liabilities under assigned leases had been deleted. The trial judge found that if the solicitor had advised the purchaser about the effect of the warranty having been deleted, the purchaser would have taken steps to obtain such a warranty from the vendor. In these circumstances, the defendant contended that the claimant had to prove on a balance of probabilities that the vendor would have agreed to provide such a warranty. The Court of Appeal rejected this argument. They held that where a client's loss depends on the hypothetical action of a third party, either in addition to action by the client or independently of it, his loss should be assessed by evaluating the chance that the third party would have acted in a manner which would have resulted in the client's loss being avoided.

As the Court of Appeal emphasised in the *Allied Maples* case, it is important to draw a distinction between questions of causation and questions of assessment of damages in cases involving a lost opportunity. A claimant must always prove, on the balance of probabilities, that had the defendant not been negligent he himself would have taken a course of action which would have avoided the loss. This is a matter of causation. However, once he has established how he himself would have behaved, he does not need to prove on a balance of probabilities that the third party would have acted in a manner which would have avoided the loss. He need merely show that there was a substantial, rather than speculative, chance that the third party would have so acted. The evaluation of that chance is a matter of quantification of damages.

3.7.2.4   Damages for mental suffering and inconvenience

Where the object of the retainer is to provide peace of mind or freedom from distress, damages for mental suffering may be recoverable. Thus in *Heywood v Wellers* [1976] QB 446, the Court of Appeal held that such damages were recoverable where the solicitor had been retained to obtain a non-molestation order against his client's former boyfriend but negligently failed to do so. On the other hand, in *Hayes v James & Charles Dodd* [1990] 2 All ER 815, the Court of Appeal held that such damages were not recoverable where the solicitor had been retained to act on the purchase of a site which was to be used for a motor repair business. The object of that retainer was not to provide peace of mind or freedom from distress, but to enable the clients to carry on a commercial activity with a view to a profit.

Damages for physical inconvenience may also be awarded in appropriate cases. In *Wapshott v Davies Donovan & Co* [1996] PNLR 361, the solicitor acted on the claimants' behalf when they purchased a flat. Later, when they decided to have a larger family, they decided to sell the flat and purchase larger premises. However, they were unable to do so because of a defect in title which the solicitor had failed to discover when they purchased the flat. The Court of Appeal held that the claimants were entitled to damages from the solicitor for the inconvenience of having to live in over-crowded conditions.

3.7.3   Mitigation

The general law as to mitigation of damages applies to solicitors. As in any other context, the courts are generally reluctant to judge a claimant's actions following a breach of duty as having been unreasonable, but in appropriate cases they will do so. An issue which sometimes arises in actions against solicitors is whether or not the client should have commenced proceedings against a third party before suing his solicitor. In *Pilkington v Wood* [1953] Ch 770, the defendant solicitor acted for the claimant when she purchased her house. The solicitor negligently failed to discover a defect in title, but he contended that his former client had failed to mitigate his losses by suing the vendor under the implied covenant for title. Harman J held that the duty on the client to mitigate his losses did not extend as far as obliging him to embark on complicated and difficult litigation against a third party. However, each case must be judged on its own facts and where the litigation against a third party would have been more straightforward the court may find that a failure to embark upon it amounts to a failure to mitigate. In *Dickinson v Jones Alexander & Co* [1993] 2 FLR 521, the defendant solicitor acted for the claimant in ancillary relief proceedings. As a result of his negligence, the claimant and her children received an inadequate settlement from the claimant's former husband. The court reduced the claimant's damages on the grounds that she had failed to mitigate her losses by failing to pursue an application to vary the maintenance order which had been made in favour of the children.

The courts may also be more willing to find that an experienced client has failed to mitigate its losses. For example, in *Western Trust & Savings Ltd v Clive Travers & Co* [1997] PNLR 295, a solicitor failed to report to his mortgagee client that the security property was owned not just by the borrower, but also by the borrower's wife. The borrower defaulted on the loan and the mortgagee sued the solicitor. The court declined to award the mortgagee any damages, because it had taken no steps to enforce the security against the husband's share of the equity, which would probably have been sufficient to clear his indebtedness. This failure was unreasonable.

Other professional negligence claims

4.1 Introduction

Professional negligence litigation can involve claims against professions other than solic-itors and medical practitioners. This chapter is concerned with claims other than those involving solicitors and medical practitioners. Amongst the defendants most frequently being sued in other professional negligence claims are accountants, architects, barristers, engineers, insurance brokers and surveyors. However, other professional negligence claims are not confined to the above professions. In recent years there has been an expan-sion in the range of professions being sued, and claims against other professionals such as stockbrokers, IT professionals, actuaries, notaries public and patent agents are becoming much more frequent.

As in litigation involving solicitors and medical practitioners, the last two decades have seen a dramatic increase in the volume of other professional negligence claims. One reason for the dramatic increase in claims generally may have been the change in social conditions, particularly an increasing reluctance by the public to defer to the judgment of professionals and a greater preparedness by it to sue. Changes in the economic climate may also be another partial explanation: the collapse of the property market in the late 1980s generated massive litigation by both lenders and purchasers against surveyors (as well as solicitors); the problems in Lloyd's in turn generated further substantial litigation by dissatisfied 'Names'. In addition, periods of recession have caused many clients to turn against their own advisers and, because they were covered by insurance, to treat them as 'deep pockets'.

Sometimes other professional negligence claims (like solicitors' negligence litigation) involves suing professionals from more than one discipline. For example, in construction disputes a quantity surveyor, engineer and architect may all be sued together. In some cases, a professional negligence claim may be an alternative to a commercial claim. For instance, in many insurance disputes where insurers have refused to indemnify a claimant, both the insurance company and insurance broker are likely to be sued in the first instance. In the leading case of *Banque Bruxelles Lambert SA v Eagle Star Insurance Co Ltd* [1997] AC 191, HL, the first defendant was an insurance company and other defendants included a number of surveyors.

One recent phenomenon has been attempts (sometimes successful) by claimants to sue what can best be described as 'quasi-professionals'. These defendants are typically educa-tional psychologists, or social workers, or local authority officials often purporting to act pursuant to statutory powers. Attempts to fix these defendants with liability have often been based on professional negligence principles. (See, for example, *Phelps v Hillingdon*

London Borough Council [2001] 2 AC 619 and *D v East Berkshire Community NHS Trust* [2005] 2 WLR 993.)

This chapter is not intended to set out a detailed discussion of the law and practice relating to other professional negligence claims. For a more detailed consideration, reference should be made to *Jackson and Powell on Professional Negligence*, 5th edition, 2002 or *Professional Negligence and Liability*, Ed Simpson. The objectives of this chapter are:

- To consider some of the common issues which arise in many other professional negligence claims.

- To discuss the general factual background against which a selected number of professions provide their services and the potential areas of liability.

4.2   Common features of other professional negligence claims

Other professional negligence claims raise the same sort of issues as those in solicitors' negligence or clinical negligence litigation. The following are some of the issues which might require consideration.

4.2.1   Can the claim be brought in contract and/or tort?

This is an important issue because the claim may give rise to causes of action in contract, or in the tort of negligence, or both simultaneously (*Henderson v Merrett Syndicates Ltd* [1995] 2 AC 145). The claimant's rights and remedies may differ according to which of the two causes of action is pleaded. For example, the right to recover damages for negligence may survive after the corresponding right to recover damages in contract has become statute-barred. Similarly, a particular head of loss may be recoverable in contract but not in tort; and the amount of damages, which are recoverable in contract under a given head of loss, may exceed those that are recoverable in tort under the same head.

4.2.2   Does the defendant owe the claimant a duty of care in tort?

Where the claimant is unable to sue in contract or faces potential limitation difficulties, this issue will be of crucial importance. In many cases, when determining whether a duty of care is owed, the courts adopt the approach to be found in the accountant's negligence case of *Caparo Industries plc v Dickman* [1990] 2 AC 605, which requires three criteria to be satisfied, namely:

- that the damage is of a kind which the defendant ought reasonably to have foreseen as being likely to arise from his acts or omissions;

- that there is a sufficient degree of 'proximity' or 'neighbourhood' between the claimant class and the defendant class; and

- that the situation is one in which the court considers it fair, just and reasonable that the law should impose a duty of a given scope on the one party for the benefit of the other.

An alternative approach is to determine whether or not the defendant has assumed a responsibility toward the claimant (eg, see *Henderson v Merrett Syndicates Ltd* [1995] 2 AC 145). This is an objective test. In some cases the court will use both the '*Caparo*' and the assumption of responsibility approach. For a more detailed consideration, reference is made to *Clerk and Lindsell on Torts*, 18th edition, 2000, paragraph 7-05 et seq.

4.2.3   What is the appropriate standard of skill and care and has there been a breach?

In other professional negligence claims (as in claims against solicitors and medical practitioners) the usual standard of skill and care which the defendant must meet in order to discharge the obligation placed upon him is the standard of the ordinary skilled man exercising and professing to have that particular skill.

4.2.4   Is causation established?

To recover damages (other than nominal damages for the defendant's breach of contract) a claimant must establish a causal link between the breach in question and the injury or loss for which he claims to be compensated. The claimant must prove this link on the balance of probabilities. In other professional negligence claims arguments about causation may typically arise in a number of different ways. For example, there may be an issue as to whether, had the defendant acted with reasonable skill and care, the claimant would have behaved any differently and thereby avoided the injury or loss which he duly suffered. Thus in surveyor's negligence cases, for example, it may be shown that even if the surveyor had provided the appropriate advice, the claimant would have ignored it in any event and would have bought the property. Secondly, the claimant may be unable to establish, on the balance of probabilities, that the defendant's negligence had any direct effect on the incidence of loss. For example, a surveyor will avoid liability if he adopts the wrong method when valuing a property but provides a figure which is within the spectrum of acceptable values (*Mount Banking Corporation Ltd v Brian Cooper & Co* [1992] 35 EG 123).

4.2.5   Is the claimant's loss one which is recoverable in law?

This might involve considerations of foreseeability and/or scope of duty. In the case of *Banque Bruxelles Lambert SA v Eagle Star Insurance Co Ltd* [1997] AC 191 (HL), the claimant banks' ability to recover losses associated with the collapse of the property market depended upon a precise examination of the scope of the duty owed by the surveyors providing valuations.

4.2.6   Is there any contributory negligence?

Under the Law Reform (Contributory Negligence) Act 1945, s 1, a claimant's damages will be proportionately reduced where he suffers damage as the result partly of his own fault and partly of the fault of any other person. The 1945 Act applies to a claim brought in contract where the defendant's liability under the contract is the same as his liability in negligence (whether or not a claim is actually pursued in negligence); it does not, however, apply where the liability in contract is for breach of a strict duty (*Barclays Bank plc v Fairclough Building Ltd* [1995] QB 214, CA). It is doubted whether the 1945 Act applies where the liability is for breach of a contractual obligation expressed in terms of taking care (or its equivalent), but where there is no corresponding duty of care in tort (see *Forsikringsaktieselskapet Vesta v Butcher* [1989] AC 852). In recent years the defence has gained credence in claims by lenders against solicitors and valuers. In such cases findings of contributory negligence have, for example, been made on the grounds that a lender has adopted an imprudent lending practice (*Nyckeln Finance Co Ltd v Stumpbrook Continuation*

Ltd [1994] 2 EGLR 143) or has relied upon the valuation without conducting further enquiries or investigations (*BNP Mortgages v Key Surveyors Nationwide Ltd* (19 July 1994) — this point was not affected by the subsequent appeal). Contributory negligence has also been successfully raised in claims against insurance brokers (*Youell v Bland Welch & Co Ltd (No 2)* [1990] 2 Lloyd's Rep 431), accountants (*De Meza and Stuart v Apple, Van Straten, Shena and Stone* [1975] 1 Lloyd's Rep 498) and architects (*Kensington and Chelsea and Westminster Area Health Authority v Wettern Composites Ltd* (1984) 31 BLR 57).

4.3 Specific professions

Below is a discussion of the factual framework against which a number of professions provide their services and potential areas of liability.

4.3.1 Barristers

A barrister instructed by a solicitor does not normally enter into a contract either with the solicitor or with the lay client. Any claim will therefore only arise in tort. In certain limited circumstances, a barrister may be instructed directly by members of recognised non-legal professions (eg, surveyors, accountants, etc) or by foreign lawyers. This may give rise to a contractual relationship between the barrister and the person giving the instructions.

A barrister may owe a duty of care to a party who is not his client (*Mathew v Maughold Life Assurance Co Ltd* (1984) 1 PN 142). In that case, a tax barrister was instructed by a solicitor acting for Maughold Life Assurance to advise on a scheme to minimise estate duty payable on the death of Mr Mathew. The judge found that the barrister owed a duty to Mr Mathew, who was present at the conference, to give an explanation of the scheme notwithstanding that his instructions were to advise Maughold Life Assurance.

It is a factual question whether a barrister has in the circumstances of the case acted with reasonable skill and care. The nature of the barrister's instructions and the information he is given when instructed are highly relevant. The fact that a barrister has made a mistake or is guilty of an error of judgement is not sufficient to justify a finding of negligence unless it is an error that 'no reasonably well informed and competent member of that profession would have made' (*Saif Ali v Sydney Mitchell & Co* [1980] AC 198).

Claims against barristers may arise in the context of non-contentious work (eg, advice on tax schemes or conveyancing) or of contentious work. Barristers can no longer rely upon the doctrine of advocate's immunity (*Arthur J S Hall v Simons and Co* [2002] 1 AC 615). In addition, barristers face a potential liability for wasted costs (Supreme Court Act 1981, s 51; Prosecution of Offences Act 1985, s 19A).

4.3.2 Surveyors

The majority of reported cases involving surveyors are concerned with the provision of valuation and/or surveying services. Typically the claimant is either a purchaser who buys a property relying upon a valuation and/or survey provided by the surveyor, or it is a financial institution lending money to a borrower and the surveyor values property, which is to be the security for the loan.

In many cases a contractual duty to take reasonable care will arise as a result of a contract between the surveyor and the claimant. Where there is no contract, a tortious duty may arise where reliance can be shown. In *Smith v Eric S Bush* [1990] 1 AC 831, the House of

Lords decided that a valuer, who was instructed by the mortgagee, also owed a tortious duty of care to the prospective mortgagor of the property being valued because he knew that his report would probably be relied upon by the mortgagor.

Expert evidence will usually be required to determine whether the surveyor has been negligent. In the surveyor's case of *Zubaida v Hargreaves* [1995] 1 EGLR 127, Hoffmann LJ describes the test for negligence as 'whether (the valuer) has acted in accordance with practices which are regarded as acceptable by a respectable body of opinion in his profession'. In forming a view, the expert has to consider both the relevant RICS or ISVA guidelines at the time and the type of report being provided (eg, a simple valuation, a house buyer's report, a survey, etc). It is of crucial importance to analyse the type of service which the surveyor agreed to provide, eg, a valuation or a valuation plus survey. This is because the functions of valuing a property and surveying it are quite distinct and criticisms as to condition may be irrelevant to the question of value.

In surveyors' negligence claims, causation/reliance arguments are often raised by defendants. These might include the argument that the claimant would have proceeded with the purchase (and paid the same price) had he known the true state of the property. Another argument, often raised by defendants in the context of valuation disputes, is that the surveyor's final figure is within a permissible range of values (*Mount Banking v Brian Cooper* [1992] 35 EG 123). Such range may often be as much as 15% either side of the 'true value' of the property in question.

4.3.3 Insurance brokers

The insurance industry is a large and complex one. Within it operate a large number of different professionals, including brokers, agents (including members' agents and managing agents at Lloyd's), adjusters and assessors. It is beyond the scope of this Manual to analyse each of the different types and therefore this section is only concerned with claims against insurance brokers. Many claims against insurance brokers will be connected with claims against the insurer on the policy where the insurer has argued that it is entitled to avoid liability. The insured typically claims against the broker on the alternative basis that if the insurer is entitled to avoid liability, that is the result of a (negligent) failure on the part of the broker.

The broker is presumed to be the agent of the insured (*Rozanes v Bowen* (1928) 32 Ll L Rep 98, CA). The relationship between broker and his client is assumed to be a contractual one. Where a client pays no fee to the broker, the consideration for the contract is the broker's opportunity to draw commission from insurers in return. There will always be a term, whether express or implied, that the broker will exercise reasonable skill and care in the performance of his duties under the contract. In addition, the parties may agree further more onerous obligations. In any event, the broker will owe his client a concurrent duty of care in tort (*Youell v Bland Welch (No 2)* [1990] 2 Lloyd's Rep 431, *Henderson v Merrett Syndicates Ltd* [1995] 2 AC 145). Given the contractual relationship between client and broker, a claim in tort is unlikely to add anything to the claim unless there are limitation problems.

Often brokers will be called to give evidence as to the reasonableness (or otherwise) of the defendant broker's actions. Such experts are likely to make reference to relevant codes such as the code of conduct of the Insurance Brokers Registration Council. The courts often regard such codes of practice as being highly relevant (see *Harvest Trucking Co Ltd v Davis* [1991] 2 Lloyd's Rep 638).

The most common situations in which brokers find themselves being sued relate to the failure to obtain suitable, or indeed any, insurance cover (*Smith v Lascelles* (1788) 2 TR 187).

Other situations include failing to provide adequate advice or information to the client. This might be advice about the appropriateness of the insurer or about the extent of coverage (*Osman v J Ralph Moss Ltd* [1970] 1 Lloyd's Rep 313). A third category of cases concern the failure of the broker to disclose material facts to the insurer, or to misrepresent facts, with the result that the insurer subsequently avoids for material non-disclosure or misrepresentation (*Coolee Ltd v Wing, Heath & Co* (1930) 47 TLR 78).

4.3.4 Accountants

Accountants perform a variety of different tasks. In addition to the preparation of accounts, they investigate and audit company accounts pursuant to the provisions of the various Companies Acts. They also provide financial advice, particularly on tax matters. Accountants often carry out administrative functions, particularly in connection with insolvency and trust matters. As auditors of a company's accounts, accountants have a statutory duty (Companies Act 1985, s 235(2) as substituted by the Companies Act 1989, s 119(1)) to examine and verify the original accounting records and to give an opinion as to whether the annual balance sheet and profit and loss account have been properly prepared and whether the accounts give a true and fair view of the company's affairs. In addition, the Companies Act 1985, s 256 (as inserted by Companies Act 1989) gives statutory recognition to the existence of accounting standards by requiring companies to state whether or not their accounts have been prepared in accordance with those standards. Such standards are to be found in documents like the Statements of Standard of Accountancy Practice or Statements of Auditing Standards. Whilst a breach by an accountant or auditor of the duties set out in these documents is not conclusive, the courts are likely to regard them as being highly relevant. In *Cheyham & Co v Littlejohn & Co* [1987] BCLC 303, Woolf J stated that:

Whilst they are not conclusive, so that a departure from their terms necessarily involves a breach of the duty of care, and they are not as the explanatory forward makes clear rigid rules, they are very strong evidence as to what is the proper standard which should be adopted and unless there is some justification, a departure from this will be regarded as constituting a breach of duty.

Where there is a contractual relationship between the claimant and the defendant accountant, there will usually be no problem in establishing a contractual duty to take reasonable care. Where, however, there is no contractual relationship, the existence of a tortious duty becomes of crucial importance. In a number of accountants' negligence cases, the claimant will be a third party seeking to rely upon information provided by the accountant in its auditing capacity which it alleges was incorrect and negligently given. In the case of *Caparo Industries plc v Dickman* [1990] 2 AC 605, the House of Lords set out the three criteria required before a finding of a tortious duty was likely to occur (see **4.2.2**). This case concerned an unsuccessful attempt by a third-party purchaser to recover compensation for losses sustained as a result of acquiring shares in Fidelity plc relying on Fidelity accounts, which had been audited and prepared by the defendant accountants.

Common situations in which accountants find themselves being sued for negligence include their failure to discover fraud (*Barings plc v Coopers & Lybrand* [1997] PNLR 179), their failure to give proper tax advice (*Owen Investments Ltd v Bennett, Nash, Wolf & Co* (1984) 134 NLJ 887), missing a time limit for tax returns (*Dyck v FMA Farm Management* [1996] 3 WWR 509), and negligently valuing shares in a company (*Burgess v Purchase & Sons (Farms) Ltd* [1983] Ch 216).

4.3.5   Architects, engineers and quantity surveyors

In a typical case an owner of property will retain all or a combination of these professionals, both to provide advice before he enters into a construction contract and thereafter to supervise and administer the contract. The advice sought usually relates to the design of the works, their practicability, the preparation of preliminary drawings, costs estimates, the type of standard form contract which is most appropriate and whether variations to those standard form contracts are necessary. Thereafter, the professional will be required to secure tenders and to prepare all necessary documentation for the purposes of securing a properly founded and competitive tender. The owner will then enter into a separate contract with the contractor and will require the engineer or architect to supervise or administer the works. As supervisor or administrator, the professional will usually be required to certify the contractor's entitlement to payment, advise as to the steps to be taken in relation to defective work, and be responsible for the eventual certification of the works effected as having been executed in accordance with the contract.

There will usually be a contract between the client and the professionals whose advice he is receiving. The standard form contracts issued by the Royal Institute of Architects, the Royal Institution of Chartered Surveyors or the Association of Consulting Engineers form the basis of most retainers of the relevant professionals.

In addition, architects and other building professionals owe a tortious duty of care not to cause personal injury to whose who they could foresee might be injured as a result of their negligence (*Eckersley v Binnie & Partners* (1988) 18 Con LR 1). Although building professionals will not be liable to third parties for economic loss caused by reason of a building being defective (*Murphy v Brentwood District Council* [1991] 1 AC 398), they will be liable if the claimant can establish a tortious duty on the normal *Hedley Byrne* principles (*Hedley Byrne & Co Ltd v Heller & Partners Ltd* [1964] AC 465).

A building professional must act with reasonable skill, care and diligence to be expected of an ordinary competent and skilled member of his profession. In *Eckersley v Binnie & Partners*, Bingham LJ stated that:

a professional man should command the corpus of knowledge which forms part of the professional equipment of the ordinary member of his profession. He should not lag behind other ordinary assiduous and intelligent members of his profession in knowledge of new advances, discoveries and developments in his field. He should be alert to the hazards and risks inherent in any professional task he undertakes to the extent that other ordinary competent members of his profession would be alert. He must bring to any professional task he undertakes no less expertise, skill and care than other ordinarily competent members would bring but need bring no more. The standard is that of the reasonable average. The law does not require of a professional man that he be a paragon combining the qualities of polymath and prophet.

The standard of care is usually established by reference to the general practice of the profession in question. An unqualified professional will be judged by the standards of a reasonably competent and qualified practitioner (*Cardy v Taylor* (1994) 38 Con LR 79). Conversely, where a client pays for high skills, the relevant standard remains that of the ordinary competent and skilled practitioner (*Wimpey Construction Ltd v Poole* [1984] 2 Lloyd's Rep 499).

There are a wide range of situations in which building professionals find themselves being sued. One of the more obvious situations is where it is alleged that architects had produced a defective design (*Victoria University of Manchester v Hugh Wilson* (1984) 2 Con LR 43). Another obvious situation is where there has been an escalation in the building costs and the complaint is made that the building professional has negligently failed to control costs; this might be because the architect or engineer has failed to produce a design at a reasonable cost (*Gordon Shaw Concrete Products v Design Collaborative Ltd* (1985) 35 CCLT 100) or because the quantity surveyor has failed to check rates or consider the reasonableness of quotations (*Tyrer v District Auditor for Monmouthshire* (1973) 230 EG 973). Building professionals are often sued for failing to carry out an adequate site examination (*Gable House Estates Ltd v Halpern Partnership* (1995) 48 Con LR 1). The other two common areas of litigation concern inadequate supervision/administration of the contract and negligent certification/valuation (*Sutcliffe v Chippendale & Edmondson* (1971) 18 BLR 149).

Part II

Conduct and management of proceedings

An overview of procedure

5.1 Introduction

The more one studies procedural law, the more one realises that it is central to a living system of law. Substantive law is merely the skeleton — it is the procedure that is the flesh, blood and above all, the nervous system. (Sir Robin Jacob, a judge of the Chancery Division, *The Forensic Accountant*, KPMG).

The Civil Procedure Rules have been in force for approaching a decade now and judges and lawyers alike are well used to them. It may seem odd in this context to continue to revisit the reasons for their introduction. Nevertheless, those reasons are fundamental to the way in which the courts interpret and implement the rules and a brief look back does help to give the new advocate an understanding of the approach of the judges and more senior advocates.

The impact of the civil procedure reforms on the conduct of civil cases has been farreaching. Altering processes has changed the perception and the dispensation of justice. In certain respects we have moved away from a truly adversarial system towards a system which encourages co-operation and compromise between the parties. Perhaps this reflects a more mature society's approach to justice or perhaps it is no more than a compromise itself, based on pragmatic realism. Whatever the rights or wrongs of this, the fact is that procedure affects the outcome of cases. As counsel you must be able to take advantage of the prevailing culture, the procedural rules, the practice directions, protocols, and guidance to the maximum benefit of your client.

This part of the Manual follows the chronological path from the pre-action legal investigation of a complaint up until its resolution. This includes:

- Early identification of the issues.
- Drafting statements of case.
- Track allocation and other court directions.
- Management and use of evidence for liability and quantum.
- Certain important interim applications.

In order to understand the rules of procedure and accompanying guidance, it is important to see the context within which they came about. This will also give you an insight into the culture within which the judges are trained and encouraged to apply the rules.

5.2 Failings of the former system

It came as no surprise that the previous rules of civil procedure were to be changed. Lord Woolf's inquiry into the civil justice system identified the following key problems:

- excessive cost;
- delay;
- complexity.

He considered that these were endemic within the system because lack of court control over the process of litigation lead to an adversarial culture within which issues of cost, pace and complexity had low priorities.

5.3 Aims of the reforms

The guiding lights for the rule makers in the reform of civil procedure could be summarised as the following principles:

- accessibility;
- proportionality;
- pace.

5.4 Means of achieving the aims

In order to influence the whole culture of civil procedure the founding principles are made explicit at the outset of the rules in the Overriding Objective (CPR, Part 1). All procedural decisions made by the courts and the parties are required to be made in a way which gives effect to or furthers this rule. You will address the principles set out in it implicitly if not explicitly in every interim application, application for directions or case management conference which you attend. You should know the rule backwards:

1.1 THE OVERRIDING OBJECTIVE

(1) These Rules are a new procedural code with the overriding objective of enabling the court to deal with cases justly.

(2) Dealing with a case justly includes, so far as is practicable —

    (a) ensuring that the parties are on an equal footing;

    (b) saving expense;

    (c) dealing with the case in ways which are proportionate —

        (i) to the amount of money involved;

        (ii) to the importance of the case;

        (iii) to the complexity of the issues; and

        (iv) to the financial position of each party;

    (d) ensuring that it is dealt with expeditiously and fairly; and

    (e) allotting to it an appropriate share of the court's resources, while taking into account the need to allot resources to other cases.

In order to achieve such ends, it was considered crucial to switch the control of the conduct of litigation from the parties to the court. The court is to be the *manager* of cases. The principal ways in which the aims are designed to be met is through an insistence upon:

- early preparation of the case;
- early identification of the issues;
- early and full disclosure;
- transparency;
- issue and service of the claim *after* extensive preparation;
- fuller pleadings (now statements of case);
- court control of the pace of litigation;
- strict and early timetabling of cases;
- control of expert evidence;
- emphasis on resolution of cases by means other than trial;
- management of the trial itself.

This management of civil disputes is implemented and encouraged through a variety of means in professional negligence cases:

- Civil Procedure Rules;
- practice directions;
- protocols;
- guidance from specialist public bodies and agencies and the promotion of a new culture of risk management and dispute resolution by those bodies;
- an increasing insistence upon specialist panels of solicitors and counsel by the funding bodies.

The following chapters consider each stage of the process identified above in relation to solicitors' negligence and clinical negligence actions, making reference to the relevant rules and guidance.

6

Early identification of the issues

6.1 Introduction

As discussed in previous chapters the aim of the Civil Procedure Rules is to encourage cost-effective, proportionate and accessible dispute resolution between parties. In particular, the parties are encouraged to settle disputes or, where litigation is unavoidable, to litigate efficiently in accordance with strict and predictable timetables. Early identification of the issues between the parties is a crucial aspect of this process; some would say the most important aspect. It encourages parties to make early and informed estimates of the value of claims and the risks involved in litigation. It is hoped that this in turn leads to less adversarial posturing and to informed settlement offers or case management. Pre-action behaviour is managed in two ways:

- pre-action protocols.
- pre-action disclosure rules.

This chapter considers the application of those two aspects of pre-action conduct to professional negligence and personal injury litigation. Detailed discussion of the rules and protocols can be found in the *Civil Litigation Manual* and reference should *always* be made to the practitioners' texts of civil rules.

6.1.1 How does this affect counsel?

When advising in writing or in conference during the early stages of a case, you need to know what information is or should be made available at each point and you should understand the requirements for the conduct of the client's case. Must a letter be written now? How and when should you seek further evidence? Is a schedule of loss required? What documents can you now get from the other side?

You might be instructed to seek a court order for pre-action disclosure.

6.2 Pre-action protocols

Protocols are addressed in the Civil Procedure Rules 1998 by a specific practice direction (see **Appendix 1**). It requires parties to follow any relevant pre-action protocols which appear in its schedule. There are currently six approved pre-action protocols, four of which are relevant here: the Pre-action Protocol for Personal Injury Claims (which applies to fast track personal injury cases) (see **Appendix 2**); the Pre-action Protocol for the Resolution of Clinical Disputes (see **Appendix 3**); the Pre-action Protocol for Construction and Engineering Disputes (including professional negligence claims against architects, engineers and quantity surveyors) (see **Appendix 4**); and the Professional Negligence Pre-action Protocol (see **Appendix 5**).

Where there is no relevant pre-action protocol the Practice Direction — Protocols requires civil litigation to be conducted in accordance with the spirit of the available pre-action protocols. This requirement is set out at para 4.1:

PRE-ACTION BEHAVIOUR IN OTHER CASES

4.1   In cases not covered by any approved protocol, the court will expect the parties, in accordance with the overriding objective and the matters referred to in r 1.1(2)(a), (b) and (c), to act reasonably in exchanging information and documents relevant to the claim and generally in trying to avoid the necessity for the start of proceedings.

The protocols set out steps which the parties to the litigation are expected to follow prior to issuing proceedings. In particular, they standardise and timetable the exchange of information and evidence. Parties can be penalised for non-compliance should the matter come to court at a later date. The protocols have a discursive rather than a strict legalistic style. You should familiarise yourself with them.

6.2.1   Aims of the protocols

It is a part of the philosophy behind the new civil procedure culture to make the intentions or aims behind the rules and guidance explicit. The relevant parts are set out below:

6.2.1.1   Practice Direction — Protocols

1.4   The objectives of pre-action protocols are:

(1)   to encourage the exchange of early and full information about the prospective legal claim,

(2)   to enable parties to avoid litigation by agreeing a settlement of the claim before the commencement of proceedings,

(3)   to support the efficient management of proceedings where litigation cannot be avoided.

6.2.1.2   Pre-action Protocol for Personal Injury Claims

1.2   The aims of pre-action protocols are:
- *more pre-action contact between the parties*
- *better and earlier exchange of information*
- *better pre-action investigation by both sides*
- *to put the parties in a position where they may be able to settle cases fairly and early without litigation*
- *to enable proceedings to run to the court's timetable and efficiently, if litigation does become necessary.*

1.3   The concept of protocols is relevant to a range of initiatives for good litigation and pre-litigation practice, especially:
- *predictability in the time needed for steps pre-proceedings*
- *standardisation of relevant information, including documents to be disclosed.*

6.2.1.3   Pre-action Protocol for the Resolution of Clinical Disputes

The extract below is a summary, please refer to the actual protocol for the full text:

2.1   The general aims of the protocol are:
- *to maintain/restore the patient/healthcare provider relationship;*
- *to resolve as many disputes as possible without litigation.*

2.2   The specific objectives are:
- *openness*
- *timeliness*
- *awareness of options for resolution other than litigation.*

6.3 Identification of issues through exchange of information

The protocols encourage the early identification of issues through an exchange of letters between the potential parties and an exchange where possible of schedules of loss.

6.3.1 Letter of claim

First, the claimant should write a 'letter of claim'. (The protocols each provide a template or suggested format for a letter of claim.)

In essence the letter should contain:

- a summary (and where appropriate a chronology) of the facts;
- the main allegations of negligence or breach of contract;
- a description of the injuries or other damage;
- an outline of the financial loss and an indication of the heads of loss claimed.

Other relevant considerations for the letter of claim are:

(a) The letter should refer to and where possible include any relevant documents.

(b) The letter might come before or after some pre-action disclosure of documents. In a personal injury case, the letter is likely to come prior to the disclosure of many documents. Often the categories of documents sought are identified in this initial letter of claim. In a clinical negligence case, the letter of claim is likely to come after there has been fairly extensive consideration of disclosed documents (eg, medical notes). In other professional negligence cases, there may be an unwillingness to disclose documents until the nature of the allegations has been made clear in the letter of claim.

(c) It should give sufficient information to enable the proposed defendant to investigate the claim and to give a broad assessment of the risk.

(d) Consideration should be given to the instruction of a joint expert.

(e) Consideration as to the use of possible alternative dispute resolution should also be given at this stage.

(f) If an offer to settle is made in this letter then it should generally contain a schedule of loss, supporting documents and evidence in support of the offer, for example, an expert's report on the condition and prognosis of the potential claimant's injuries.

6.3.2 Letter of response

The potential defendant must acknowledge receipt of the letter of claim within the time prescribed by the protocol (varies between 14 and 21 days). The potential defendant then has a period to investigate the claim and must respond fully within the period stipulated by the relevant protocol (three months in the case of the Pre-action Protocol for Personal Injury Claims). In this letter the defendant must state which, if any, parts of the claim he admits and whether he intends any admission to be binding. Where he denies any part of the claim, he must give reasons for the denial commenting specifically upon the allegations of negligence or the issues of causation which he denies and setting out his own case.

In addition, the defendant would be well advised to:

- Refer to and where possible include any relevant documents.

- Seek further information or documents from the claimant if the information/ disclosure has so far been inadequate.
- Consider the instruction of a joint expert.
- Consider alternative dispute resolution.
- If appropriate, make an offer to settle.

6.3.3   Letter of settlement

The letter of settlement is only mentioned in the Professional Negligence Pre-action Protocol and may be sent as an alternative, or in addition to, the letter of response. It should identify the issues which the professional believes are likely to remain in dispute and those which are not; make an offer of settlement or identify further information required before proposals can be formulated; and provide copies of documents relied upon. Where a letter of settlement is received by a claimant the parties have six months for negotiations.

6.3.4   Status of letters of claim, response and settlement

6.3.4.1   With or without prejudice?

The specimen letters annexed to the protocols do not include a statement that they are without prejudice and so it should be assumed that these letters will normally be open letters. The only protocol to address this matter is the Professional Negligence Pre-action Protocol. This states that the letter of claim will normally be an open letter and that a letter of settlement will normally be a without prejudice letter. All letters which include an offer to settle are likely to be headed 'without prejudice'.

6.3.4.2   Are the letters like statements of case?

The letters are not intended to have the same formal status as statements of case. This is expressly stated in most of the protocols (see the Pre-action Protocol for Personal Injury Claims, para 2.9).

6.3.4.3   What happens where a party alters a case at the pleading stage?

The Pre-action Protocol for the Resolution of Clinical Disputes says that a party should not be penalised for altering the case between letter of claim and statements of case (para 3.20). The Pre-action Protocol for Personal Injury Claims says that a point should not be taken upon such an alteration unless there has been an attempt to mislead other parties (para 2.9). The Professional Negligence Protocol says that, in its discretion, the court can give sanctions for material differences between the letter and the statement of case (para B5.3).

6.3.5   Schedule of loss

It clearly assists parties to identify issues and to reach early settlement if a schedule of loss can be drafted and served on the defendant before proceedings even start. The protocols encourage this, for example, the Pre-action Protocol for Personal Injury Claims states:

SPECIAL DAMAGES

   3.13 The claimant will send to the defendant as soon as practicable a schedule of special damages and supporting documents, particularly where the defendant has admitted liability.

The Pre-action Protocol for the Resolution of Clinical Disputes is less definite in relation to the schedule but it recommends that a schedule of loss and supporting documents are sent wherever an offer to settle the case is made by the claimant (para 3.22). Neither the Professional Negligence nor the Construction and Engineering Disputes protocols specifically mentions schedules of loss, although it is clear that this information should be included in the letter of claim.

6.4 Identification of issues through voluntary disclosure

6.4.1 Documents

The protocols encourage early exchange of relevant information including all documents for which an order for pre-action disclosure could be made.

The Pre-action Protocol for Personal Injury Claims states:

DISCLOSURE OF DOCUMENTS

2.10 The aim of the early disclosure of documents by the defendant is not to encourage 'fishing expeditions' by the claimant, but to promote an early exchange of relevant information to help in clarifying or resolving issues in dispute . . .

The Pre-action Protocol for the Resolution of Clinical Disputes gives guidance as to the type of documents which a claimant should seek (medical records, X-rays, hospital reports about the patient, etc) and standard forms for the request and response to request for hospital records. The Pre-action Protocol for Personal Injury Claims gives detailed lists of relevant documents in different types of cases. See Annex B in **Appendix 2**.

Failure to comply with the protocols' requirements in relation to early disclosure can lead to costs penalties in subsequent applications to the court and is likely to result in an application for pre-action disclosure under the CPR, Part 31.

6.4.2 Experts

The use of expert evidence is discussed in detail in later chapters. It is worth noting the following here:

(a) The Pre-action Protocol for Personal Injury Claims encourages and promotes the use of jointly instructed experts or, where a claimant has instructed its own expert, the defendant is encouraged to ask questions of the claimant's expert and/or to agree the report and so avoid the need to instruct a further expert (paras 2.11, 2.12 and 3.14–3.21).

(b) The Pre-action Protocol for the Resolution of Clinical Disputes recognises the need for experts in three areas: breach of duty and causation condition and prognosis and valuing aspects of the claim. The protocol is not prescriptive about the use of experts in clinical negligence cases and it acknowledges the fact that separate experts will often be required. It encourages parties to consider the use of a joint expert in connection with condition and prognosis (para 4).

(c) The Professional Negligence Pre-action Protocol has a completely flexible attitude towards the instruction of experts (paras B.7 and C.6) and the Pre-action Protocol for Construction and Engineering Disputes does not prescribe any procedure for the instruction of experts.

6.5 Encouragement to settle

All of the pre-action protocols encourage parties and legal representatives to enter into negotiations before proceedings are commenced. The Pre-action Protocol for Construction and Engineering Disputes states that as soon as possible after receipt by the claimant of the defendant's letter of response the parties should normally meet to consider the issues and how they might be resolved (para 5.1). The pre-action protocols also encourage the parties to consider alternative dispute resolution.

The Practice Direction — Protocols sets out penalties for failure to settle where proceedings have been started without efforts being made to settle claims which could otherwise have been avoided (para 2.3).

Once the action has begun, the court has the power to stay proceedings for a period of time to allow for settlement to be explored.

6.6 Commencing proceedings

If the claimant does not receive a response to his letter of claim within the prescribed time limit then he is entitled to issue proceedings. Likewise a claimant may issue proceedings if the defendant's letter of response denies the claim. In the case of construction and engineering disputes parties should only issue proceedings after they have met to discuss the issues and have been unable to resolve them.

The protocols do not alter statutory time limits for starting proceedings and therefore a party should commence proceedings if limitation is about to expire even if the relevant protocol has not been complied with.

6.7 Failure to comply with pre-action protocols

Compliance with the relevant pre-action protocols may have a bearing on the directions made by the court and orders for costs. The protocols may be breached in a number of ways:

- in a personal injury case, by instructing one's own expert having unreasonably objected to every expert on a list of experts provided by the other party;
- by failing to provide sufficient information when requested to do so;
- by failing to respond to a letter of claim within the specified time fixed for that purpose.

It is necessary to be familiar with the requirements of the pre-action protocols in order to be able to make submissions on directions in the light of non-compliance with the relevant protocols. The following rules are important in this regard:

(a) CPR, r 3.1(4), provides that the court may take into account whether or not a party has complied with any relevant pre-action protocol when it gives directions.

(b) CPR, r 3.1(5) and (6), give the court the power to order a party to pay a sum of money into court where that party has failed to comply with a pre-action protocol without good reason.

(c) CPR, r 44.3(5)(a), provides that the court may take into consideration the extent to which a party has complied with a pre-action protocol when exercising its discretion as to costs.

(d) Practice Direction — Protocols, r 2.3, lists the following orders which a court can make against a party at fault where proceedings have been commenced or where costs have been incurred unnecessarily:

    (i) an order that the party at fault pay the costs of the proceedings or part of the costs;

    (ii) an order that those costs be paid on an indemnity basis;

    (iii) an order depriving a claimant of interest or part of the interest on the sum of damages awarded;

    (iv) an order against an unsuccessful defendant to pay interest on damages at a higher rate than would have been otherwise awarded (although not exceeding 10% above base rate).

6.8 Pre-action disclosure

6.8.1 Provisions

(See the *Civil Litigation Manual*, **Chapter 20**, for detailed discussion of the provisions.)

Pre-action disclosure is now available in all civil cases. The application must be supported by evidence and made in accordance with CPR, Part 23. Pursuant to CPR, r 31.16, the applicant must satisfy the court that:

- should an action start both the applicant and the respondent are likely parties;

- the disclosure sought would be standard disclosure within those proceedings;

- pre-action disclosure is desirable in order to dispose fairly of the proceedings, to assist in resolution of the dispute without proceedings or to save costs.

6.8.2 Rationale

Before the civil procedure reforms, pre-action disclosure was available in personal injury cases but not in other civil cases. This extension is significant and is in line with the emphasis on early identification of issues between the parties.

6.8.3 Extent of disclosure

Pre action disclosure is limited to standard disclosure which is defined in CPR, r 31.6 and discussed in the *Civil Litigation Manual* at **20.4.2**. This is as much as will be disclosed in the action for many cases and will always be sufficient to enable parties to form a view of the strengths and weaknesses of their case and the likely value of the claim.

6.8.4   How to use CPR, r 31.16, to best advantage

Don't use it if you can avoid it! If you can get what you are seeking by reminding your opponent of the requirements under the pre-action protocol and the sanctions for non-compliance then don't risk a costs order against your client by going to court. This is an application which should only be made after the protocol routes have failed.

6.8.5   Next steps

If all parties have complied with the pre-action protocols and litigation is still the only route forward you should be in a position to state your client's case fully and accurately and to comply thereafter with a fairly strict timetable.

7

Court control

This chapter discusses the control of cases by the court from the allocation stage to trial with particular emphasis on case management conferences.

7.1 Allocation

If the parties are unable to settle as a result of the pre-action protocol procedure then proceedings may be commenced. After the close of pleadings the preliminary stage of case management is allocation to one of the three tracks: small claims, fast track or multi-track, or for a disposal hearing. The rules relating to track allocation are considered in detail in the *Civil Litigation Manual*. Below is a brief reminder of how cases are allocated to the fast or multi-track (the small claims track is hardly ever relevant to cases of professional negligence).

When a defendant to an action files a defence the court will serve an allocation questionnaire on each party (CPR, r 26.3(1)). On the basis of the allocation questionnaire the court will allocate the case to one of the tracks or for a disposal hearing.

7.1.1 The fast track

Under CPR, r 26.6(4) and (5), the fast track is for claims which:

- do not qualify for the small claims track;
- have a value of not more than £15,000;
- the court considers are likely to last for no longer than a day; and
- the court considers do not require expert evidence in more than two fields (each party is limited to one expert in each field).

The majority of personal injury claims are allocated to this track. Professional negligence claims and certainly clinical negligence claims tend not to be allocated to this track.

7.1.2 The multi-track

The multi-track sweeps up all other claims which have not been allocated to either the small claims or the fast track. This tends to be the normal track for professional negligence claims as they are frequently complex.

7.2 Case management

7.2.1 Fast track

Under CPR, r 28.2(1) the court will give directions for the management of the case when it allocates it to the fast track setting a timetable for steps to be taken between the giving of the directions and the trial. The Pre-action Protocol for Personal Injury Claims is designed to ensure that a considerable amount of the preparation for a fast track case is undertaken before proceedings are commenced so that the strict timetable provided for on the fast track can be adhered to. It is intended that directions be given without the need for a hearing. However, PD 28, para 2.3, provides that the court will hold a hearing to give directions whenever it appears necessary or desirable to do so. In practice, directions hearings are frequently held.

7.2.2 Multi-track

When a case is allocated to the multi-track the court may either give directions for the management of the case setting a timetable up to trial or it may fix a date for a case management conference or pre-trial review (CPR, r 29.2(1)).

7.2.3 Case management conference

7.2.3.1 Purpose of the CMC

The case management conference will be used by the court to exercise its powers of management (as set out in CPR, r 3.1) in order to further the overriding objective. The case management conference provides it with an opportunity to identify the issues, dispose summarily of others, encourage the parties to co-operate with one another, fix a timetable and deal with as many aspects of the case as it can on one occasion (see CPR, r 1.4).

Proposals for the management of proceedings may be agreed between the parties. However, in accordance with CPR, r 29.4(1), the court will only approve the parties' proposals without a hearing if it considers that the proposals are suitable.

PD 29, para 5.3, sets out topics which the court is likely to consider at the case management conference:

(1) whether the claimant has made clear the claim he is bringing, in particular the amount he is claiming, so that the other party can understand the case he has to meet . . .

This presents an opportunity for one party to put pressure on another to clarify his case. An application may be made that a party clarify his case in order to expose a weakness. In some cases it may not be clear exactly what claim is being brought. In others, the claimant may not have set out his case on quantum: in personal injury actions or clinical negligence claims the claimant may have been speculative or vague in setting out special damages or future loss. In solicitors' negligence cases this would be the time to clarify, for example, how the claimant quantifies its loss of a chance claim (eg, what does it say were its chances of success in the previous case?)

(2) whether any amendments are required to the claim, a statement of case or any other document . . .

It may be that in the light of expert evidence there is a need to amend a statement of case. Thus a claimant may wish to amend a schedule of loss on the basis that future loss is likely to be greater than initially anticipated or a defendant may wish to amend its defence in the light of expert evidence to allege, for example, that a claimant is malingering.

(3) what disclosure of documents, if any, is necessary . . .

The aim of the pre-action protocols is that disclosure should have taken place at a much earlier stage. However, pre-action protocols only exist in a limited number of areas and as the case progresses it can become apparent that further documentation will be needed.

(4) what expert evidence is reasonably required in accordance with rule 35.1 and how and when that evidence should be obtained and disclosed . . .

In practice a considerable amount of time and attention is given to the question of experts, for example:

(a) A party may seek permission to instruct a further expert. Reasons for this may include:

(i) dissatisfaction with answers given by an expert to written questions under CPR, r 35.6;

(ii) matters arising from an existing expert's report — thus, for example, an orthopaedic surgeon may be of the opinion that there is no organic cause of a disability but that there may be a psychiatric explanation and therefore a psychiatrist should be instructed;

(iii) a desire to bolster evidence with a further report.

In giving the directions the court will be guided by CPR, r 35.1 (that expert evidence should be restricted to what is reasonably required to resolve proceedings) and the overriding objective (in particular the principle of proportionality (CPR, r 1.1(2)(c)) and the requirement of saving expense (CPR, r 1.1(2)(b)). Thus a court will be reluctant for a party to instruct a psychiatrist, psychologist, neuropsychologist and a neurologist in a relatively small personal injury claim. However, where a single joint expert has been instructed, a court may be ready to allow a party to call its own expert where, for genuine reasons, he or she wishes to obtain further information before making a decision as to whether or not he may wish to challenge the single joint expert's report (*Daniels v Walker* [2000] 1 WLR 1382 (CA)).

(b) The court will require experts of like disciplines to meet or otherwise discuss issues. In cases where two experts have been instructed rather than a single joint expert, the court has power under CPR, r 35.12 to direct that the experts meet to reach agreement where possible and where they are unable to agree, to identify the issues in the proceedings. At the case management conference the parties and legal advisers often assist the judge in giving directions as to which issues the experts should discuss and how their agreements or disagreements should be recorded.

(c) A party may seek a direction that the experts attend trial for oral examination. Lord Woolf has made it clear that wherever possible a joint expert should be instructed. If there is disagreement over the report a party may either pose questions to the expert or be permitted to instruct his own expert. If after meeting the experts are unable to agree then as a last resort experts may give oral evidence before the court (*Daniels v Walker*).

(d) A party may have acquired video evidence of a claimant and want experts to reconsider their conclusions in the light of it.

(e) When setting the timetable for exchange of experts' reports, supplementary reports and meetings the court will need to know the expert's availability. If the court gives an expert two weeks to produce a further report and that expert is away on holiday for that two weeks then the party in concern will fail to keep to the set timetable and may be penalised in costs.

(5) what factual evidence should be disclosed . . .

The issue of what witness statements the parties are intending to rely on and when they should be disclosed will be dealt with at the case management conference. As with expert evidence, the issue arises whether or not it is necessary for all witnesses to attend trial to give evidence orally or whether or not their evidence can be agreed.

(6) what arrangements should be made about the giving of clarification or further information and the putting of questions to experts . . .

Parties may use the case management conference as an opportunity to apply to the court for an order to require a party to clarify a matter or give additional information in relation to a matter in accordance with CPR, r 18.1. A party may also seek permission to put written questions to another party's expert in accordance with CPR, r 35.6. In both cases the court will be concerned with the timetabling of responses.

(7) whether it will be just and will save costs to order a split trial or the trial of one or more preliminary issues.

Under CPR, r 3.1(2)(e) the court has the power to direct that part of any proceedings be dealt with as separate proceedings and under r 3.4(2)(i) to direct a separate trial of any issue. In personal injury actions courts will often order that the issues of liability and quantum should be decided separately, ie in 'split trial'. This will usually be the case if the issues of liability and quantum can be decided separately. Clearly the advantage of the split trial is that liability can be decided/apportioned without the need for all parties to prepare a case on quantum. In appropriate situations this may facilitate settlement and save costs.

The trial of a preliminary issue may be suitable where that preliminary issue is fundamental to a case and can be dealt with swiftly. Limitation is frequently dealt with by way of a preliminary issue: this obviates the need for undergoing preparation for a full trial which would be unnecessary if the parties were to find that the case is time barred. Another example of a matter which is frequently dealt with as a preliminary issue is the interpretation of contracts in construction disputes.

7.2.3.2   Narrowing the issues and striking out

Under the Civil Procedure Rules 1998, the court is under a duty to identify issues at an early stage (r 1.4(2)(b)) and to decide promptly which issues need investigation and trial whilst disposing of others summarily (r 1.4(2)(c)). The case management conference gives both the court and the parties the opportunity to carry out these duties. One means of summarily disposing of issues is the striking out procedure set out in r.3.4(2)(a) and (b) (r 3.4(2)(c) is dealt with at **8.2.5**). This enables the court to strike out a statement of case on the following grounds:

- where it appears to the court that a statement of case discloses no reasonable grounds for bringing or defending the claim (r 3.4(2)(a)); and
- where it appears to the court that a statement of case is an abuse of the court's process or is otherwise likely to obstruct the just disposal of the proceedings (r 3.4(2)(b)).

The court may strike out of its own initiative at the case management conference where as the parties should make an application in accordance with Part 23 (PD 3, para 5).

A striking-out application will need to be put succinctly and with clarity. Whether required by the judge or not, a skeleton argument is likely to assist him and should be prepared and sent to the court and the other side in advance. Applications under CPR, r 3.4(2) may be made without evidence in support although careful consideration should be given as to whether facts need to be proved and therefore whether evidence in support of an application for summary judgment should be filed and served.

7.2.3.3   Preparation

The master or district judge holding the case management conference will want to deal with matters quickly and efficiently and will expect parties to have conferred before the hearing. Given the pressure on court time it may be the case that the party who makes it easy for the master or district judge to give directions in his favour will succeed in getting what he wants.

7.2.3.4   Case summary

PD 29, paras 5.6 and 5.7, suggest that if it is thought that a case summary will assist the court to understand and deal with the questions before it then the claimant should provide one. If you are acting for a defendant and the claimant is not intending to provide a case summary, then it may be advisable to provide one – if you are able to assist the judge and create a good impression it can only assist you in obtaining the directions you seek. PD 29, para 5.7 states that the case summary should not exceed 500 words in length. It should set out a brief chronology of the claim, the issues of fact which are agreed or in dispute and the evidence needed to decide them.

7.2.3.5   Draft directions

Draft directions are another means of assisting the judge and making it easier for him to make the directions you are seeking. Form PF 52 (contained in the *White Book* and obtainable from the Royal Courts of Justice) is a useful guide. Arrive at the court early in order to discuss the draft directions with your opponent — the judge is likely to take a dim view of parties who have not discussed directions between themselves. If draft directions have not been prepared, the judge may decide what directions should be given and then send the parties out to fill in Form PF 52 and return later when he has dealt with other matters.

7.2.4   Sanctions

PD 29, para 5.1(1), provides that at the case management conference the court is to review the steps which the parties have taken in the preparation of the case, and in particular their compliance with any directions that the court may have given. Delays were identified in the Access to Justice report as one of the evils of the old civil justice system. This problem was addressed in the Civil Procedure Rules 1998: first by making it a part of the overriding objective that cases are to be dealt with expeditiously; and secondly by giving the courts the following powers to penalise parties for failing to keep to timetables:

> (a) Under r 3.4(2)(c) the court has the power to strike out a case if it appears to the court that — 'there has been failure to comply with a rule, practice direction or court order'.

This draconian power was considered in *Biguzzi v Rank Leisure plc* [1999] 4 All ER 934 at 940. It was held that where the Civil Procedure Rules applied, pre-CPR authorities on matters of civil procedure were no longer generally of any relevance. Under the Civil Procedure Rules the courts had a series of alternative powers which could be used to make it clear that they would not tolerate delays. In many cases it would be more appropriate to use these alternative powers as they would produce a more just result.

The issue was revisited by the Court of Appeal in *UCB Corporate Services Ltd v Halifax (SW) Ltd* The Times, 23 December 1999, where a professional negligence claim against surveyors was struck out on the basis that there had been a wholesale disregard by the claimant of the rules and court orders which amounted to an abuse of process. Lord Lloyd of Berwick commented that Lord Woolf would not have intended *Biguzzi* to lead judges to treat cases of delay with greater leniency than under the old procedure. He concluded that 'there were lesser sanctions in less serious cases but in more serious cases striking out was appropriate where justice required it'. Lord Justice Ward commented that while Lord Woolf had stated in *Biguzzi* that earlier authorities are no longer of any relevance under the Civil Procedure Rules he was not saying that the underlying thought processes that informed those judgments should be completely overturned.

With reference to both *Biguzzi* and *UCB* May LJ commented in *Purdy v Cambran* [1999] CPLR 843, that there are no hard and fast theoretical circumstances in which the court will strike out a claim or decline to do so: 'rather it is necessary to concentrate on the intrinsic justice of a particular case in the light of the overriding objective'. However, he confirmed Lord Justice Ward's comments on earlier authorities and the test applied was that which had applied under the old rules, namely: 'if the matter goes to trial will the claimant be caused or have suffered serious prejudice by the claimant's unwarranted delay?'. It was held that the claimant's delay had been inordinate and that after ten years and the death of the defendant's orthopaedic expert a fair trial of the issue was no longer possible.

The issue of whether striking out a case is contrary to art 6(1) of the European Convention on Human Rights was considered in *Arrow Nominees Inc v Blackledge* [2000] 1 BCLC 709. In this case it was held that to strike out a claimant's case solely because he had been found to be in contumacious breach of the rules or an order of the court was an improper exercise of the court's powers. However, where acts which constituted a contempt led to a real risk that a fair trial could not take place, it would not be a breach of art 6(1) to strike out the contemnor's case.

(b) Under r 44.3 the court has discretion as to whether costs are paid by one party to another; the amount of those costs; and when they are to be paid. CPR, r 44.3(4)(a) provides that the court is to take parties' conduct into consideration when deciding what order to make about costs. Where the court does not consider it just to strike out a claim as a consequence of a party's breach of a rule, practice direction or court order, it may nonetheless punish a party by an award of costs against it. CPR, r 44.3(6) gives the court scope to make orders that a party must pay:

(i)   a proportion of another party's costs;

(ii)   a stated amount in respect of another party's costs;

(iii) costs from or until a certain date only;

(iv) costs incurred before proceedings have begun;

(v) costs relating to particular steps taken in proceedings;

(vi) costs relating only to a distinct part of the proceedings; and

(vii) interest on costs from or until a certain date, including a date before judgment.

The court also has discretion as to whether or not it awards costs on the standard or indemnity basis. The assessment of costs on an indemnity basis means that the court will resolve any doubt which it may have as to whether costs were reasonably incurred or were reasonable in amount in favour of the receiving party (r 44.4(3)). When assessing costs on the standard basis the court will only allow costs which are proportionate to the matters in issue (r 44.4(2)) and will resolve any doubt which it may have as to whether costs were reasonably incurred and proportionate in amount in favour of the paying party. In *Biguzzi* (at 941), Lord Woolf suggested that the power to award costs on an indemnity basis may be an appropriate sanction in cases where there has been disregard of timetables.

(c) A further sanction at the court's disposal is the discretion to order a party to pay a sum of money into court. The court may make such an order pursuant to its powers under CPR, r 3.1(3) and (5). Where the court orders a payment into court that payment acts as a security for any sum payable by that party to any other party in proceedings (r 3.1(6)).

In *Mealey Horgan plc v Horgan* The Times, 6 July 1999, it was held inappropriate to order a party to give security where the party's default had not prejudiced the trial and had not significantly prejudiced the other party. Buckley J thought that it might be appropriate where there was a history of repeated breaches of timetables or court orders or where the conduct of a party gave rise to the suspicion that it was not bona fide and the court thought that it should therefore be protected.

However, striking out a statement of case because a party has failed to comply with a court order for payment of a sum of money which is beyond his means to pay, may in some circumstances amount to a breach of the ECHR Article 6(1) right of access to a court (see *Ford v Labrador* [2003] 1 WLR 2082).

Part III

Drafting statements of case

Drafting professional negligence particulars of claim

8.1 Introduction

The usual rules and conventions of drafting statements of case apply to professional negligence cases as to any other contractual or tortious claims and you should refer to the *Drafting Manual* and to the relevant Civil Procedure Rules and the Practice Directions accompanying them.

The purpose of this chapter is to highlight some important aspects of drafting the particulars of claim in relation to professional negligence cases and to give you the opportunity to read and analyse several examples taken from practitioners' drafts. All examples are taken from clinical or solicitors' negligence cases. Other professional negligence cases are the same in principle. The chapter considers the structure and then particular aspects of particulars of claim. At each stage, examples are given.

8.2 Structure

Professional negligence cases often involve fairly complex facts and legal issues. You need to set out the relevant facts clearly and make the issues explicit. In order to do so you will need to structure your statement of case carefully. The usual shape of particulars of claim in a professional negligence/breach of contract case is:

- introduce the parties and background;
- duty/contract;
- defendant's knowledge (where relevant);
- contract terms;
- performance (what the professional did in pursuance of the duty/contract);
- breach of duty/contract;
- causation;
- loss and damage;
- interest;
- remedies sought.

It is not always appropriate to stick rigidly to this pattern. In order to put the case most effectively you might find that you need to alter the conventional pattern.

For example: C is suing D (solicitors) for failing to issue proceedings in time against XY for injuries sustained in a road traffic accident. The previous case against XY is an integral part of this claim. The story is probably best told chronologically:

- introduce the parties to this claim (C and D);
- set out the facts of the road traffic accident;
- XY's breach of duty and causation of C's injury;
- duty/contract (C and D);
- defendant's knowledge;
- contract terms;
- performance;
- breach of duty/contract;
- causation;
- loss (of chance).

In a clinical negligence claim you might have lengthy background information about the treatment history and this will usually need to be set out after the introductory paragraph. Where the allegations involve more than one NHS clinician, the shape of the particulars of claim might look like this:

- introduce the parties;
- duty of care owed by defendant hospital trust;
- the claimant's relevant background medical history;
- what took place between GP and claimant;
- particulars of negligence alleged against GP;
- what took place between nurse and claimant;
- particulars of negligence alleged against nurse;
- what took place between hospital doctor and claimant;
- particulars of negligence alleged against hospital doctor;
- causation;
- loss.

In some circumstances it is easier for the reader to understand the allegations being made when the claimant states a positive case as to what the professional ought to have done prior to stating the particulars of negligence.

Sometimes it helps to set out the case on causation prior to the allegations of negligence.

Some practitioners will even state the injuries and loss prior to the particulars of negligence in a clinical negligence case.

An example is set out below:

2.   At midday on the 3 May 2000, the Claimant developed meningitis which caused her to feel unwell. She telephoned [the surgery] and was visited at home by the Defendant at 12.30 pm. She described her symptoms to him [particularise].

3.   The First Defendant told the Claimant that she had 'flu' and to go to bed and take paracetamol, which advice the Claimant followed.

4.   At 3.00 pm, the Claimant's husband came home and found the Claimant almost unconscious and saw that she had developed a rash with purple patches on her chest and arms and hands. He rushed her to hospital.

5. The Hospital diagnosed viral meningitis and administered the following treatment [set out details of treatment and duration of her stay].

6. The Claimant developed septicaemia in her fingers and toes which resulted in the amputation of all toes on her right foot, the small toe on her left foot and her right index finger.

7. It is the Claimant's case on causation that had the First Defendant correctly diagnosed the Claimant's condition as viral meningitis at the time of his visit, he would have:

    (a) administered an injection of [drug] immediately; and

    (b) referred her to hospital as an emergency admission immediately.

Had he done so, the Claimant would not have developed the septicaemia and consequent injuries.

8. The diagnosis made and the treatment given by the Defendant was negligent. [set out particulars of negligence].

As you can see, pleading these more complex claims requires a degree of flexibility and confidence. As a general rule, you should stick to the conventional and chronological structure unless you have good reason to deviate from it. If in doubt, remember the purpose of your statement of case: to set out all material facts and to identify the issues in the case as clearly and concisely as possible.

8.3 Introducing the parties

There is no magic in the way parties are introduced in professional negligence claims but certain situations can cause confusion and so are discussed below.

8.3.1 Clinical negligence

8.3.3.1 NHS hospital treatment

If the treatment was carried out at a hospital under the National Health Service, the appropriate defendant is the relevant hospital trust. The trust is vicariously liable for all of its employees, be they doctors, nurses or auxiliary staff. It is not usual to sue the individuals although their names will appear in the particulars of claim, where known, as a part of telling the story. A typical introductory paragraph would be:

The Defendant is and was at all material times the National Health Service Trust with responsibility for the administration, management and control of the hospital at [address] and the employer of all medical, surgical and other staff working there.

An NHS general practitioner will be sued in his own name and/or in the name of the partnership. If the claimant is alleging negligence against the GP and the hospital, you can still introduce both defendants in the opening paragraph. For example:

At all material times the First Defendant was a National Health Service General Practitioner practising from his surgery at [address] and the Second Defendant was the National Health Service Trust with responsibility for the administration, management and control of the hospital at [address] and the employer of all medical, surgical and other staff working there.

8.3.3.2 Private treatment

A typical introductory paragraph would be:

At all material times the Defendant was a consultant dermatologist in private practice at the [. . .] Hospital at [address]. The Claimant was a patient of the Defendant and had attended monthly appointments with him since [date].

8.3.2 Solicitors' negligence

It is usual to sue the firm of solicitors and to name the relevant partner(s) or employees who had conduct of the case in the body of the particulars of claim. For example:

1.   The Defendant is and was at all material times a firm of solicitors practising at [address].

2.   On [date] the Claimant instructed and retained one Mr Smith, a solicitor, who was an employee or partner of the Defendant firm.

8.3.3 Other professional negligence

This is as in solicitors' negligence. If the firm (or individual) held itself out as having a certain skill, this can be a good place to set that out. For example:

The Defendants are a firm of chartered accountants carrying out their practice from [address] and at all material times held themselves out to be experienced, skilled and competent accountants specialising in forensic accounting.

8.4 Duty and standard of care

8.4.1 Between professional and client or patient

The duty and standard of care are the foundation of all professional negligence claims. Too often they are stated by the use of stock phrases. With some thought, you can make a precise and persuasive case by being very specific as to the extent of the duty and standard of care alleged. Stating a full and accurate duty of care will assist you later in formulating the breaches of duty. Ask yourself how the defendant or individual partner or employee 'sold' himself to the claimant? Did he claim to specialise in a particular area of the profession? If so, include that in your plea of duty of care. Rather than just setting out an obligation to act as a reasonably competent member of the profession, spell out the higher duty. For example:

Instead of:

At all material times the Claimant was a patient in the care of the Defendant. In the premises [name of doctor] was under a duty to exercise all due skill and care to be expected of a competent medical practitioner.

Try:

At all material times the Claimant was a patient in the care of the Defendant. In the premises [name] was under a duty to exercise all due skill and care to be expected of a skilled and competent Consultant Surgeon [or eg, Commercial Solicitor].

Can you make your case still clearer? It sometimes helps to be explicit as to the different tasks which you allege ought to have been carried out by the professional with that due skill and care. For example:

At all material times the Claimant was a patient in the care of the Defendant. In the premises [name] was under a duty to exercise all due skill and care to be expected of a skilled and competent Consultant Surgeon *when advising pre-operatively, performing the operation and in providing postoperative care.*

8.4.2 Duty of care to third parties

Where the claimant was not the client or patient of the professional, the existence of the duty of care will be more difficult to establish. You must ensure that you state sufficient facts upon which to base your case that such a duty of care did exist between the parties. See **Chapters 2** and **3** above. For example:

At all material times the Defendant knew or ought to have known of the existence of the Claimant and that he was a dependant of the deceased. In the premises the Defendant owed the Claimant a duty to take care to protect the Claimant's interests when conducting proceedings on behalf of the deceased's estate.

8.4.3 Concurrent duties in contract and tort

In professional negligence claims the same facts often give rise to a cause of action in both contract and tort (eg, between solicitors and clients and between privately-paying patients and clinicians). The outcome under either cause of action is usually identical but there are (rare) times when it is not (see the *Remedies Manual*). You should plead both causes of action together and in the alternative so as to enable the claimant to avail himself of the most advantageous remedy at trial.

Where the only contractual term upon which you rely is an implied term to take care, that term and the tortious duty of care can usually be pleaded together in one paragraph. For example:

It was a term of the Defendant's retainer with the Claimant that the Defendant would, at all material times, use the proper skill, care, diligence and competence to be expected of an experienced conveyancing solicitor. Further or alternatively, the Defendant owed the Claimant a like duty of care in tort.

Or:

It was a term of the Defendant's retainer, or in the alternative it was his duty, that he would at all material times exercise the reasonable skill, care and diligence to be expected of a consultant surgeon when advising pre-operatively, performing the operation and providing post-operative care.

When relying on more terms of the contract it is clearer to set those out first and then to add a separate paragraph pleading the duty of care in tort. For example:

6.   The following were, among others, the express, or alternatively implied terms of the Retainer:
  (1) The Defendant would take all necessary steps to protect the Claimant's position as the proposed mortgagee of the property.
  (2) The Defendant would advance the money to the borrower only in accordance with the Claimant's written instructions.
  (3) The Defendant would inform the Claimant of any fact or matter known to its partners, servants or agents, which might reasonably affect the Claimant's decision as to whether to advance the money to the borrower.
  (4) The Defendant would exercise the care, skill and diligence to be expected of a competent conveyancing solicitor.
7.   Further and alternatively, the Defendant owed the Claimant a duty of care at all material times, to use the proper skill, care, and diligence to be expected of a competent conveyancing solicitor.

8.5 Knowledge

You sometimes need to rely upon the defendant's knowledge in order to show that the losses claimed were within the defendant's contemplation and are therefore not too remote. For example, where a client wishes to purchase a factory building in order to turn it into a residential flat, the conveyancing solicitor would only be liable for the losses resulting from his failure to discover that planning applications for such conversions in the particular area were routinely refused, if it could be established that he knew (or ought to have known) that the purchaser wished to change the use of the building. For example:

It is the Claimant's case that at all material times the Defendant knew that the Claimant intended to convert the building to a residential apartment. In particular the Claimant will rely upon the letter of [date] served with these particulars of claim.

8.6 Contract terms

8.6.1 Express terms

Set out in full any express terms upon which you rely (ie any which the defendant is alleged to have breached).

Remember the requirement to attach to the particulars of claim and/or serve with them a copy of any written contract or documents setting out the agreement (PD 16, para 7.3).

If relying on an oral agreement, you are required to set out in the particulars of claim the relevant contractual words used and to state by whom, to whom, when and where they were spoken (PD 16, para 7.4).

For example:

2.   On or about [date], at a meeting in the Defendant's offices, the Claimant retained the Defendant for a fee to act on her behalf in relation to all aspects of advice, investigation and prosecution of her claim against XYZ Bank Plc. The terms of this agreement were recorded in a letter from the Defendant to the Claimant dated [date] and attached and served with these particulars of claim.

3.   In particular the Claimant will rely upon the following express terms of the agreement:[set out relevant terms].

8.6.2 Implied terms

Before you draft the particulars of claim, you should be absolutely clear in your own mind which facts you will rely on to establish the breaches of contract and duty of care. If the express terms cover an obligation in relation to each of those facts then your task is fairly straightforward; you state each of those express terms. Frequently, however, you will know, from your expert's report or the profession's guidelines, that there has been a failure to meet the requisite professional standard (eg, a solicitor's failure to write a letter before claim, to seek necessary pre-action disclosure and to issue proceedings in time) but the contract documents are silent as to the specific obligations. You need to formulate an implied term of the contract to reflect that duty. Should you state an implied term to 'match' every single breach or should you rely on a more general 'catch-all'?

For example, is it better to state:

The following were, among others, implied terms of the retainer:
- (a)   the Defendant would write a letter before claim to XY;
- (b)   the Defendant would seek all appropriate pre-action disclosure from XY;
- (c)   the Defendant would issue proceedings within the limitation period allowed by statute for personal injury claims.

Or:

It was an implied term of the retainer that the Defendant would, at all material times use the proper skill, care and competence to be expected of a skilled personal injury solicitor.

The answer is that it is a matter of judgment in each case. Remember that particulars of claim are a persuasive tool and will probably be the first document to which the judge turns. There is a balance to be struck. On the one hand, the claimant's case is made simple and explicit by setting up a specific term to anticipate every breach. On the other hand, that process can make the statement of case long, repetitive and arduous to read.

In this case, and in many, there is a 'halfway' position which is tighter than the 'catch-all' but more concise:

5.   It was an implied term of the retainer that the Defendant would, at all material times use the proper skill, care and competence to be expected of a skilled personal injury lawyer.
6.   In particular it was an implied term of the retainer that the Defendant would comply with all current Civil Procedural Rules, Practice Directions and Protocols.

As a general rule, the more unusual the term you seek to imply, the more specific you need to be when stating it.

8.7   Performance of the duty/contract

It is important to include all facts relevant to the breaches alleged. You will find some professional negligence claims involve a complex series of events. Try to be concise but do include all necessary facts even if your particulars of claim are lengthy as a result. For example, it is not unusual to see several paragraphs (or even pages) setting out a long history of medical treatment or a series of detailed actions over a short period of time (eg, during a woman's labour). However, not every consultation with the doctor will be relevant nor will every aspect of the treatment. Use the expert's report to help you to analyse the relevant facts. Ask yourself whether each fact you state is necessary to establish the cause of action or the loss.

8.8   Breaches of contract/duty of care

This is the heart of your case and involves the allegations against the defendant's professionalism. You must be very careful to formulate the breaches:

- particularly (ie, separating and detailing each allegation);
- accurately;
- on the basis of sound evidence.

The claimant needs to demonstrate that the professional defendant fell below the standard of the competent professional practising in his field. Consequently, the particulars of claim must reflect not only what the defendant did but also, at least implicitly, what the claimant says he ought to have done. For example, it is not usually sufficient to say 'negligently failed to diagnose the condition', you need to go further to show how that diagnosis ought to have been made. For example:

(a)   failed to take a proper history from the Claimant,
(b)   failed to examine the Claimant's foot,

(c) failed to investigate the Claimant's condition by taking a blood test to determine the level of uric acid in her blood,

(d) failed to diagnose the Claimant's condition,

(e) failed to refer the Claimant for further investigation.

Or:

(a) Failed to discover that the existing fence (marked green on the plan annexed hereto) was erected 2 metres into the neighbouring property and that it did not reflect the true boundary between the properties (marked red on the plan).

(b) Failed to make any or any adequate investigations at the land registry or otherwise as to the title of the land between the coloured lines on the plan.

(c) Failed to make any or any adequate pre-contract inquiries from the vendor as to the title of the land or as to the existence or status of any disputes over the title of that land.

(d) Failed to advise the Claimant in writing or orally that the fence was not erected along the true boundary line of the property.

(e) Permitted the Claimant to proceed with the purchase of the property without giving any or any adequate advice as to the extent of the property.

In most professional negligence cases the evidence of what the professional ought to have done, and so of the breach, will come from an expert in the relevant field. It might also come from a review of the relevant professional guidelines/rules/codes of conduct or protocols. In solicitors' negligence it is also likely to come from Law Society guidelines, from statutes and procedural rules. As discussed in **Chapter 7**, you will usually have this evidence prior to pleading the statements of case.

8.8.1 Breaches of concurrent duties of care in tort and contract

Where there is breach of a concurrent duty in contract and tort do not repeat the facts under each cause of action but set them out together. For example:

The Defendant acted in breach of the terms of the retainer, and/or negligently, in that:

(a) He advanced the money to the borrower without the Claimant's instructions.

(b) He failed to inform the Claimant of the fact that the borrower had lost his employment.

(c) In the premises he failed to exercise the care, skill and diligence to be expected of a competent conveyancing solicitor.

8.9 Causation and loss

8.9.1 Pleading a positive case on causation

In a case where causation is very straightforward, eg, a road traffic accident, causation is usually dealt with in the same paragraph as loss. For example:

By reason of the matters set out above, the claimant suffered injury, loss and damage.

PARTICULARS OF INJURY

As discussed elsewhere in the Manual, professional negligence claims often involve complex issues of causation. Because of that it is usually necessary to state the claimant's case on causation very clearly and explicitly. For example:

It is the Claimant's case on causation that had the Defendant given him the correct dose of [drug] on [date] he would have made a full recovery by [date].

The law and the issues on causation are different in clinical negligence cases and solicitors' negligence cases and are considered separately below.

8.9.2   Causation and loss in clinical negligence

For a full discussion of causation and measure of loss in clinical negligence cases refer to **Chapter 2**. You must remind yourself of the law before you attempt to plead the case on causation. For example:

Failure to diagnose:
It is the Claimant's case that had the Defendant diagnosed appendicitis on [date] at [time], the Claimant would have been operated on timeously and the appendix would not have ruptured.
    As a result of the negligent misdiagnosis the Claimant sustained injury, loss and damage:

PARTICULARS OF INJURY

(a)   An additional 6 hours of pain and suffering.
(b)   Peritonitis.
(c)   Increased pain as a result of the ruptured appendicitis.
(d)   A longer operation.
(e)   Worse scarring from the operation than she would otherwise have had.

Failure to warn:
It is the Claimant's case, that had she been warned of the risk that the operation might cause her symptoms to deteriorate, she would not have consented to the operation.
    As a result of undergoing the operation, the Claimant's condition has deteriorated in the following ways: [set out Particulars].

8.9.3   Causation and loss in solicitors' negligence

It is tactically stronger to adopt a less explicit approach when pleading causation and the loss of a chance in solicitors' negligence cases. Take, for example, the case where a solicitor has failed to issue proceedings within the limitation period and the claimant has lost the chance of succeeding in a claim for personal injury damages. Rather than attempting to be precise as to chances of success which you say the claimant has lost (eg, 60%), be simple and factual as to the level of damages which would have been claimed:

By reason of the matters set out above, the Claimant has suffered loss and damage

PARTICULARS OF LOSS

1.   The Claimant has lost the opportunity to recover damages from ABC. The damages would have comprised the following:
    (a)   damages for pain, suffering and loss of amenity [particularise injuries];
    (b)   financial losses [particularise].
2.   Wasted costs of the first claim.

8.9.4 Schedules of loss and interest

You are referred to the *Remedies Manual* and the *Drafting Manual*.

8.10 Statement of truth

You are referred to the *Drafting Manual* and the *Civil Litigation Manual*.

Drafting professional negligence defences

9.1 Introduction

It has already been said that the usual rules and conventions of drafting statements of case apply to professional negligence cases as to other contractual and tortious claims and reference should be made to the *Drafting Manual* and to the relevant rules and practice directions. In particular, you should note CPR, r 16.5(1) and (2), which provides:

CONTENTS OF DEFENCE

(1)   In his defence, the defendant must state —

(a)   which of the allegations in the particulars of claim he denies;

(b)   which allegations he is unable to admit or deny, but which he requires the claimant to prove; and

(c)   which allegations he admits.

(2)   Where the defendant denies an allegation —

(a)   he must state his reasons for doing so; and

(b)   if he intends to put forward a different version of events from that given by the claimant, he must state his own version.

PD 16 adds the following relevant requirements:

(a) The defendant must give details of the expiry of any limitation period upon which he relies (para 13.1).

(b) Where the claim is for personal injury and the claimant has attached a medical report in respect of his injuries to the particulars of claim, the defendant must according to para 12.1:

(1)   state in his defence whether he:

(a)   agrees,

(b)   disputes, or

(c)   neither agrees nor disputes but has no knowledge of,

the matters contained in the medical report,

(2)   where he disputes any part of the medical report, give in his defence his reasons for doing so, and

(3)   where he has obtained his own medical report on which he intends to rely, attach it to his defence.

The medical report referred to is likely to be the report concerning condition and prognosis (ie, quantum) and not concerning liability in a clinical negligence case (there is no requirement that the claimant should attach a liability report to the particulars of claim, although he could choose to do so).

(c) Where the claim is for personal injury and the claimant has included a schedule of past and future expenses and losses the defendant should according to para 12.2:

> . . . *include in or attach to his defence a counter-schedule stating:*
>   *(1) which of those items he:*
>   *(a) agrees,*
>   *(b) disputes, or*
>   *(c) neither agrees nor disputes but has no knowledge of, and*
>   *(2) where any items are disputed, supplying alternative figures where appropriate.*

In addition, PD 16 states that the defence may:

- make reference to any point of law on which it is based;
- include names of witnesses whom the defendant proposes to call; and
- attach documents essential to the defendant's case.

9.1.1 A comprehensive defence

Before the advent of the Civil Procedure Rules 1998, defendants frequently responded to particulars of claim with what became known as a 'holding defence'. This was usually a fairly skeletal document containing short and unexplained denials and non-admissions. It gave the claimant little, if any, detail of the defendant's positive case and did not deal with the detail of the claimant's medical report. The rationale for this approach was that the defendant needed to respond to the particulars of claim in a short time and that it therefore had inadequate time to investigate the claim. The holding defence was therefore supposed to buy the defendant time in which to investigate before amending to plead a fuller defence. In practice, the defence was often left unamended in this form. With the advent of the new Rules, and in particular of the pre-action protocols, the parties are expected to have exchanged sufficient information and documentary evidence prior to the issue of proceedings to obviate the need for this approach. The new Rules as set out above require a fully reasoned, comprehensive defence. There will in practice still be times when there have been insufficient investigations to enable you to plead full reasons for each issue. For example, where the defendant does not yet have a medical report, you will need to reserve your position in relation to parts of the claimant's medical report or schedule of loss. You should be clear and explicit about doing so. For example:

The Defendant is not yet in a position to admit or deny paragraphs [indicate paragraphs] in the Claimant's medical report dated [date] but requires the Claimant to prove the same. Without prejudice to the generality of the non-admission, the Defendant contends that the same paragraphs contain the following inaccuracies [set out inaccuracies].

9.2 Structure

The structure of a professional negligence defence normally reflects the structure of the particulars of claim; setting out the response to each matter stated and adding the necessary additional facts or allegations at each stage before responding to the next paragraph.

9.2.1 Preliminaries

Where it is intended to rely on a specific legal defence (which is likely to form the basis of a summary judgment application under CPR, Part 24, or of a strike-out application under CPR, r 3.4), it is usually clearest to set that matter out first or immediately after the paragraph concerning the parties. Thereafter the body of the defence will follow the usual structure.

9.2.2 Length

An interesting aspect of professional negligence cases is that the defence is often much longer than in a straightforward breach of contract or negligence case. Whilst you should strive for conciseness, you should not be surprised if your defence is longer than those which you have previously drafted. Situations which require full and often lengthy pleading include:

- setting out the defendant's version of the detailed history of the professional relationship and the content of relevant communications;
- setting out the defendant's case on causation (see later examples in this chapter);
- setting out the defendant's case on the claimant's loss of a chance particularly in loss of a chance of litigation (see example given below);
- setting out the defendant's case distinguishing the claimant's pre-existing injuries and those caused by the alleged negligence/breach of contract.

9.3 Parties and background

The defendant will normally be in a position to admit the introductory paragraph as to the parties and background of the case. However, you should be alert to an allegation that the defendant held himself out to be a specialist in any given field. Check the accuracy of that before admitting to it.

9.4 Specific legal defences

9.4.1 Limitation

This is usually very straightforward for the defendant to plead, for example:

The Claimant's cause of action arose more than [3 or 6] years prior to this action and it is therefore barred by operation of section . . . of the Limitation Act 1980.

Whilst the issue of limitation can involve complex issues (such as the date of knowledge under s 14 of the Act), all the defendant needs to do at this stage is to invoke the operation of the Limitation Act and thereafter it will be for the claimant to show how he intends to bring himself within the relevant period.

9.4.2 Collateral attack

Where a claimant sues his solicitor or barrister for the negligent conduct of a trial or application, the defendant will sometimes be able to rely upon the doctrine of collateral attack (see **3.6.2** above). For example:

> The Claimant's case is an abuse of the process of the Court in that it involves a collateral attack on the decision of a court of competent jurisdiction, namely the decision of HHJ [...] sitting at [...] court on date [...] in the case of [...].

9.5   Duty of care

9.5.1   No duty owed

In those unusual cases where the defendant's case is that he owed no duty of care to the claimant, the defence must expressly plead that and it must be supported by facts relevant to the legal tests of: proximity; foreseeability; whether it would be fair, just, and reasonable to impose such a duty; and the defendant's voluntary assumption of responsibility.

9.5.2   Limits to the duty

The claimant's experience can have an effect on the extent of the duty of care owed:

> If, which is denied, the Defendant would have owed a duty to give detailed advice as to the commercial implications of the merger to an inexperienced client, the Defendant will contend that no such duty was owed to the Claimant which is a limited company employing its own financial advisor.

9.6   Contract terms

9.6.1   Express terms

The particulars of claim should annexe any written contractual documents and any pleaded terms which were reduced to writing are unlikely to be contentious. However, you should set out any terms upon which you rely whether they are written or oral which do not appear in the particulars of claim.

9.6.2   Implied terms

As set out in relation to drafting the particulars of claim, the implied terms are likely to come from a variety of sources such as experts' reports, your client's instructions, professional guidelines, and (in solicitors' negligence cases) from Civil Procedure Rules, practice directions and protocols. Ensure that you plead any additional terms upon which your client will seek to rely at trial.

For example, in response to particulars of claim alleging negligent conduct of litigation against a solicitor which pleads (in paragraph 3) only the implied term to act with ordinary skill and care in the conduct of litigation, the defendant might respond:

> Paragraph 3 of the Particulars of Claim is admitted. It is further contended that it was an implied term of the contract that the Claimant would cooperate with the Defendant's reasonable requests to provide information necessary for the conduct of the case.

9.7 Breaches

It is not sufficient to respond to the claimant's particulars of negligence/breach of contract with a one-line denial. You are required to set out the reasons for your denials. The allegations of breach of duty can be denied for very different reasons, which will require different responses. Be sure in your own mind before you plead the defence what the defendant's case is in relation to each alleged breach. Is it:

(a) Inaccuracy: the events did not take place as alleged.

(b) The facts alleged are incomplete or taken out of context which distorts the picture; the full facts will show that the professional's acts were not negligent (eg, misdiagnosis or solicitor's failure to advise in relation to a certain aspect of the client's affairs).

(c) The facts alleged are correct but the acts or omissions accorded with good practice.

(d) The facts are correct and the error occurred but it was not negligent (eg, small accidental slip in keyhole surgery).

Once you have analysed the case in relation to each breach you will be in a position to respond appropriately (ie, with reasons for the denial) and to include all relevant facts.

For example, in answer to these allegations:

3. The Defendant was negligent in that he:
    (a) failed to take a proper history from the claimant,
    (b) failed to examine the Claimant's foot,
    (c) failed to investigate the Claimant's condition by taking a blood test to determine the level of uric acid in her blood,
    (d) failed to diagnose the Claimant's condition,
    (e) failed to refer the Claimant for further investigation.

the defence might be set out as follows:

It is denied that the Defendant was negligent as alleged in paragraph 3 of the Particulars of Claim or at all. In particular the Defendant pleads to each allegation as follows:
    (a) The Defendant sought, took and recorded a full history from the Claimant in relation to her foot pain. The same is set out in the GP notes dated [. . .].
    (b) The Defendant looked at the Claimant's foot but she did not allow him to touch it.
    (c) It is admitted that no blood test was taken but in the circumstances and given the history of [details] it is denied that the failure to do so was negligent.
    (d) It is admitted that [describe condition] was not diagnosed on [date] but it is contended that the presenting symptoms were non-typical [particularise] and that the failure to diagnose was not negligent.
    (e) It is further contended that the Defendant's advice to the Claimant to return in three days if the condition deteriorated was proper advice in the circumstances.

9.8 Specific factual defences in solicitors' negligence cases

9.8.1 Acting on counsel's advice

After having dealt with the allegations of negligence, set out the facts and matters relied upon to demonstrate that the solicitor was in fact relying upon counsel's advice where it was proper to do so. For example:

The Defendant instructed specialist Counsel [name] to advise in the case and was properly acting on the advice of Counsel set out in his Opinion dated [. . .] at all relevant times. In the premises if, which is denied, the allegations set out in paragraph [. . .] of the Particulars of Claim are proved and/or found to constitute negligence, the Defendant denies that he is liable.

9.8.2 Acting on the client's instructions

For example:

It is admitted that the Defendant compromised the action on behalf of the Claimant as set out in paragraph [. . .] of the Particulars of Claim. It is contended that he did so on the express instructions of the client given [orally/in writing] on [date] at [place] in the following terms [set out].

It is the Defendant's case that the instructions were given by the Claimant after the Defendant had given full and proper advice as to the true chances of success and the likely award of damages in the case [set out particulars of the advice and the dates and manner in which it was given].

In the premises it is denied that the Defendant was negligent as alleged or at all.

9.9 Contributory negligence

There is no reason why a defendant in a professional negligence case should not rely upon the full or partial defence of contributory negligence. However, it is not relied on as often in professional negligence cases as in many other forms of negligence cases such as personal injury. The reason is that courts are reluctant to find that an inexperienced client has contributed to a negligent error by a professional whose services the client has usually engaged precisely because of his own inexperience. See **3.6.5** for examples of contributory negligence findings in solicitors' cases. It is even more unusual to have contributory negligence in a clinical negligence case although not unheard of. Remember to set out facts which demonstrate the special experience or knowledge of the claimant upon which you rely. For example:

Such loss and damage as the Claimant may have suffered was caused or contributed to by her own negligence:

PARTICULARS

The Claimant, who was an experienced forensic accountant, failed to take any or any adequate notice of the following entries in the company accounts, which the Defendant had sent to her [set out].

9.10 Causation

Causation in professional negligence cases is often complex. Your statement of case must make the client's case on causation very clear and explicit.

9.10.1 Causation in clinical negligence

There can be many reasons to deny causation in clinical negligence cases as discussed in **2.6** above. You must analyse the defendant's position carefully before pleading it to ensure that you have covered each aspect and set out a positive case. Two examples are included below.

9.10.1.1   Denial of causation in a case of a negligent misdiagnosis

This is a case where the defence is factual:

> If, which is denied, the Defendant was negligent as alleged, causation is denied. It is the Defendant's case that, had the casualty nurse diagnosed the deceased as suffering from arsenic poisoning on his arrival at the hospital at [time], he would have died from such poisoning at [time he in fact died] in any event.

9.10.1.2   Denial of causation in a case of a negligent failure to attend a patient

This presents more difficulties as the defendant must demonstrate that:

- even if the doctor had attended his actions (or inactions) would not have altered the course or outcome of the illness or injury, and
- those hypothetical actions (or inactions) would not have been negligent.

It is therefore insufficient to plead that had the doctor attended (ie, had not been negligent as alleged), the outcome would have been the same. You must go further and set out what the doctor would have done had he attended, the fact that such acts would have been in accordance with a responsible body of approved medical practice and that the outcome would have been the same in any event. For example:

> Causation is denied. The Defendant's case as to causation is set out below:
>
> (a)   Had Dr [name] attended the Claimant, she would not have intubated him or have taken any other action at that time.
>
> (b)   Her decision not to intubate him or not to act otherwise would have been based upon the following factors [particularise].
>
> (c)   In the premises, such a decision would have been in accordance with practices accepted by a responsible body of medical opinion.
>
> (d)   Consequently, the outcome for the Claimant would have been unaltered by the attendance of Dr [. . .].

9.10.2   Causation in solicitors' negligence cases

Again, it is important to set out the full, particularised case on causation where it is in issue. For example, in response to an allegation that the claimant would not have purchased a property had the conveyancing solicitor warned her that there was a public footpath over the garden, it is less persuasive to state:

> It is denied that the Claimant would have pulled out of the sale as alleged or at all.

than it is to state:

> It is the Defendant's case that the Claimant was determined to purchase the property and that she would have done so even if she had been informed about the footpath. In particular the Defendant will rely upon the following facts and matters:
>
> (a)   The Claimant had been looking for a property for [time] and was delighted to find this property.
>
> (b)   The Claimant told the Defendant on [date] that she considered the property to be 'a complete bargain' and that it was her 'dream home'.
>
> (c)   The footpath cannot be seen from the house because of a large hedge which runs across the bottom of the garden.

9.11   Loss of a chance

See **8.9.3** as to pleading a claim for the loss of a chance to succeed in litigation. For reasons discussed there, the particulars of claim are often very short on this point. It falls to the defendant to plead a full case in this regard. It is best illustrated by example.

Assume in this case that the solicitor has admitted negligently failing to issue proceedings against X within the limitation period in a personal injury action.

Further and alternatively, the Claimant's loss is to be assessed on a loss of opportunity basis, taking into account, among other things:

(a) the fact that X would have defended the claim;

(b) the risk or likelihood that at trial the judge would have:

(i) made a finding that the Claimant was driving too fast for the road conditions;

(ii) made a finding that the Claimant was paying no or no adequate attention to the oncoming traffic when he began his right turn;

(iii) made a finding that the Claimant was not wearing a seatbelt;

(iv) dismissed the claim against X or alternatively reduced it to take account of contributory negligence;

(c) the risk that the Claimant would have failed to establish his full loss of earnings claim having regard in particular to his lack of business accounts for the preceding years;

(d) the risk that the judge would have rejected or reduced the Claimant's other claims of loss including the claims for housekeeping and gardening;

(e) the likelihood that the Claimant, even if successful, would have suffered irrecoverable costs;

(f) the fact that had the Claimant lost his claim or failed to beat any payment in to court, there would have been a costs order made against him;

(g) the likelihood that the claim would have settled for a lesser amount than that claimed;

(h) the risks inherent in litigation.

9.12 Failure to mitigate

It is for the defendant to raise the issue of mitigation. You should set out the allegation that there was a failure to mitigate and then set out the facts upon which you will rely to show that the claimant could have but did not lessen his losses.

For example:

The Claimant failed to take any or any adequate steps to mitigate her loss.

PARTICULARS

(a) Failed to pursue an application to vary the order made by District Judge [name] on [date] at [court].

(b) Failed to put the house on the market with local estate agents.

9.13 Particulars of injury, loss and damage and the medical report

The medical reports attached to the statements of case are likely to be in relation to quantum (ie, concerned with condition and prognosis) rather than liability. You should set out in the defence the areas of agreement or dispute between the claimant's medical reports and any report which is to be attached to the defence. You can separate these into factual inaccuracies and difference of opinion or hypothetical arguments if appropriate. This part of the defence can sometimes be lengthy. Try to be concise and to refer to paragraphs within the attached reports rather than regurgitating large portions of them.

A counter-schedule should be included with the defence and served as set out in the Civil Procedure Rules discussed at the beginning of this chapter.

It is good practice to end this part of the Defence with a general non-admission as to the allegations of loss and injury and the parts of the reports not expressly dealt with:

As to paragraph [. . .] of the Particulars of Claim:

(a) Save as set out in this Defence, the Defendant is unable to admit or deny and has no knowledge of the alleged pain, injury, loss and damage set out in paragraph [. . .] of the Particulars of Claim. The Claimant is put to strict proof thereof, in particular the cause, nature and extent of the alleged injury, loss and damage and of each and every step taken in mitigation thereof.

(b) Save as set out in this Defence the Defendant neither agrees nor disputes but has no knowledge of the matters contained in the medical reports of [name] dated [. . .] served with the Particulars of Claim and the Claimant is put to strict proof thereof.

(c) Save as set out in this Defence and in the Counter-Schedule of past and future expenses and losses attached, the Defendant neither agrees nor disputes but has no knowledge of the matters set out in the Schedule of Special Damage and the Claimant is put to strict proof thereof.

9.14 Statement of truth

You are referred to the *Drafting Manual*.

Part IV

Evidence

Non-expert evidence in clinical negligence cases

10.1 Introduction

In clinical negligence cases a good deal of evidence needs to be gathered and considered before an expert is involved. A particular difficulty experienced by many patients who have had an unexpected and adverse outcome to clinical treatment, is finding out whether they were the victim of a medical mishap at all. Has something gone wrong or are their symptoms simply caused by the illness or injury with which they presented, an underlying medical condition, or a natural, perhaps extreme, reaction to the treatment rightly given? It may not be only the claimant who is in the dark. The defendant clinician might not know the answer to the question. The legal advisors also need to see a full picture of the surrounding circumstances.

Once evidence has been gathered to enable a determination of this issue, consideration needs to be given to evidence which will establish the blameworthiness (negligence) or otherwise of the mishap.

In order to determine whether there has been negligence, the judge will need to know (a) what happened (facts), and (b) what should have happened (hypothesis). Invariably in clinical negligence cases, expert evidence is needed to establish (b) and it is usually required to interpret and explain (a), the facts. However, before the expert can do so evidence needs to be obtained in relation to the following:

- What was the health of the patient prior to the clinical treatment?
- What was the expected outcome of the treatment?
- What is his or her health now?
- What in fact happened to the patient during the treatment?

As counsel you need to know what documentary evidence is or should be available to help to answer these questions, where the evidence comes from and when and how your client can get it. Once the evidence is obtained, you should know what to look for within it. You should be able to notice where there are or might be gaps in the evidence and be able to advise as to seeking further evidence, and as to what evidence should be seen by an expert. You should also be in a position to formulate questions to be put to the expert or to notice which areas he has considered or failed to consider in his report.

10.2 Types of evidence

First, you need to be aware of the types of documents which are available. These will include documents which record relevant events or which inform (or should inform) the clinical practice. Below is a list of relevant types of evidence which might be available in a clinical negligence case:

- Medical records (hospital and general practice notes).
- Dental records.
- Associated records (eg, nurses' notes, physiotherapy).
- X-rays, scans, test results.
- Ambulance records.
- Alternative therapy records (eg, osteopathy, acupuncture, homeopathy).
- Hospital protocols.
- Department of Health circulars.
- General Medical Council circulars.
- Clinical Governance Strategy documents from the relevant hospital or other clinical practice.
- Internal investigations surrounding the adverse outcome.
- Witness statements from patient and all relevant clinicians.
- Evidence concerning any incident which caused the patient's original medical complaint.

Once you know what to look for you need to know what to seek and how to get it. Once you have got it, you need to know whether you have got all of it (ie, what it should look like) and what to do with it. These matters are discussed below in relation to broad categories of different types of evidence.

10.3   Medical (and associated) records

10.3.1   What to seek

The general practice is for both sides to obtain all of the potential claimant's medical records. Obviously the notes concerning the particular treatment under question are needed. The notes thereafter can assist in showing any after-effects of the treatment or other intervening injuries or illness which has affected the claimant's lifestyle. The past notes are crucial to give a full picture of the claimant's health prior to the relevant incident. Was he pre-disposed to this injury? Should the previous history have indicated a certain course of treatment to the treating doctor? Would this claimant have ceased to work in any event at some future date because of a pre-existing medical problem? Think laterally to make sure that you are seeking all relevant notes from the hospital, general practitioner, alternative health practitioners, etc.

10.3.2   How to get them

Notes and records should be sought and given in accordance with the Pre-action Protocol for the Resolution of Clinical Disputes and the normal rules of pre-action disclosure and disclosure which are discussed in **Chapter 6** and in the *Civil Litigation Manual*, **Chapters 20 and 21**.

10.3.3   What to expect in GP notes

You will see photocopies not originals of notes. GP notes tend to be kept in cardboard envelopes. The front cover can contain much relevant information such as a summary of the main complaints or the medical allergies of a patient. Make sure that this has been copied for you. The majority of notes are usually handwritten on cards with only recent years being computer generated. Any hospital referral letters or test results will be kept with the notes. You should arrange and paginate the notes in a chronological order if that has not already been done. Ensure that you have clear photocopies. Check for any gaps in the notes. Wherever there is mention of a referral, follow that through if at all relevant. You should find a letter from the relevant referral doctor detailing his appointment with the patient.

Likewise when tests (eg, blood tests) have been requested, check to see that you have the results. If the notes are computerised, ask for an audit trail to demonstrate that they have not been altered.

10.3.4   What to expect in hospital notes

The type of notes will obviously depend upon where the claimant entered the hospital system, whether he was an in-patient or an out-patient and what kind of treatment he received. You might find an Admission Record sheet, out-patient notes, in-patient notes, operation notes, nurses' notes and drug records. There might also be X-rays, pathology reports, blood test results, etc. Think about each stage of what happened to the patient in hospital and what notes you would expect to see. Follow through references within the notes you do get to other departments or other treatment and check that you have received the relevant notes from there.

10.3.5   Dental notes

These tend to be more straightforward but check as you would GP notes for evidence of previous referrals, tests, etc.

10.3.6   Alternative practitioner notes

These can be a very useful source of information in relation to pre-existing problems or for detailed explanations of the current medical problem. Often you will find a much fuller history is given by an alternative practitioner than by a conventional doctor partly because of methodology and partly because of time.

10.3.7   Understanding notes

Once you have got all of the notes you need, make them your own. Photocopy a bundle for you to mark. Put them in chronological order and paginate them. Make sure that you can read them. It is tempting to skim-read parts of notes which are difficult to decipher. It might be that the handwriting is the problem, but more often than not it is the doctor's use of unfamiliar medical terms and shorthand which makes the notes hard to read. In time you will become familiar with many terms. To begin with you may need to refer to other members of chambers. Your first port of call however should be a medical dictionary or textbook or a medico-legal text such as Powers and Harris, *Clinical Negligence* (3rd edn, Butterworths). The *Case Preparation Manual*, **Appendix 1**, includes a useful glossary of medical terms.

10.3.8   Understanding the problem

Whilst you must be careful not to assume medical expertise yourself, you do need to have a basic understanding of the medical problem if you are to approach the case with a useful forensic mind. Invariably in contested clinical negligence cases you will need to have the help of an expert as will the court. You will be much better equipped to ask pertinent and focused questions if you are at home with the relevant terminology and you understand the nature of the injury or other sickness with which the patient was suffering. Make sure that you can visualise what the medical problem was. Use pictures, eg, a Body Atlas, or if you are better working in 3D use a CD-ROM Body Atlas; use a medical dictionary. Do not try to research the matter in depth through the Internet, though it is a useful resource for definitions, pictures and initial understanding of unfamiliar medical conditions.

10.3.9   Understanding the clinical procedures

Equally you need to understand the procedures and treatment employed by the clinicians. If the notes mention a particular diagnostic tool such as a CT scan, an MRI scan, or a laparoscopy, you must know what that means. What did it entail for the patient? When considering an operation, be sure that you can visualise, at least diagrammatically, what the surgeon did. Some internet sites provide films of common operations (eg, gall bladder removal). Likewise you should have looked up any relevant drugs given and know how they are administered (orally, intravenously, intramuscularly) and what they were expected to accomplish. Reading the notes carefully along with a good medical dictionary, a drug dictionary and a basic body atlas will usually provide all of the information which you need to form a sufficient understanding prior to meeting the expert.

10.3.10   What to look out for

You will usually be guided by your instructions and by the issues clearly raised in the case as to what to be alert to when reading the notes. In particular, you should always:

- Notice the precise sequence of events. Make a detailed chronology of all relevant times.
- Note any delays.
- Note any change of medical staff or change of drugs.
- Note any relevant pre-existing injuries/illnesses.
- Note any reference to time off work.
- Note any inconsistencies between the medical records and the witness statements/ medical reports and protocols or other guidelines which you have access to.

Flag or highlight these parts of the notes.

Go through the relevant parts of the notes carefully with your client and expert. Ask the expert if there is anything else he might expect to see in the notes.

10.4   Internal clinical documents

10.4.1   What to seek

Many hospital departments, GP practices and other clinical practices work increasingly to internal protocols and other guidelines produced with the intention of promoting good practice and managing risk. Sometimes these are produced by the individual hospital trusts or even hospital departments, sometimes the GP practice will have devised their own guidance. On other occasions, the documents will come from independent bodies, eg, NICE (National Institute for Clinical Excellence) provides guidance to the NHS in connection with the use of certain treatments (see www.nice.org.uk) and the British Association for Accident and Emergency Medicine has produced 'Clinical Governance Safeguards' which deal with prioritising patients in A & E departments. The Department of Health publishes and issues guidelines on many aspects of clinical practice, eg, immunisations and drugs contraindications. Osteopathic and homeopathic associations also issue guidance to their members. You cannot be expected to know of the existence of all relevant protocols and guidelines but you should:

- be alert to the possibility of their existence;
- ask your expert what he would expect to see;
- ask the proposed defendants if they have any relevant publications.

10.4.2 How to get them

Many of these documents are in the public domain and your expert should provide them or reference to them. Alternatively, these documents should be sought and given in accordance with the Pre-action Protocol for the Resolution of Clinical Disputes and the normal rules of pre-action disclosure and disclosure which are discussed in **Chapter 6** and in the *Civil Litigation Manual*, **Chapters 20** and **21**.

10.4.3 How to use protocols and guidelines

(a) Analyse the sequence of events which actually took place in the light of the available clinical guidance for procedures in the relevant hospital.

(b) Show them to your expert.

(c) Departure from guidance or protocol does not necessarily mean negligence. The test of *Bolam v Friern Hospital Management Committee* [1957] 1 WLR 582 remains. However, it gives the claimant ammunition in cross-examination and so in negotiation.

(d) The absence of a protocol when you would usually expect to see one might also assist the claimant in establishing a case in negligence. At a relatively recent (unreported) Inquest hearing, a private hospital's standard of care was called in to question for the failure to have a protocol for the monitoring of patients after they had undergone a caesarean section when, it was said, all NHS hospitals had such a protocol. Ask the expert in the case whether he would expect to see published guidance to cover the relevant procedures.

10.5 Internal investigative documents

10.5.1 What to seek

The GMC's 'Good Medical Practice' requires doctors to inform patients when something has gone wrong. Moreover, after an adverse outcome in a hospital or where there has been a near miss, most hospitals will have a system of reporting and investigating what occurred. Different trusts have different procedures for this and call them different names, eg, 'adverse outcome reports' or 'serious incident reporting'.

10.5.2 How to get them

It is likely that the defendant will claim privilege in respect of certain internal investigation documents. The claimant is entitled to see such documents unless the dominant purpose for which the document was prepared is litigation. (See the *Civil Litigation Manual*, **20.5**.) In *Lask v Gloucester Health Authority* (1991) 2 Med LR 379, the health authority produced affidavits from its solicitors to the effect that a confidential accident report which was required by the National Health Service Circulars to be prepared to prevent further accidents was also prepared in case of litigation and, they argued, should therefore attract privilege. However, the Court of Appeal held that the dominant purpose was not litigation and it should therefore be disclosed.

10.5.3 How to use the internal investigative documents

You should:

- Show them to your expert.
- Look out for any references to documents which you have not got.
- Build a fuller picture of the events.
- Look at the documents closely — they might even contain admissions.
- Look for any inconsistencies between these and the witness statements or clinical notes.

10.6 Witness statements

Your instructing solicitor is likely to have prepared the witness statements. You should satisfy yourself that they contain all of the information relevant to any issue on each element of the cause of action or defence. They should cover the relevant parts of the medical notes, records and other documents. Any issues as to the contents of the medical notes should be raised. All aspects in relation to the quantum of the claim should also be included in detail.

10.7 Conclusion

Once you have sought and considered the relevant evidence you will be in a position to formulate pertinent questions to your expert in order to elicit his opinion as to whether the acts or omissions of the clinicians fell below the proper standard of care owed by them.

Expert evidence in clinical negligence cases

11.1 Introduction

Expert evidence is central to almost all contested clinical negligence cases. Reports can be required in relation to standard and duty of care, breach of duty, causation, condition and prognosis and often the cost of future care. Expert evidence is also expensive and so often offends against the principle of proportionality now enshrined in the Civil Procedure Rules 1998.

The intention behind the rules governing the use of expert evidence is clearly set out in the preamble to PD 35:

Part 35 is intended to limit the use of oral expert evidence to that which is reasonably required. In addition, where possible, matters requiring expert evidence should be dealt with by a single expert. Permission of the court is always required either to call an expert or to put an expert's report in evidence.

The control of the court over the use of expert evidence is fundamental to the Civil Procedure Rules. Parties have to seek permission to use expert evidence. Not only can the court limit the number of experts but it can also limit the issues covered in the report. The PD 35 partially dictates the contents and form of a report and failure to comply can result in the evidence being ruled inadmissible. In fast track cases it will be the norm not to allow parties to call expert evidence so that only the written report(s) will form a part of the evidence.

As ever, the general rules sat uneasily in some respects with clinical negligence and consequently the Pre-action Protocol for the Resolution of Clinical Disputes recognises that parties will require 'flexibility in their approach to expert evidence'. In particular it states (para 4.2):

Decisions on whether experts might be instructed jointly, and on whether reports might be exchanged sequentially or by exchange, should rest with the parties and their advisers.

This approach is reflected in the pre-action protocols for other areas of professional negligence.

However, most of the rules and requirements concerning experts will still apply to clinical negligence cases.

The practice and procedure governing the use of expert evidence comes from many sources: substantive law, Civil Procedure Rules, practice directions, Code of Guidance, protocols and conventions of practice. This part of the Manual will help you to understand and navigate those sources when deciding how to make best use of expert evidence to maximise your client's chances of success. It starts by describing the expert's role, status, rights and duties then goes on to consider all of the stages of working with an expert on liability and quantum. In particular, the following aspects are discussed: obtaining the court's permission, choosing an expert, briefing him, getting a comprehensive report, meeting in conference, practical handling of your expert generally, questioning the other side's expert in writing, setting up a meeting of all parties' experts and examining and cross-examining the experts at trial. Another important aspect of the law which informs many of your dealings with an expert in practice is the operation of legal professional privilege and its waiver, which is discussed at **11.4** below.

11.2   Role, status, rights and duties of an expert

11.2.1   Role of the expert

The heart and the battleground of a clinical negligence case is usually the expert evidence. It is fairly unusual for there to be an issue as to the factual sequence of events which are normally fully recorded. Instead, the issues tend to be about the nature of acceptable practice, the risks and benefits of certain treatments, causation and future care requirements. Before he can form his judgment as to the negligence or otherwise of the defendant, the judge needs help in the form of medical expertise to assist him in the interpretation of the facts which he finds. The general rule is that opinion evidence is inadmissible in court proceedings. An exception to the rule applies to expert evidence where two things are satisfied: first, the evidence must be given by an appropriately qualified witness; and secondly, it must be given in relation to a matter which requires expertise. It has long been established that scientific or medical matters require expertise and therefore, when given by an appropriate expert, such evidence is admissible.

11.2.2   Status of the expert evidence

A judge is not obliged to accept the expert evidence presented to him. He is obliged to take it into account but ultimately it is only there to assist him in reaching his own independent judgment. In the case of *Bolitho v City and Hackney Health Authority* [1998] AC 232, HL, Lord Browne-Wilkinson illustrates this point powerfully when considering the judge's application of the expert evidence to the *Bolam* test:

... the court is not bound to hold that a defendant doctor escapes liability for negligent treatment or diagnosis just because he leads evidence from a number of medical experts who are genuinely of the opinion that the defendant's treatment accorded with sound medical practice ... the court has to be satisfied that the exponents of the body of opinion relied upon can demonstrate that such opinion has a logical basis.

In the case of *Stevens v Simons* [1998] CLY 1161, the Court of Appeal considered the judge's rejection of expert evidence in relation to causation. It held that the fact that an agreed medical report contained the opinion that the symptoms suffered by the claimant were not attributable to the injuries sustained in the relevant accident, did not prevent the judge from concluding otherwise after hearing evidence and reading the reports.

However, where departing from medical evidence the judge should say so and give his reasons. A failure to do so is grounds for appeal and in some cases the Court of Appeal has referred the matter back for a retrial on those grounds (*Flannery v Halifax Estate Agencies Ltd* [2000] 1 WLR 377; *Dyson v Leeds City Council* (1999) LTL 22/11/99). Where there is conflicting medical evidence (as in many clinical negligence cases), the judge will have to decide which expert's evidence he prefers. He should take into account the experience, qualifications and credibility of the expert, and the basis of the evidence he has heard when making this decision.

11.2.3   Witness of fact who is also an expert

One of the interesting aspects of clinical negligence cases is that one or more of the witnesses of fact are likely to be medical experts (eg, the defendant doctor). Is that witness entitled to give expert opinion evidence? In law he is entitled to give opinion evidence if appropriately qualified. The risk is that in doing so the party will offend against the procedural rules. Was the evidence disclosed in the proper way? How many expert witnesses are allowed? In tactical terms, there is limited use in allowing your witness of fact to give such expert evidence as it is likely to be self-serving and so to lose the judge's interest. In practice, the defendant clinician and/or supporting medical team will give a fair amount of opinion evidence when explaining their own actions and clinical decisions. For example, the defendant clinician might want to say: 'I checked the patient's blood pressure at four-hourly intervals because that accorded with the approved practice at my hospital and in my opinion that was sufficiently often.' He might wish to stray further in to the domain of the expert by relying on the hospital protocol documents to support that statement. That is all part and parcel of his explanation for his actions and nobody would be likely to object to that. He should probably not go the extra step to say, 'a responsible body of medical opinion would do as I did'. In practice, the line between his evidence and the expert's might be a little blurred, but common sense really dictates where to stop with the witness of fact and where to begin with the expert. The Court of Appeal recognised the overlap of expert evidence and evidence of fact and gave the claimant permission to rely upon two experts of the same discipline in order to put it on an equal footing with the defendant in a case where the defendant's witnesses of fact would inevitably stray in to giving expert opinion (*ES v Chesterfield North Derbyshire Royal Hospital NHS Trust* [2003] EWCA Civ 1284).

11.2.4   Expert's duty to the court

Cresswell J in *National Justice Compania Naviera SA v Prudential Assurance Co Ltd* [1993] 2 Lloyd's Rep 68) listed the duties of the expert. They are summarised below:

- Expert evidence should be independent and uninfluenced by the exigencies of litigation.
- An expert witness should not assume the role of the advocate but should give objective, unbiased assistance to the court.
- Facts or assumptions upon which the opinion is based should be stated as should material facts which could detract from the conclusion.
- An expert should make it clear when a matter fell outside his expertise.
- If the report was incomplete for reasons of time or otherwise qualified that should be stated in the report.
- If the expert changed his mind after exchange of reports about a matter contained within it that should be communicated to the other side (through lawyers) without delay and, where appropriate, to the court.

- Documents referred to in the report should be provided to the other parties at the same time as the report.

The Civil Procedure Rules 1998 make the expert's duty to the court explicit and clear. There is no longer room to consider the expert as a hired gun. CPR, r 35.3 states:

> *(1)   It is the duty of the expert to help the court on the matters within his expertise.*
>
> *(2)   This duty overrides any obligation to the person from whom he has received instructions or by whom he is paid.*

The expert is required to state in his report that he understands this duty and has complied with it (r 35.10).

The Expert Witness Institute's Code of Guidance on Expert Evidence (see **Appendix 6**) re-emphasises the impartial role of the professional expert (para 14).

11.3   Expert evidence of liability and quantum

Expert evidence in relation to liability will concentrate on the duty and standard of care owed by the relevant clinician and will detail the specific breaches of the duty owed. It will also deal with all issues of causation. The expert medical evidence in relation to quantum deals with the extent of the injury and the future implications (condition and prognosis). Further expert evidence is frequently required in relation to the financial claim, for example, care reports assessing and valuing the special needs of an injured claimant or accountants' reports valuing the loss of earnings claim. These aspects are beyond the scope of this Manual and reference should be made to the *Remedies Manual* and appropriate practitioners' texts.

This part considers when and how to go about getting expert medical evidence and how to use it in the preparation and conduct of your case as well as how to attack the other side's expert evidence.

11.3.1   At what stage should you involve an expert on liability?

Before you are in a position to advise your client as to whether there is a good cause of action or defence, you are likely to need the help of an expert. You may receive the papers prior to the instruction of an expert and be asked to advise what expert evidence is required. You will need to be clear as to the type of expert needed, the issues which he needs to consider, the documents which he should see and whether or not he needs to examine the potential claimant. You should ask that he gives his opinion in the form of a letter or draft (not final) report. This is for many reasons; not least because the expert may alter his opinion as the case progresses, for example, after seeing the witness statements, discussing it in conference, seeing correspondence or reports from the other side. You may well need a conference after seeing the draft report and before settling the particulars of claim or defence. The advice received from the expert will form the basis of your pleaded allegations or defence. It does not have to be attached to the statement of case (whereas the report as to condition and prognosis does) and it is unlikely to be so. You should be conscious that the instructions you now give will form the basis of the final report and will therefore have to be disclosed to the other side at a later stage if you use the expert's evidence at trial.

11.3.2   At what stage should you involve a medical expert on quantum?

The short answer is early! The claimant is required to attach a report as to condition and prognosis to the particulars of claim. The defendant needs to plead to that report setting out areas of agreement and disagreement and can, but is not obliged to, annexe a report to the Defence. (For detailed discussion of these provisions, see the *Drafting Manual*.)

11.3.3   Permission to adduce expert evidence

Having used the expert to assist you to settle the statements of case, you will now need permission to rely upon his evidence. As set out above, parties no longer have the right to adduce expert evidence without the permission of the court. In fast track cases, expert evidence will normally be limited to written reports unless attendance is required in the interests of justice (CPR, r 35.5(2)). The court can also limit the issues addressed and the recoverable fees. CPR, r 35.4 sets out what needs to be done when applying to the court for permission to rely upon expert evidence:

> (1)   No party may call an expert or put in evidence an expert's report without the court's permission.
> (2)   When a party applies for permission under this rule he must identify:
>> (a)   the field in which he wishes to rely on expert evidence; and
>> (b)   where practicable the expert in that field on whose evidence he wishes to rely.
> (3)   If permission is granted under this rule it shall be in relation only to the expert named or the field identified under paragraph (2).
> (4)   The court may limit the amount of the expert's fees and expenses that the party who wishes to rely on the expert may recover from any other party.

How will the court exercise its discretion under this rule? You should be ready to persuade the judge that the issues you wish to be addressed are material and that the expert you wish to call is the appropriate one. It is possible that you will need to demonstrate that your expert is objective, perhaps that he acts for as many claimants as defendants in his medico-legal practice, that he is a specialist in the relevant field, that his fees represent good value for money and so on.

11.3.4   Will the court insist on appointing a single joint expert?

CPR, r 35.7(1), provides:

> Where two or more parties wish to submit expert evidence on a particular issue, the court may direct that the evidence on that issue is to [be] given by one expert only.

The practice direction for the management of cases on the fast track (PD 28) provides at para 3.9:

> Where the court is to give directions on its own initiative and it is not aware of any steps taken by the parties other than the service of statements of case, its general approach will be: . . .
>> (4)   to give directions for a single joint expert unless there is good reason not to do so . . .

And at para 3.7:

> Directions agreed by the parties should . . . where appropriate contain provisions about: . . .
>> (4)   the use of a single joint expert, or in cases where the use of a single expert has not been agreed, the exchange and agreement of expert evidence . . . and without-prejudice discussions of the experts.

If the court disagrees with separate instruction it can insist upon the joint instruction of a single expert under CPR, r 35.7(1) as set out above.

The multi-track practice direction (PD 29, para 4.13) provides:

Where the court is proposing on its own initiative to make an order under rule 35.7 (...that evidence... is to be given by a single expert) or under rule 35.15 (which gives the court power to appoint an assessor), the court must, unless the parties have consented in writing to the order, list a case management conference.

Practically all clinical negligence cases will be allocated to the multi-track because of the complexity of the issues and the likelihood of evidence taking more than one day. Moreover, as discussed at **11.1**, it has been recognised that clinical negligence cases will require flexibility in relation to expert evidence. It will largely be left to the parties and their legal advisers to decide whether there should be joint or separate experts. On the whole, each party will call its own medical experts on liability in clinical negligence cases. However, in relation to quantum, there is more scope for the appointment of a joint expert.

11.3.5   Finding the right expert

First, you must ensure that you choose experts who are qualified in the right discipline and appropriately specialised. An oncologist's evidence that a cancer should have been diagnosed by a general practitioner on a certain date is not as compelling as an experienced and well-qualified general practitioner's evidence to that effect. Equally, whilst a general surgeon is qualified to give his opinion as to bowel surgery, if the surgery in question was carried out by a specialist surgeon or if the other side's expert is such a specialist then your client's case would be stronger if a specialist bowel surgeon was instructed to give evidence. Beyond that there are some general pitfalls to avoid:

- The expert's evidence should be based on experience not just a reading of research papers. Check the extent of the relevant experience and that it is recent and continuing if possible.

- Does the expert have connection with the claimant or defendant witnesses which might detract from the objectivity of his evidence?

- Make sure that the expert is not a known 'claimant's (or defendant's) expert' which will also detract from the impact of his evidence.

- Make sure that the expert is prepared to come off the fence and is able to stand his ground under cross-examination.

Secondly, you must find the expert. At first, you will need to rely on recommendations from your solicitors, colleagues in chambers, chambers' database or expert witness organisations such as the Expert Witness Institute.

11.3.6   Brief for the expert

Your instructing solicitor will instruct the expert witness but might ask for your guidance before doing so. Consider the following:

(a) The Expert Witness Institute's Code of Guidance on Expert Evidence sets out on guidelines to those instructing an expert in para 6 (see **Appendix 6**).

(b) The expert needs to know the extent and purpose of the instructions.

(c) Ask your solicitor to tell the expert what is expected: are you seeking interpretation of the medical notes, a preliminary advice, a conference, a draft report, a final report for use in court proceedings, meetings with other experts, an examination of the client, a response to the other side's evidence?

(d) Set out the questions the expert needs to address fully and clearly.

11.3.7   Medical examination for report

Your expert might well need to examine the potential claimant and/or carry out investigative tests before giving advice. If you act for the claimant, you will probably have no difficulties in arranging this. If you act for the defendant, you may meet objections from the claimant. If the claimant unreasonably refuses to be examined, the court has powers to stay proceedings (*Edmeades v Thames Board Mills* [1969] 2 QB 67, CA). See the **Civil Litigation Manual, 29.3**, for a full discussion of this issue.

11.3.8   Which documents should the expert see?

The expert should see all documents in the case which are relevant to the issues upon which you are asking him to comment. These might include:

- Statements of case if proceedings have begun.
- All medical notes. (In good order with copies for him to keep wherever possible. You should ask him to interpret any relevant parts of the notes which you have difficulty understanding.)
- Associated records (eg, nurses' notes, physiotherapy).
- X-rays, scans, test results.
- Ambulance records.
- Alternative therapy records (eg, osteopathy, acupuncture, homeopathy).
- Hospital protocols or other healthcare guidance.
- Internal investigations surrounding the adverse outcome.
- Witness statements from patient and all relevant clinicians.
- Evidence concerning any incident which caused the patient's original medical complaint.
- The other side's witness statements/medical reports if you have them.

The expert should not be shown previously obtained expert evidence upon which you do not intend to rely. If he has seen it, he will need to set that out in his statement of material instructions. See *Lucas v Barking, Havering and Redbridge Hospitals NHS Trust* [2003] EWCA 1102.

11.3.9   Issues of liabiilty for the expert to consider

The expert's advice or report to you will form the basis of the allegations or defence to allegations in the Statement of Case which you draft. You need to ensure that the expert considers every element of the cause of action or defence which is in issue. In order to do so, you need to have thoroughly understood the law relating to each issue. This has been considered in **Chapter 2** and will not be discussed here in any detail. You will also need to refer to practitioners' texts such as Jackson & Powell, *Professional Negligence*; Powers & Harris, *Clinical Negligence* and Pittaway and Hammerton, *Professional Negligence Cases*.

11.3.9.1 The duty and standard of care

The duty of care needs to be addressed on the basis of the *Bolam* test as developed in *Bolitho v City and Hackney Health Authority* [1998] AC 232. In other words, the expert needs to comment upon (a) whether the defendant acted in accordance with the practice of a responsible, reasonable and respectable body of medical opinion, and (b) whether that body of opinion was based upon a logical and sound analysis of the risks and benefits of the relevant practice.

11.3.9.2 Breach of duty

It is not enough to have a general statement about a clinician's incompetence. Each and every aspect of the treatment which is alleged to have fallen below the requisite standard must be identified and the reasons why it was or was not adequate explained. These separate breaches will form the backbone of the Particulars of Claim.

11.3.9.3 Causation

Some experts deal with issues of breach of duty and standard of care and fail to go on to deal with causation. It is of no assistance to the claimant to prove, for example, that the clinician failed to operate timeously if the injuries she suffered would have occurred in any event. When considering causation remember:

(a) Be conscious when asking questions of the expert of the relevant tests of causation in clinical negligence cases (*Hotson, Wilsher, Bolitho*) (see **Chapter 2** above).

(b) In relation to each separate allegation of breach of duty, causation must be considered and explained and the consequences of the breach set out.

(c) Causation can be the most difficult aspect of the case and the expert is being asked to deal in both factual and hypothetical situations. You will need to ask clear and explicit questions and sometimes quite a lot of questions to elicit all of the information which you need.

For example, it would be insufficient to ask: 'What would have happened if the cancer had been diagnosed earlier?'

You would need to ask many more questions. In relation to each date on which the claimant alleges the diagnosis ought to have been made you would need to ask at least the following questions. If the diagnosis had been made on [date]:

- What stage is it likely the cancer would have reached?
- What course of treatment would have been carried out?
- What would the outcome have been (on the balance of probabilities)?
- What would the chances of successful treatment have been in those circumstances?

You would also need to understand the evidence or reasoning upon which the expert based the answer to those questions: for example, was his opinion based upon statistical findings or upon his own clinical judgment?

11.3.9.4 Quantum

The expert must consider the condition of the claimant prior to and since the incident complained of. The likely prognosis of the current condition with particular reference to the extent to which that condition has been exacerbated or accelerated by alleged negligence. The report also needs to deal with any medical incapacity of the claimant's in relation to past, current or future earnings (eg, in relation to the person's ability to sit, stand, lift, or drive or in relation to specific vulnerabilities to environmental factors). The likely course of future treatment (eg, drugs/operations/counselling) and its possible impact on the claimant's lifestyle.

11.3.10   Conference

11.3.10.1   Beforehand

Know the papers, know the legal issues, understand the medical background, look up any medical terms which you do not understand. Familiarise yourself with your expert's qualifications and experience. Work out and, if appropriate, send an agenda of the areas to be covered to the expert through your instructing solicitors.

11.3.10.2   Purpose

The purpose of the conference is to:

- analyse and interpret the evidence in the case together from a medical and a legal point of view;
- identify with precision the acts or omissions which form the basis of a negligence action;
- analyse the consequence of each breach to the patient;
- discuss possible defences to those acts or omissions;
- consider the other side's evidence if you have it;
- meet and assess the expert witness prior to calling him to give evidence in court. Check the areas of the witness's expertise, the qualifications and the experience;
- discuss the form and content of the final report;
- assess the strengths and weaknesses of the client's case and advise the client accordingly.

11.3.10.3   At the conference

Be sure to get a very good note of the conference which might form the basis of your statement of case and/or of your next opinion.

11.3.11   The report

The Civil Procedure Rules 1998 and accompanying practice directions, and the Code of Guidance on Expert Evidence under the Rules, dictate fairly strict requirements as to the reports. These are set out below:

11.3.11.1   Written report: CPR, r 35.5

Expert evidence must be given in a written report:

> *(1)   Expert evidence is to be given in a written report unless the court directs otherwise.*
> *(2)   If a claim is on the fast track, the court will not direct an expert to attend a hearing unless it is necessary to do so in the interests of justice.*

Many clinical negligence cases will be allocated to the multi-track because of the complexity of the issues and the likelihood of evidence taking more than one day.

11.3.11.2   Limits: CPR, r 35.1

Expert evidence shall be restricted to that which is reasonably required to resolve the proceedings.

You are unlikely to recover costs for evidence which goes beyond the contested issues in the case so ensure that the report does not go beyond them.

11.3.11.3   Contents: CPR, r 35.10 and PD 35, para 2.2

Full compliance with these provisions ought to ensure that the expert has included in his report everything which he regards as relevant to the opinion which he has expressed and that anything which would affect the validity of that opinion has been drawn to the attention of the court (see the note to the rule in the *White Book*).

Under CPR, r 35.10:

- The report must comply with the relevant practice direction.

- The report must include a statement at the end by the expert that he understands and has complied with his duty to the court.

- The report must state the substance of all material instructions, whether written or oral, on the basis of which the report was written.

PD 35, para 2.2, provides:

An expert's report must:

    (1)   give details of the expert's qualifications,

    (2)   give details of any literature or other material which the expert has relied on in making the report,

    (3)   contain a statement setting out the substance of all facts and instructions given to the expert which are material to the opinions expressed in the report or upon which those opinions are based;

    (4)   make clear which of the facts stated in the report are within the expert's own knowledge;

    (5)   say who carried out any examination, measurement, test or experiment which the expert has used for the report, give the qualifications of that person, and say whether or not the test or experiment has been carried out under the expert's supervision;

    (6)   where there is a range of opinion on the matters dealt with in the report:

        (a)   summarise the range of opinion, and

        (b)   give reasons for his own opinion,

    (7)   contain a summary of the conclusions reached;

    (8)   if the expert is not able to give his opinion without qualification, state the qualification; and

    (9)   contain a statement that the expert understands his duty to the court, and has complied and will continue to comply with that duty.

Paragraphs 2.3 and 2.4 state that the report should contain a statement of truth in the following form:

I confirm that in so far as the facts stated in my reports are within my own knowledge I have made clear which they are and I believe them to be true, and that the opinions I have expressed represent my true and complete professional opinion.

11.3.11.4   Code of Guidance on Expert Evidence

The Expert Witness Institute's guide for its members: *The Law and You: Code of Guidance on Expert Evidence* is an important document. It gives guidance on all aspects of instructions to an expert and the contents of an expert's report. The full code is set out in **Appendix 6**. Of particular note are paras 14, 16 and 17:

THE EXPERT'S REPORT

    14. In preparing their reports, experts:

        (a)   should maintain professional objectivity and impartiality at all times;

(b)   in addressing questions of fact and opinion, should keep the two separate and discrete; and

(c)   where there are facts in dispute:

(i)   should not express a view in favour of one or other disputed sets of facts, unless, because of their particular learning and experience, they perceive one set of facts as being improbable or less probable, in which case they may express that view, and should give reasons; and

(ii)   should express separate opinions on every set of facts in dispute.

(CPR, r 35.3)

CONTENT OF REPORT

16.   In providing a report experts:

(a)   must address it to the court and not to any of the parties;

(b)   must include a statement setting out the substance of all instructions (whether written or oral). The statement should summarise the facts and instructions given to the expert which are material to the opinions expressed in the report or upon which those opinions are based;

(c)   where there is a range of opinion in the matters dealt with in the report, give:

(i)   a summary of the range of opinion; and

(ii)   the reasons for his own opinion.

(d)   must express any qualification of, or reservation to, their opinion;

if such opinion was not formed independently, should make clear the source of the opinion;

(f)   must declare that the report has been prepared in accordance with this Code and the requirements of the Civil Procedure Rules; and

(g)   must include a statement of truth, as required by PD 35.

AMENDMENT

17.   Experts:

(a)   must not be asked to, and must not, amend, expand or alter any part of the report in a manner which distorts the expert's true opinion; but

(b)   may be invited to amend or expand a report to ensure accuracy and internal consistency completeness, relevance to the issues and clarity.

A persuasive report will have the following attributes:

- Comprehensive; considering all issues separately and fully.
- Not overstating the client's case.
- Meeting the difficulties in the client's case.
- Clear structure.
- Written in clear terms, avoiding or explaining technical medical terms.
- Based on few assumed facts.
- Well-qualified/experienced author.
- Research well explained within the body of the report.

11.3.12   Failure to disclose the report on time: CPR, Parts 29 and 35

CPR, r 35.13, states:

A party who fails to disclose an expert's report may not use the report at the trial or call the expert to give evidence orally unless the court gives permission.

For an example of a case where permission to rely on the report was refused, see *Stevens v Gullis* [2000] 1 All ER 527.

11.3.13   Written questions to the other side's expert

Under the Civil Procedure Rules 1998, a party may put written questions to another party's expert or a joint expert about the report (CPR, r 35.6(1)). Unless the court gives permission or the other party agrees, these questions can only be put once, must be put within 28 days of the receipt of the report and must be for the purpose of clarification of the report (CPR, r 35.6(2)). The purpose of the rule is no doubt to make it harder for a party to justify the need to call an expert to give evidence in court as many issues can be clarified at this stage. This provision is used frequently to fill in gaps where experts have not addressed important issues. It also limits the need to have separate experts for each party (see *Daniels v Walker* [2001] 1 WLR 1382). The expert's responses are treated as a part of his written report. The Expert Witness Institute's Code of Guidance on Expert Evidence, para 24, states that the expert should respond within 28 days. Where an expert does not respond to questions put in accordance with the rule, the court may make an order that the party who instructed the expert may not rely upon him and/or that the expert's fees may not be recovered by that party from any other party.

11.3.14   Changing Expert

Sometimes a party is disappointed with its own expert and wishes to use a different expert in the same field. The courts are very reluctant to allow this practice, which has been described as 'expert shopping'. In certain circumstances, it is possible to persuade a court to allow a party to change expert but such permission will usually only be given on the condition that the party discloses its first expert's reports. See *Beck v Ministry of Defence* [2003] EWCA Civ 1043, *Carlson v Townsend* [2001] 1 WLR 2415 and *Hajigeorgiouv Vasiliou* [2005] EWCA Civ 236.

11.3.15   Joint meeting of experts

Under CPR, r 35.12, the court has the power to direct a discussion between experts at any stage of the proceedings. The discussion is for the purpose of requiring the experts to identify issues and to reach agreement upon those issues where possible.

The purpose of this discussion is to limit the issues upon which expert evidence will be needed at court. This enhances the prospect of settlement, limits costs and shortens any trial which is necessary. The meeting should take place as early as possible in order to define the issues before unnecessary costs are incurred.

The discussion can take place at a meeting or by telephone or other electronic means. The Expert Witness Institute's Code of Guidance on Expert Evidence states that it may take place face to face or otherwise, proportionate to the circumstances and the allocated track.

At a case management conference the court should not only direct a discussion but will also, with the help of the parties and their legal representatives, specify the subject matter to be discussed (*Access to Justice Final Report*, p 148). Agendas for the meetings should also be worked out. As counsel you are likely to be involved at the case management conference and might well be asked to assist in formulating questions for the agenda of the meeting. See the Code of Guidance on Expert Evidence, para 26, which provides:

The parties, their lawyers and experts should cooperate to produce concise agendas for any discussion between experts, which should, so far as possible:

    (a) be circulated 28 days before the date fixed for the discussion;

    (b) be agreed seven days before the date fixed for the discussion;

    (c) consist of questions which are clearly stated and apply, where necessary, the correct legal test;

(d)   *consist of questions which, by their nature, are closed, that is to say, capable of being answered 'yes' or 'no'; and*

(e)   *include questions which enable the experts to state the reasons for their agreement or disagreement.*

The guidance also states that experts must not be given and must not accept instructions not to reach agreement on any areas within their competence. However, the experts cannot bind the parties in relation to any agreement without the parties' express consent to be bound (this is recognised in CPR, r 35.12(5)).

At the meeting the experts can be required by the court to draw up a statement of the areas of agreement or disagreement and a summary of their reasons for disagreement. This statement is for the court. However, contents of the discussion between the experts cannot be referred to at trial without the agreement of the parties (CPR, r 35.12(4)).

11.4   Privilege and the expert

11.4.1   Legal basis

Legal professional privilege attaches to two classes of documents:

(a) Communications between lawyer and client in relation to legal advice.

(b) Communications between lawyer and or client and third parties where the dominant purpose of the communication is use in pending or contemplated litigation.

As a result of this second type of legal professional privilege, communications between experts and parties have always been protected from disclosure. Thus, letters of instruction, draft reports, supplementary letters, telephone attendance notes, notes of conference, etc have always passed between lawyers, clients and experts without fear of being seen by the other side.

11.4.2   The civil reforms

In his *Interim Report* considering the civil procedure reforms, Lord Woolf considered that the attachment of privilege to the communications with experts was contrary to the new principles of transparency in litigation and possibly ran counter to the overriding duty of the expert to the court. He wanted to prevent parties from suppressing 'relevant opinions or factual material which did not support' their case. Consequently, he recommended:

Once an expert has been instructed to prepare a report for the use of a court, any communication between the expert and client or advisers should no longer be the subject of privilege.

The effect of this would be to make all draft reports and many other communications disclosable which would alter clinical negligence litigation very significantly. By the time of Lord Woolf's *Final Report* this had been modified:

I accept . . . that it would not be realistic to make draft experts' reports disclosable. I do not however consider that privilege should apply to the instructions given to experts.

Instead he recommended that all written instructions and a note of all oral instructions should be annexed to the report as a pre-requisite of its being admissible. This would no doubt include letters and attendance notes of conversations between the lawyers/client and the expert which would refer to other privileged documents containing advice such as draft reports, etc. Perhaps to avoid this effect, the final rule is modified still further than the recommendation.

CPR, r 35.10, provides:

> *(3)   The expert's report must state the substance of all material instructions, whether written or oral, on the basis of which the report was written.*
>
> *(4)   The instructions referred to in paragraph (3) shall not be privileged against disclosure but the court will not, in relation to those instructions—*
>
> > *(a)   order disclosure of any specific document; or*
> >
> > *(b)   permit any questioning in court, other than by the party who instructed the expert, unless it is satisfied that there are reasonable grounds to consider the statement of instructions given under paragraph (3) to be inaccurate or incomplete.*

PD 35 adds that cross-examination in relation to the instructions will be allowed where it is in the interests of justice to do so.

11.4.3   What constitutes 'material instructions'?

The answer would be simple if instructing solicitors wrote one letter of instruction to an expert prior to his writing one report which was relied upon in court. In reality, however, there is a good deal of communications back and forth between lawyers and experts with letters, phone calls, supplementary letters, meetings, draft reports, comments upon draft reports, comments upon the other side's reports and so on.

The notes to *The White Book* (*Civil Procedure*) draw a distinction between instructions to an expert before and after the court has given permission for expert evidence:

> This [CPR, r 35.10(3)] can only relate to the reports prepared for the use of the court on which the evidence would be based. It cannot relate to reports prepared by an expert for a party before leave was granted by a court and thus the expert's status changed from that of expert advising a party to that of expert witness both advising a party and with an overriding duty to the court under the rules.

The Court of Appeal has recently considered the question of material instructions in the case of *Lucas v Barking, Havering and Redbridge Hospitals NHS Trust* [2003] EWCA 1102. It was held that the provision of a medical report by another expert and a witness statement of the claimant in the letter of instruction to the expert, were a part of the instructions for the purpose of CPR, r 35.10(3). Thus privilege did not attach to those documents, as is clear from CPR, r 35.10(4). However, disclosure of such documents will be restricted to the situation where 'there are reasonable grounds to consider the statement of instructions given . . . to be inaccurate or incomplete'. The Court went on to remind us that the obligation under CPR, r 35.10(3) is to make an accurate and complete statement in the report of the *material* instructions and not an obligation to set out or disclose all the material supplied.

11.4.4   *Ultra vires?*

The effect of the rule considered above appears to be (as was expressly intended) to alter the law of legal professional privilege. Can the rules of court do that or is it *ultra vires*? The rules came into force under the Civil Procedure Act 1997. The Act allows (Sch 1, para 4) the rules to modify the rules of evidence. Is that all legal professional privilege is or is it a 'substantive legal right which . . . is beyond the power of the Civil Procedure Rule Committee to abolish or limit'? Toulson J considered that question in *General Mediterranean Holdings SA v Patel* [1999] 3 All ER 673 in connection with CPR, r 48.7 which allowed the court to order the disclosure of privileged documents (between lawyers and clients) in relation to wasted costs orders. The rule was declared *ultra vires* on the basis that privilege is a substantive right which cannot be overriden by subordinate legislation. The same arguments could be applied to CPR, r 35.10(3). The Court of Appeal recently considered this question in the case of *Jackson v Marley Davenport Limited* [2004] 1 WLR 2926. The claimant served an expert report on the defendant which made it clear that the expert had changed his mind since writing an earlier report. The defendant sought disclosure of the first report and the claimant claimed privilege. The Court of Appeal held that CPR 35.15 did not abrogate privilege and that references to the disclosure of experts' reports in 35.10(2) were references to the actual expert's evidence and not references to earlier, draft reports.

11.4.5   Practical interpretation

To minimise the risk of having to disclose sensitive documents you might:

(a) Instruct a shadow expert (ie, one who is not later asked to prepare a report). This could only be justified in very large claims and fees are unlikely to be recoverable from the other side.

(b) Attempt to make a clear break between the advisory and the reporting roles of the expert by giving formal instructions immediately after the permission of the court is granted to adduce evidence from the expert.

(c) Avoid difficulties by being clear what you want to ask from the expert at all times, avoiding asking questions to which you do not want the answer, discouraging side letters and telephone conversations which contain or might elicit views which contradict the report.

(d) Be careful not to send previously obtained expert reports upon which you do not wish to rely, to your expert.

11.5   The expert at trial

11.5.1   Evidence-in-chief

Remember that all parties will have had a copy of the report and that the judge is likely to have read it prior to the trial either because it is the most important evidence as to liability or because it is annexed to the statements of case (particularly the condition and prognosis report). The ostensible purpose of eliciting evidence from your medical expert is to clarify, explain, expand or update the report. Of course it is also a chance for you to put the expert at relative ease prior to cross-examination and to begin to persuade the court of your case through emphasising the strong parts of the report.

Where possible, you should ensure that the expert covers the following areas, in a logical order, emphasising the most important or persuasive aspects:

(a) Introductions: including a description of the expert's particular specialisation, current post, qualifications and experience. You should aim to highlight the relevance and length of experience.

(b) The report:

(i)   The instructions.

(ii)   The evidential basis of the report. This is the opportunity to lay a sound factual basis for the opinion. For example, any examination of the claimant, any tests undertaken, X-rays seen, which notes he has read and which hospital protocols or other documents were available.

(iii) The methodology and research basis of the opinions formed in the report.

(c) State his opinion in relation to each issue:

(i)   Explain how he supports his opinion (ie link the opinion to the evidential or research basis of the report).

(ii)   Give reasons as to why his opinion is sound and should be relied upon in preference to others.

(iii) Ask him to turn to relevant parts of the other party's expert report and deal with disputed matters.

11.5.2   Cross-examination

This part has been written by an experienced professional negligence practitioner. You are also encouraged to read the *Advocacy Manual*, **19.7**, which considers cross-examination of expert witnesses in general.

Throughout your time in practice you will observe many different styles of cross-examination, a few good, a few bad, and most only partially effective. From your observation you will see how other advocates set about strengthening their case or weakening their opponent's case. You will find that you cannot adopt another advocate's cross-examination style. Advocates develop their own style. It is personal to the advocate. Behind the style there are, however, a number of fundamentals required to be a good cross-examiner. This section is concerned with expert evidence in clinical negligence cases but much of it would apply to cross-examination of expert and factual witnesses in other cases.

Preparation for written work or a conference is very different from preparation for a trial. When you receive papers shortly before trial, you should have the trial bundle from which to work. You may also have other papers, which you have built up over the period of time or are with your brief, eg, pre-trial bundles, conference notes, and correspondence. Start by going through all the papers to identify any information that may be useful to your case. A thorough understanding of the facts and issues of the case at an early stage will make the case much easier to prepare. Sometimes it may be prudent to mark with flags any documents that you consider relevant in the pre-trial bundles, and cross-refer to the trial bundle to make sure that they are included. If they are not, prepare a list of documents that you want inserted into the trial bundle or in a supplementary bundle. In clinical negligence cases you should read all the medical records and the literature attached to the expert's reports. Mark and flag the passages you consider may be relevant or that you do not understand. You can ask your expert about them later. These days the preparation of statements of issues, chronologies and skeleton arguments help focus your attention on the issues in the case. Before you prepare your skeleton argument make sure that you have read all the papers thoroughly. Make sure that you sort out and put to one side all the papers that you are not likely to use at trial.

In most cases there will have been directions by the QBD Master or District Judge for an experts' meeting and a statement of issues agreed and not agreed signed by the experts. This document should be examined carefully. It is by no means unknown for experts to go back on the joint statement at trial or seek to qualify concessions that have been made once the consequences of that concession have been drawn to their attention by the party who instructed them. If there is sufficient time you may be able to put questions to the other party's expert, the answers to which may help you decide whether you require an expert to attend court. While the expert's overriding duty is to the court, you should always remember that the other party is paying for their expert. Where concessions have been made you may be better off with those concessions than running the risk of the expert at trial qualifying his position.

When you have prepared your skeleton argument you should have in mind the factual and expert issues in the case. Once you have the issues in mind you can start to prepare your cross-examination. Some advocates may wish to use their notebooks or a separate file or a computer. I prefer to bring all the information together on the blank page opposite each page of the experts' report, supplemented by other documents if necessary. It makes it less likely that you will miss out issues on which you need to cross-examine. If you use a pencil you can always erase your comments and re-write your cross-examination. Go through the other party's expert's report carefully identifying the areas of agreement and disagreement. Where there are areas of agreement, consider whether there are any questions that you might ask which help your case. Where there are areas of disagreement, examine the factual basis upon which those opinions have been given. Look back at the cross-examination you have prepared for the factual witnesses to see if it covers an area where you might be able to make some headway. Once you have isolated the areas which are in dispute, consider how you are going to attack the opinion being expressed.

Look at the qualifications of the expert. Is he appropriately qualified to give the evidence? There should be a copy of his curriculum vitae in the trial bundle. In clinical negligence cases you might also look him up in the Medical Directory to check that all his publications are listed. Examine carefully the dates of his appointments. Was he in practice at the relevant time and at what level of seniority? If he is a young consultant he may not have been sufficiently qualified in a particular discipline at the relevant time to give useful evidence. If he is a retired consultant he may not have been in practice at the relevant time. Medical practice can change rapidly. What is acceptable practice in an obstetric unit in one decade may not be in the next. He may not be familiar with medical practice at the relevant time. In either case an expert who is familiar with the standards in a London teaching hospital may not be familiar with a typical District General Hospital. His publications may show that his principal areas of interest are not those of the case in which he is instructed. Careful thought needs to be given as to how these issues can be broached at trial. Trial judges are not impressed by unmeritorious attacks on the qualifications and experience of experts but where there are good grounds to make such an attack it may give them sufficient material to reject their evidence.

You will have the material that is contained in your expert's report and in the conference notes. You should see your expert in conference before the trial and discuss the issues. You should discuss the weaknesses and strengths of all the experts' arguments. Get your expert to identify those parts of the literature that you can use in cross-examination, highlight the relevant parts and flag the pages. Ask him to explain those parts you do not understand and to interpret any part of the medical records you do not follow. Sometimes you may find references in the medical records that have not been referred to and which you think may be relevant. Ask the expert about them. Summarise the information you require on the opposite page of the other party's expert's report in the trial bundle so that you can refer the trial judge and witness easily to the passages either in the witness statements, medical records or literature that you want to draw attention to.

It is important to think carefully about the structure of your cross-examination. It is generally unnecessary to write out each question, however, in your early years it may give you self-confidence to write out important questions. Generally, it is sufficient to identify the issues that you want to address. How you precisely phrase the question may best wait until you have heard how the witness gives evidence but you should always have a basic structure to your cross-examination. You should work out what you are seeking to achieve on each issue in the case. In most cases it is probably sensible to deal with matters in a chronological fashion — qualifications, matters arising from the factual history, and matters of opinion. In cases where the expert has taken a bullish position in examination-in-chief you may want to use a strong point early on. Most medical experts do not enjoy giving evidence in court or being cross-examined. Although they may have written many reports most clinical negligence cases settle and their actual court experience may be small.

When you rise to your feet, remember that you are dealing with a professional person. As I said earlier, advocates have many different styles, I believe that a polite but firm approach to cross-examination rather than an aggressive and hectoring tone is more productive. Unnecessary aggression may lead to the trial judge having sympathy for an expert that he did not have before you began.

Clinical negligence cases often deal with complex issues. A trial judge may not have been in this type of case at the Bar or tried many of them. He needs to be helped to understand the issues involved. Check with your experts that you understand the terminology involved and that you know how to pronounce the technical words. Nothing looks less impressive than an advocate who fluffs the pronunciation of a common word in medical practice or who does not know what a particular acronym means. A basic understanding of the medicine involved will assist the trial judge and reduce the likelihood of the other party's expert bamboozling you whilst you are on your feet. Ideally, your expert should be sitting right behind you to help with technical points as they arise.

On your feet you should have all the information either written up in the other party's expert's report or in a separate file and it should be at your fingertips. Occasionally you may have the transcript of evidence that an expert has given in a previous case. Take the expert through the points you wish to raise with him. Unless there are particular benefits to be gained, do not take the expert laboriously through all his report. You have identified the issues that arise, and there may be other issues that arise during the trial, concentrate on those issues. Ask questions politely and firmly of your expert. Seek to achieve your objects in cross-examination but do not enter into unprofitable arguments with the expert. If you obtain a concession from one expert that is not dealt with by a subsequent expert settle for the concession that you have obtained. Do not try and improve on it with the next expert. He will have been sitting in court and you might not like the answer. Invariably there will be points that you have forgotten to ask. If the expert has not left the witness box stand up and tell the trial judge that you have forgotten to ask about a particular point. Most will show understanding to young advocates.

To many advocates cross-examination is the most enjoyable part of the job. It is a privilege to cross-examine distinguished members of another profession, remember not to abuse that privilege.

David Pittaway QC

Evidence in solicitors' negligence cases

12.1 Introduction

The subject of this chapter is evidence in the context of solicitors' negligence cases. Solicitors' negligence cases are in many respects no different from any other civil cases, and the ordinary rules and principles relating to evidence apply to each equally. For a comprehensive treatment, therefore, reference should be made to the standard text books on the subject.

The application of the Civil Procedure Rules, practice directions and protocols to the use of evidence and in particular expert evidence is discussed in **Chapters 10** and **11** and you should refer to those in relation to procedural aspects.

If you are asked to advise on evidence in such a case, you will find it helps to set out each of the elements of the cause of action in turn, and to consider the kind of evidence you will need to prove (or, as the case may be, refute) that element of the claim, how you might go about acquiring that evidence, and the rules of practice and procedure which you will have to observe in order to ensure that the evidence is properly before the court. This chapter follows that approach by considering:

- the scope of the solicitor's duty;
- the standard of care;
- breach of the duty;
- causation of loss;
- quantification of loss.

In many of the cases you are asked to look at, not all of these elements of the claim will be contentious. You will need to scrutinise the statements of case carefully to establish exactly what is in issue. Be ready, however, to anticipate likely amendments in the other side's case, and tailor your advice on evidence accordingly.

This chapter is written primarily from the viewpoint of counsel instructed on behalf of the lay client, and references to 'the client' should be interpreted accordingly. But you will find most of the commentary equally applicable to defending a professional negligence claim as well.

12.2 Scope of the solicitor's duty

The importance of ascertaining the scope of the duty has been reaffirmed by the House of Lords in *South Australia Asset Management Corp v York Montague Ltd* [1997] AC 191.

claimant who sues for breach of a duty imposed by the law must do more than prove that the defendant failed to meet the requisite standard of conduct. He must show that the duty was owed to him and that it was a duty to safeguard him from the kind of loss which he has suffered.

12.2.1   Written retainers

Your first recourse must always be to the retainer, since this defines the scope of the solicitor's contractual obligations towards the client. Where there is a written retainer the basic parameters of the solicitor's duty will rarely be in dispute. Nonetheless, issues may still arise as to the precise extent of the solicitor's obligations, particularly in relation to the commercial implications of the work carried out under the retainer. In this area evidence as to the client's own experience may be relevant in assessing the scope of the duty owed. In *Carradine Properties Ltd v D J Freeman & Co* (1982) 126 SJ 157, Donaldson LJ observed that 'an inexperienced client will need and will be entitled to expect the solicitor to take a much broader view of the scope of his retainer and of his duties than will be the case with an experienced client'.

So you may need to find out:

- the client's own professional qualifications;

- whether the client has previous experience of the sort of transaction which is the subject-matter of the proposed negligence action;

- whether this particular solicitor has acted for the client in the past and, if so, the subject of those previous dealings and the scope of the solicitor's retainer on those occasions.

12.2.2   Oral retainers

Oral retainers, whether or not evidenced by an exchange of correspondence, are commonplace in solicitors' negligence cases, and you should not be surprised to encounter them. You should bear in mind, however, that the absence of a written retainer immediately puts the solicitor at a disadvantage. It has been said that where there is a dispute between solicitor and client as to the terms of any retainer, prima facie it is the client's version which should prevail (*Crossley v Crowther* (1851) 9 Hare 384, *Re Payne* (1912) 28 TLR 201). In *Gray v Buss Murton* [1999] PNLR 882, QBD, the basis for this principle was said to be that it is the client who actually knows what he wants the solicitor to do, and so it is the solicitor's business to ascertain the client's wishes accurately, bearing in mind the possibility that the client, through ignorance of the correct terminology, may not have correctly expressed it. Similarly, in *Griffiths v Evans* [1953] 2 All ER 1364, Lord Denning stated that:

the client is ignorant and the solicitor is, or should be, learned. If the solicitor does not take the precaution of getting a written retainer, he has only himself to blame for being at variance with his client over it and must take the consequences.

A further difficulty, from the solicitor's point of view, is that since it is the solicitor and not the client who is expected to commit the agreement to paper, any departure from the normal scope of a retainer will be harder for the solicitor to establish than the client. If the solicitor is alleging that his obligations are narrower than might ordinarily be expected in the given situation, the court is likely to ask itself why there is no written evidence to show it; whereas if the client maintains that his instructions were broader than normal, the same criticism cannot be so readily made of him. In this context, note that the *Guide to the Professional Conduct of Solicitors*, 1999, states at para 12.08:

...It is essential at the outset for a solicitor to agree clearly with the client the scope of the retainer...If a solicitor limits the scope of the retainer it is good practice for the limits of the retainer to be precisely defined in writing to the client.

In addition, in some instances you may be able to rely upon the lack of a carefully worded retainer as indicative of general sloppiness and lack of attention to detail on the part of the solicitor; and that in turn may assist you in persuading the court to prefer the client's evidence on other contentious issues of fact in the case.

12.2.3 Holding out

There may be cases where a solicitor has no particular professional expertise on a subject, but where he has held himself out as being so qualified. This may be relevant in defining the scope of the duty (as well as the appropriate standard of care). Care should always be taken when acting for the client to find out what the solicitor may have said in any pre-contractual meetings, in case the ostensible level of expertise offered at the time differs from the actual level professed by the solicitor in defence of the claim.

12.2.4 No retainer: duties owed to third parties

Different considerations apply in those cases where a solicitor is alleged to owe a duty to someone other than a client in a contractual relationship. Evidence will be directed to issues such as the assumption of responsibility, reliance, and whether it is fair, just and reasonable to impose a duty — all matters which do not arise where there is a retainer.

In practice, in most cases the question of whether a duty is owed, and the scope of the duty, will be a matter of decided law. Either the claimant/defendant relationship you are dealing with will fit into one of the categories in which a duty has been held to exist (for example, the relationship between a testator's solicitor and an intended beneficiary, as in *White v Jones* [1995] 2 AC 207), or it will not. The role of evidence-gathering in such cases is therefore necessarily limited.

12.3 Standard of care

12.3.1 Sources of evidence

The standard of care is usually said to be that which is ordinarily exercised by reasonably competent solicitors who profess the same speciality (if any) as the defendant (see *Jackson & Powell* at 1–99). How is that standard to be established evidentially? The main sources of evidence are:

- professional guides and codes of conduct;
- textbooks;
- expert evidence;
- previous decisions of the court.

12.3.2 Guides and codes of conduct

Apart from the particular terms agreed between the solicitor and his client and embodied in the retainer, you can often find additional evidence as to the applicable standard of care in the various rules, guides and codes of conduct which govern the solicitors' professional duties. The Law Society (of which all practising solicitors must be members) issues a number of such publications, including:

- *Civil Litigation, a Guide to Good Practice*;
- *Client Care, a Guide for Solicitors*;
- *The National Protocol*;
- The 'Green Card' (guidance regarding potential mortgage frauds).

A number of these appear as annexes to the Law Society's *Guide to the Professional Conduct of Solicitors*.

Although these provide useful indicators of the sorts of standards and practices which are likely to be followed in the profession, you should not equate them with the standard of care itself. In *Johnson v Bingley* [1997] PNLR 392, QBD, the judge held that a client suing her former solicitor did not necessarily prove negligence on the solicitor's part by establishing that the solicitor breached the Law Society's Guide to Professional Conduct of Solicitors. The Guide set out a code of proper and accepted practice, but its provisions were not mandatory. Negligence would continue to be determined according to the principles established in *Donoghue v Stevenson* [1932] AC 562.

When considering evidence of this kind you should also be alert to the danger of anachronism. Guides and codes of conduct evolve over time, and you must be strict in applying only those which were in force at the time of the act or omission which is alleged to constitute the negligence. You may well find that you have ready access only to the most up-to-date material, and some detailed research may therefore be called for.

The point is illustrated by the case of *Searles v Cann and Hallett* [1999] PNLR 494, QBD, where the claimant sought to establish the defendant solicitor's negligence in the handling of a property transaction by reference to guidance given in the Law Society's *Conveyancing Handbook*, 1997 edn, as to what a prudent solicitor would do in the given circumstances. The court rejected the argument, in part because the transaction took place in 1990, and there was evidence that general practice in this area had significantly changed in the intervening seven-year period. (Incidentally, the court was also not satisfied that the yardstick of the 'prudent solicitor' equated with that of 'every competent solicitor': a point which reinforces the importance of applying the *Bolam* test in solicitors' negligence cases.)

Similarly, in *Martin Boston & Co v Roberts* [1996] PNLR 45, CA, the Court of Appeal emphasised that the test was what the reasonably competent practitioner would do having regard to the standards normally adopted in his profession, and that this test must be based on events in prospect and not in retrospect.

12.3.3 Textbooks

In *Bown v Gould & Swayne* [1996] PNLR 130, CA, the claimant sued his former solicitors for failing to discover the defective title to a property which he had purchased, and sought to adduce the evidence of a conveyancing expert so as to establish best practice in conveyancing matters. The Court of Appeal dismissed his appeal against an order refusing permission to call such evidence, holding that were it necessary to assist with an understanding of the deduction and investigation of title the proper recourse was to the standard conveyancing textbooks rather than to the evidence of conveyancing solicitors.

Many of the standard textbooks will already be familiar to you from your own studies. However, when asked to advise on evidence in a solicitor's negligence action, you may find yourself instructed to advise on evidence in an area of the law with which you are not very familiar. Often you will find that there is a single authoritative practitioner's textbook on that subject. Where there are a number of such books available, be guided by your instructing solicitors as to which are the preferred texts in their profession.

12.3.4   Expert evidence

An unsurprising consequence of the fact that judges are themselves trained lawyers is that the courts are generally slower to admit expert evidence in relation to solicitors' negligence claims than to those dealing with the practice of other professions. Expert evidence of the accepted standard of conduct amongst solicitors can and should be received in appropriate cases (*Midland Bank Trust Co v Hett, Stubbs & Kemp* [1979] Ch 384, QBD). But unlike clinical negligence cases, where experts are invariably deployed to assist the court in determining liability, admitting such evidence in solicitor's negligence actions remains very much the exception, rather than the rule.

Expert evidence should in any case be restricted to that which is reasonably required to resolve the proceedings (CPR, r 35.1). Judicial reluctance to admit evidence in determining the liability of solicitors is illustrated by the case of *May v Woollcombe Beer & Watts* [1999] PNLR 283, QBD, where the court observed that the general judicial experience was that expert reports were frequently served at great cost but contributed little to the elucidation of the matters in dispute. Accordingly, before making an order for expert evidence, a court should be fully satisfied that an issue had arisen on which evidence of proper practice was necessary to allow the court to make its decision (applying *Bown v Gould & Swayne* [1996] PNLR 130).

12.3.4.1   Evidence of what?

In *Midland Bank Trust Co v Hett, Stubbs and Kemp* [1979] Ch 384 Oliver J distinguished three types of evidence:

(a) evidence of some accepted standard of conduct which is laid down by a professional institute or sanctioned by common usage;

(b) evidence 'which really amounts to no more than an expression of opinion by a particular practitioner of what he thinks that he would have done had he been placed, hypothetically and without the benefit of hindsight, in the position of the defendants'; and

(c) evidence of the witness's view of what, as a matter of law, the solicitor's duty was in the particular circumstances of the case.

These three types of evidence are considered further below.

Evidence of accepted standard practice

In the *Midland Bank* case, it was held that evidence of this type can and ought to be received in appropriate cases. Such evidence may still be admitted, notwithstanding the decision in *Bown v Gould & Swayne* [1996] PNLR 130. In *May v Woollcombe Beer & Watts* [1999] PNLR 283, the defendant solicitors acted for the claimants in relation to the purchase of their home in Barton. Prior to the purchase, a modification order had been made by the local authority in respect of two rights of way near the house. The defendants had been informed by the vendor's solicitors of the details of the modification order, but they did not make an optional enquiry of the local authority concerning the status of the confirmation request with the Secretary of State. Following completion of the purchase, a public inquiry was held and the rights of way were confirmed as byways open to all traffic. In the course of the negligence action, the claimants sought an order allowing for expert evidence to be obtained from a solicitor experienced in conveyancing on the issue of whether further enquiries should have been made, and if so, what enquiries. The judge held, distinguishing *Bown v Gould & Swayne*, that expert evidence was not required on the straightforward issue of whether the solicitors should have made an optional enquiry of the local authority. The next question was whether, having discovered the existence of the modification order, they should have enquired whether the local authority had sought confirmation of the order from the Secretary of State. That question could not be answered through textbooks or Law Society guidance, and it was a matter on which the court would be assisted by evidence from an experienced conveyancer of proper practice.

Evidence of what the expert would himself have done
In the *Midland Bank* case, Oliver J dismissed evidence of this kind as being of little assistance to the court. The Court of Appeal confirmed in *Bown v Gould & Swayne* that such evidence is inadmissible because it is irrelevant, the test being not whether the defendant departed from the recommended practice of one particular expert (however eminent) but whether he acted in a way which no ordinarily competent solicitor would have done.

Evidence of what, in the expert's view, was the solicitor's duty and whether, in the expert's view, the solicitor was in breach
In the *Midland Bank* case, this type of evidence was held to be inadmissible, as being the very question which it is the court's function to decide. The Court of Appeal endorsed this view in *Bown v Gould & Swayne*.

But the Court of Appeal has held otherwise in other cases, by reference to s 3, Civil Evidence Act 1972 which states:

> *(1)   Subject to any rules of court made in pursuance of ... this Act, where a person is called as a witness in any civil proceedings, his opinion on any relevant matter on which he is qualified to give expert evidence shall be admissible in evidence ....*
>
> *(3)   In this section 'relevant matter' includes an issue in the proceedings in question.*

In *Re M and R (Minors) (Sexual Abuse: Expert Evidence)* [1996] 4 All ER 239, the court observed *obiter*, 's. 3 makes clear that [relevant expert] evidence is admissible whether or not it goes to an issue or even in appropriate circumstances the ultimate issue in the litigation'. A similar conclusion was reached in *United Bank of Kuwait v Prudential Property Services Ltd* [1995] EGCS 190, CA. These two decisions were applied in *Archer v Hickmotts* [1997] PNLR 318, where the county court judge allowed evidence to be given, by a solicitor with long-standing experience in conveyancing matters, of how he would expect a reasonably competent solicitor to discharge the duty of care imposed on the defendant solicitors.

However, Jacob J in *Routestone Ltd v Minories Finance Ltd* [1997] 1 EGLR 123 suggested that solicitors' negligence cases were an exception to the rule that 'expert evidence may be admissible on the issue of whether the legal test has been breached, even if that question is the ultimate question in issue or to establish the primary factual matrix on which the court makes its decision as to the legal test to be applied'.

The practice and procedure relating to: the instruction of experts, the form and content of reports, questions to experts, and meetings of experts, is covered in detail in **Chapter 11.**

12.3.5   Previous decisions

Usually the standard of care which the court will require of a solicitor depends on all the facts of the particular case. On occasion, however, some guidance may be obtained from decided cases in which the courts have held that a given practice (or the omission to follow it) is negligent. Thus in *Martin Boston & Co v Roberts* [1996] PNLR 45, CA, the client retained solicitors to defend him in an action brought against him by a limited company. The solicitors applied for security for costs against the company but withdrew the application in return for a personal guarantee executed by one of the company's directors for £200,000 secured on the director's freehold property. The client was successful in the action, but was unable to enforce the guarantee because the property had been subject to a prior legal charge and was subsequently repossessed by the chargee. On appeal, the Court of Appeal held that there was a foreseeable risk of the guarantor not meeting the liability for costs, a risk that could have been avoided either by entering a restriction under the Land Registration Act 1925 or by allowing the company to bring the action only if it brought money into court as security. In failing to obtain security for costs by either of these methods, the solicitors had not acted to a standard to be expected of reasonably competent litigation solicitors and had therefore been negligent.

12.3.6   Local standards

The Court of Appeal has recently stated the importance of the role of trial judges in assessing standards of care to be expected of solicitors practising in the locality of their courts. In *Balamoan v Holden & Co* (1999) 149 NLJ 898, a supermarket was constructed near to the claimant's home and he retained the defendants as his solicitors to advise him on a claim for damages for nuisance. The solicitors assessed the claim as worth less than £3,000, which in due course led to the discharge of the claimant's legal aid certificate. He continued his claim as a litigant in person and ultimately settled for £25,000 and costs. He claimed damages for professional negligence against the solicitors. On appeal against the dismissal of that claim, the Court of Appeal held that when seeking to assess the appropriate standard of care to be exercised by a solicitor in a small rural town, it was of paramount importance that the court should not seek to impose too high a standard of care. The court should always place great emphasis upon the opinion of the local circuit judge as to the appropriate standard to be expected from local solicitors. Nonetheless, it was clear on the particular facts in the instant case that the solicitors had breached their duty of care to the client, and the appeal was therefore allowed.

12.4   Breach of duty

In many cases, the issue of breach is uncontroversial. Once the scope of the retainer and the requisite standard of care have been established, proving a breach is a simple matter of looking at agreed facts to discern whether the solicitors' conduct did or did not meet that standard. Most disputes concerning breach turn on simple issues of fact. For example: Did the client pass on the critical piece of information? Did the solicitor give the particular advice? Did the solicitor make the correct enquiries? What answer did he receive?

As when establishing the scope of the retainer (see above), the quality of the solicitor's record-keeping often proves crucial in resolving these issues. Solicitors who keep comprehensive attendance notes are in a vastly better position to defend proceedings than those who rely on their own memories, on assertions of normal practice, or on inferences which they say can reasonably be drawn from agreed primary facts.

12.4.1 Obtaining the documents

Ordinarily, copies of any relevant documents from files still in the possession of the solicitors will be provided to your client in the course of standard disclosure, and vice versa. Sometimes, however, the solicitors will refuse to disclose documents. This may be because of alleged legal professional privilege; or it may be upon the exercise of the solicitor's lien. Equally, you may be called on to advise whether documents in your own client's possession can and should be withheld on grounds of privilege.

12.4.2 Privilege

The issue of privilege can arise in various different ways. Some examples are given below.

The client may wish to assert privilege in respect of documents arising from the retainer which is the subject-matter of the litigation. Here there is no room for argument: a client who brings proceedings against his former solicitors is deemed to have waived privilege in respect of documents and information concerned with the particular retainer in issue (*Lillicrap v Nalder & Son* [1993] 1 WLR 94, CA).

The client may assert privilege in respect of documents arising from a retainer with another firm of solicitors, or from previous retainers involving the defendant solicitors. The test for disclosure here is essentially whether the documents are necessary for the just resolution of the dispute. In *Paragon Finance plc v Freshfields* [1999] 1 WLR 1183, the claimant mortgage lender brought an action for damages for professional negligence against solicitors who had previously represented them in respect of insurance claims stemming from mortgage defaults. After the defendants had ceased to act for the claimant, another firm of solicitors had been instructed in the litigation. The defendants, in seeking to refute the claims of negligence, applied for disclosure of confidential communications between the claimant, its new solicitors and counsel relating to the insurance claims litigation. The Court of Appeal allowed an appeal against an order allowing the application, holding that since the claimant had not asked the court to determine any issue stemming from its confidential relationship with its new solicitors, the privilege prevailed. See also *Kershaw v Whelan* [1996] 1 WLR 358, QBD, and *Lillicrap v Nalder & Son* (see **12.5.1**).

The solicitors may assert privilege in respect of documents arising from a retainer by a third party. In such a case the privilege will prevail unless what is alleged is that the privilege is being used to further or conceal some form of wrongdoing or iniquity. So, in *Abbey National plc v Clive Travers & Co* [1999] PNLR 819, the defendant solicitors acted on a property purchase financed by a mortgage provided by the claimant. The claimant sued for negligent failure to report certain matters, and alleged a fraud between the purchaser, his mortgage broker, and a legal executive employed by the solicitors. The Court of Appeal upheld an order requiring the solicitors to give disclosure of the purchaser's file and of correspondence passing between the broker and the legal executive, on the basis that the allegations were sufficient to assert a degree of wrongdoing to give rise to a duty on the solicitors' part to examine the files.

12.4.3 Liens

You may find yourself instructed by a client who wishes to sue his former solicitors, and who has withheld payment of some or all of the solicitors' fees in protest. It is likely in those circumstances that the solicitors will be claiming a general or retaining lien. The lien entitles a solicitor to retain all papers of his client, which come into his possession as the client's solicitor, until all his costs and charges are paid.

A solicitor exercising a lien is entitled to be given every security for payment, which includes preventing the making and sending of copies of the documents retained, but subject to the important proviso that retention of the documents should not be 'inconsistent with the progress of the cause' (see *Bentley v Gaisford* [1997] QB 627). The overriding principle is that the court should make such order as is most conclusive to the interests of justice by weighing up (a) the fact that the litigant should not be deprived of material relevant to the conduct of his case, and (b) that litigation should be conducted with due regard to the interests of the court's own officers who should not be left without payment for what was justly due to them (*Ismail v Richards Butler* [1996] QB 711, QBD). Your client may therefore be required to pay the outstanding fees into court as security for release of the documents, but only if he has the means to do so.

12.5   Causation

Causation proves a fertile ground for defendants in solicitors' negligence cases. No doubt this is because so often the service provided by the solicitor is merely a preliminary link in a further chain of events which is intended to culminate in a completed transaction, or in litigation. In those circumstances there is frequently scope for questioning whether the transaction would ever have happened, or whether the litigation would have gone as planned.

12.5.1   Negligent advice

Where the alleged negligence consists of giving the wrong advice, or of failing to give advice altogether, you should ask yourself whether you have the necessary evidence to show that the client would have heeded the advice which should have been given. In *Etridge v Pritchard Englefield* [1999] PNLR 839, the trial judge had found that the claimant wife, who had sued the defendant solicitors for failing to advise her in such a way as to free her of her husband's undue influence, would have entered into the transaction even if she had been properly advised by the solicitor. The Court of Appeal refused to overturn that finding and made clear that there is no presumption that if a solicitor gives correct advice it will be followed by the client.

The evidence you will require will vary greatly according to the facts of the individual case. Often it will be a matter of the client's own affirmation as to what he would have done if properly advised, in which case you must take care to ensure that the point is fully dealt with in his witness statement. On other occasions, you will be relying mainly on inferences which can be drawn either from common sense and/or from all the surrounding circumstances. It may be instructive to explore with the client whether he has been faced with analogous situations in the past, so that some evidence of consistency can be established.

This approach can work for the defendants as well. In *Lillicrap v Nalder & Son* [1993] 1 WLR 94, the claimant, a property developer, sued his former solicitors for negligence in failing to advise him on rights of way material to the title of a property. The solicitors admitted negligence but denied causing loss. They sought permission to add as further particulars of denial matters relating to previous retainers where, in similar transactions, their advice had been ignored. The judge refused the application but the Court of Appeal allowed the appeal, holding where a client sued his solicitor he impliedly waived his claim to privilege and confidence in respect of all matters which were relevant to an issue. The particulars were relevant to the issue of causation and loss, and the solicitors were entitled to particularise them in their defence.

12.5.2 Failure to secure a benefit

Where the negligence consists of a failure on the part of a solicitor to secure an apparent benefit for your client, you must positively prove that the benefit of which he has been deprived had some actual value. Again, the court will not assume that much in your favour. The following cases illustrate the problem:

(a) In *Searles v Cann and Hallett* [1999] PNLR 494, QBD, the defendant firm of solicitors failed to obtain a charge over the property of the borrower in favour of the claimant lender. The court found that the defendants had owed a duty of care in tort to the claimant, and that their failure had been negligent, but dismissed the claim on the basis that there was insufficient evidence to establish that there would have been any equity left in the property at the relevant time upon which for the charge to bite.

(b) In *Green v Collyer-Bristow* [1999] Lloyd's Rep PN 798, the claimant wife sued the defendant solicitors, who had been acting for her in ancillary relief proceedings, for failing to advise her to accept a favourable offer from her husband. In dismissing the claim the court held that no loss had been established by the claimant, because by the earliest date when the solicitors would have advised her to accept the offer it would have been withdrawn in any event.

In *Casey v Hugh James Jones & Jenkins* [1999] Lloyd's Rep PN 115, QBD, the defendant solicitors had acted for the claimant in a personal injury action under a legal aid certificate. The Legal Aid Board asked the claimant to show cause why legal aid should continue. The solicitors did no more than pass on counsel's opinion, legal aid was withdrawn, and the case was subsequently struck out for want of prosecution. The judge held the solicitors to have been negligent in not making proper representations to the Board, but found that even if they had there would have been no realistic prospect of legal aid being continued. Accordingly, the claimant was entitled to nominal damages only.

12.6 Quantum

12.6.1 Loss of a chance

It is a peculiarity of solicitors' negligence cases that the claimant's loss has often to be characterised as a loss of a chance — that is, as the loss of the opportunity to achieve some benefit or to avoid some detriment through the relevant transaction or litigation. As has already been discussed (see **Chapter 3**), the law distinguishes between acts of the claimant, which are regarded as matters of causation to be decided on the balance of probabilities, and acts of the third party, which go to quantum (see *Allied Maples Group Ltd v Simmons and Simmons* [1995] 1 WLR 1602).

This distinction has particular implications for the gathering of evidence in such cases. Broadly speaking, when setting out to prove that the client would have done a particular thing in the hypothetical situation, the balance of probabilities must weigh in the client's favour. Possibilities will not be enough. By contrast, when considering what the third party might have done, the only requirement is that the prospect be more than merely speculative. It will be therefore in the client's interest to adduce relatively slight evidence in the hope of surmounting this much lower threshold. See, for example, *Lloyds Bank plc v Parker Bullen* [2000] Lloyds Rep PN 51, ChD: damages assessed on basis of loss of 15% chance of favourable outcome.

In an appropriate case concerning loss of a chance, evidence may be required on a large number of issues. By way of illustration, in *Harrison v Bloom Camillin* [2000] Lloyd's Rep PN 89, ChD, the judge considered the following issues to be relevant. Detailed evidence was adduced in respect of each of them:

- whether the claimants would have proceeded with their action against the third party;
- the prospects of establishing a duty of care owed by the third party;
- the prospects of establishing breach of the duty;
- the prospects of establishing reliance;
- the prospects of contributory negligence being established against them;
- the likely level of damages;
- set-offs and counterclaims.

12.6.2   Notional trial date

It is important to establish the notional trial date because of possible changes in the law or the factual situation between notional trial date and the date of the actual hearing. On the whole, the law and the facts as at the date of the notional trial will be taken and evidence as to any later developments will be inadmissible. But note that in some circumstances evidence only coming to light *ex post facto* may yet be relevant and admissible. In *Charles v Hugh James Jones & Jenkins* [2000] 1 All ER 289, the defendant solicitors appealed against an assessment of damages made against them in a professional negligence action following the automatic striking out of the claimant's personal injury claim. They argued that the date for assessment of damages was the notional trial date and that medical evidence made available thereafter should be inadmissible in the assessment of damages hearing. It was held, dismissing the appeal, that the date for assessment of damages for loss of opportunity was the date of a notional trial of the personal injury action. Although evidence relating to a completely new head of damage arising after the notional trial date might have to be refused, medical evidence coming to light after the notional trial date which related to an existing head of damage could be of assistance to the judge and could be considered in an appropriate case.

12.6.3   Mitigation of loss and evidence relating to compromise

Where a claimant sues his solicitor in respect of a transaction with a third party and, prior to the issue of proceedings, reaches a settlement with that third party which reduces the losses claimed against the solicitor, disclosure of documents relating to that settlement (including evidence of 'without prejudice' negotiations) may be ordered if the reasonableness of the settlement is put in issue (see *Muller v Linsley & Mortimer* [1996] PNLR 74).

Be aware of the possibility of a shortcut. What if there was evidence that the third party had anticipated legal proceedings being brought against it and had made plans, say, to pay a particular sum into court. If the claimant gives credible evidence that it would have accepted that amount, that ought to be an end of the matter, and no further enquiry into the value of the claim ought to be necessary (*Harrison v Bloom Camillin* [2000] Lloyd's Rep PN 51). But how would such evidence be obtained? There is no reason why your instructing solicitors could not approach the third party and invite it to give voluntary disclosure, or even to provide a witness statement.

Notwithstanding the burden of proof, the court is likely to proceed, in the absence of evidence to the contrary, upon certain assumptions: eg, that the parties, if they had settled, would have settled for what the claim was objectively worth; and that a judgment would have been satisfied. So claimants will want to look for concrete evidence that indicate those assumptions are unduly pessimistic. Defendants will want to look for evidence which shows the reverse. For example, you may have evidence that the third party was impecunious.

Part V

The practical context

Who's who in professional negligence claims

13.1 Introduction

Most professions have their own professional bodies and related institutions such as trade unions, defence societies and insurers, which support their members in a variety of ways. This can be through disseminating information, continuing education, publishing recent research, issuing guidance about procedures, writing and implementing codes of conduct, disciplining members and funding or otherwise assisting in any litigation arising out of a member's work. A basic understanding of the various bodies and their roles is necessary in practice. As defence counsel, the decision to instruct you may well depend upon your being on a list of approved counsel assembled and kept by the relevant body and you are likely to meet its representative in conference or in court. You should also know who is funding the litigation, ie who is paying your fees. You are likely to come across correspondence on file with the relevant bodies. Knowledge of the role of the relevant institutions will alert you as counsel for the claimant or the defendant to various lines of enquiry. You might wish to consider what professional guidance, if any, was available to the defendant in relation to any issue and to consider his performance as against that.

A further complicating issue in claims against the medical profession is the existence of the National Health Service. It can be confusing to work out who is the correct defendant: the individual doctor, the local NHS trust, the GP partnership?

Set out below is an overview of some of the most important players within the medical profession and the solicitors' profession. You will feel more confident when you meet your professional client if you are armed with at least this information.

13.2 The medical profession

13.2.1 General Medical Council (GMC)

The GMC is the professional body which regulates doctors. It is responsible for registering and for disciplining doctors. It describes itself as existing to protect patients not the medical profession, whose interests are 'protected by others'. It promotes good practice through issuing statements. These can be general, eg, 'Good Medical Practice' or specific to certain issues, eg, 'Consent (1999)'. You are unlikely to come across the organisation in a clinical negligence case although it might help you to be aware of any statements issued relevant to your case (see www.gmc-uk.org).

13.2.2   National Health Service (NHS)

The NHS is Europe's biggest healthcare organisation with over one million people in the workforce. The government decides how much money overall goes to the NHS each year. There are 29 strategic health authorities which oversee the performance management of NHS Trusts and Primary Care Organisations, ensuring that they adhere to annual 'accountability agreements'. The Trusts provide hospital and community health services. GPs are members of Primary Care Organisations.

13.2.2.1   NHS trusts

In cases involving negligence at NHS hospitals or in community-based services the correct defendant is usually the relevant trust. As an employer, it is vicariously liable for the actions of its employees. Consequently, the individual clinician(s) might be named in the body of the statements of case, but will not be named as individual defendants.

13.2.2.2   NHS general practitioners

General practitioners are not employed by the hospital trusts and must be sued in their own name or as partner or employee in a GP partnership. The partnerships will be vicariously liable for the actions of their employees such as nurses and locum doctors.

13.2.2.3   NHS litigation authority (NHSLA)

The NHSLA was set up in 1995. Broadly speaking, its purpose is to minimise the incidents of clinical risk and to spread the financial consequences in such a way as to reduce the impact on the provision of healthcare. It tries to achieve those ends through a variety of means. In particular, it administers schemes which effectively act as mutual insurers of NHS trusts. In other words, when a hospital trust is the defendant the money behind the defence is administered by the NHSLA.

The NHSLA has lists of approved solicitors and counsel and only those who appear on the lists will be instructed to defend clinical negligence claims involving NHS hospital trusts. The NHSLA often sends a representative to conference with counsel and to court. See www.nhsla.com for useful information.

13.2.3   Private hospitals and clinics

Consultant doctors working in private hospitals will have their own indemnity policies and should be sued in their own names. Other clinicians and staff will usually be the employees of the hospital or clinic or of the consultant and will be covered by their insurance. Care should be taken when deciding precisely who to sue. It is often safest to sue the clinician in his own name as well as suing the trust or company which runs the establishment and/or the consultant head of the team.

13.2.4   British Medical Association (BMA)

The BMA is an independent trade union and a scientific and educational body and publisher. Eighty per cent of doctors are registered with the BMA. It will act for members in relation to industrial relations litigation but it is of less relevance in relation to negligence actions.

13.2.5   Defence organisations

Doctors are required by their professional rules to be insured. Where a clinician is not employed by an NHS trust (eg, a national health service GP or a private clinician) he will have a policy of professional indemnity with a defence organisation such as the Medical Defence Union (MDU) or the Medical Protection Society.

13.3 Claimants' organisations

13.3.1 AVMA — Action *against* medical accidents

This charitable organisation offers support, investigative and legal assistance to victims of medical accidents. It assists clinical negligence lawyers through training programmes, literature and discussion groups. It also offers a subscription service giving advice to lawyers on all aspects of clinical negligence litigation including lists of appropriate experts. Since 1999 the Legal Aid Board (and now the Legal Services Commission) has restricted funding for clinical negligence cases to those solicitors who appear on the AVMA and Law Society Panels of specialist solicitors.

13.4 The solicitors' profession

13.4.1 The Law Society

The Law Society is the representative and regulatory body for solicitors of England and Wales. It regulates the members of the profession by requiring solicitors to be qualified and to act in accordance with the professional rules laid down by the Society in the 'Guide to Professional Conduct of Solicitors'. Solicitors can only practise if in receipt of a Practising Certificate issued by the Law Society annually. Issues of conduct and discipline are investigated and pursued through the Society's Office for the Supervision of Solicitors and the Solicitors' Disciplinary Tribunal. Solicitors can be rebuked or struck off the register for misconduct. The Society supervises the provision of training for solicitors both prior to entry to the profession and afterwards through continuing professional development training. The Law Society informs its members of recent legal and professional developments and represents them in relation to law reform and other relevant issues.

13.4.2 Solicitors' professional indemnity

Solicitors are required by the Law Society to be insured. For many years, until September 2000, the insurance was arranged through a central fund called the Solicitors' Indemnity Fund (SIF). Contributions were set annually by the Law Society. In an attempt to move to a more competitive market place, from September 2000 firms can arrange their own compulsory Professional Indemnity Insurance from approved insurers. One of the newly approved insurance companies will administer its policies through an organisation called the 'Managing General Agency' (MGA) which will use the expertise and infrastructure of the SIF. The SIF had its own lists of approved solicitors' firms and counsel which it would instruct in relation to solicitors' negligence cases.

Funding professional negligence claims

14.1 Introduction

Professional negligence actions are expensive and financially risky to litigate. The defence is almost invariably funded by the state (NHS) or by an insurance company. The professions and their insurers and advisors are experienced at conducting defence litigation and are in a position to take tactical advantages. The funding options for a claimant intending to bring a professional negligence action are less straightforward. They include:

- private means;
- insurance;
- trade union backing;
- the Community Legal Service (formerly legal aid);
- conditional fee arrangements.

The last two are discussed below.

14.2 Community legal service

Schedule 2 to the Access to Justice Act 1999 sets out the type of claims for which Community Legal Service funding is not available. All applications for funding by the Legal Services Commission must meet the tests set out in a document called the 'Funding Code'. The Code has been approved by Parliament and it replaces the previous civil merits test. Below is a summary of the position in relation to State funding for clinical negligence and solicitors' negligence claims.

14.2.1 Clinical negligence

The government's intention was to withdraw State funding for clinical negligence cases along with all personal injury cases under the Access to Justice Act 1999. However, after strong representations were made (largely by the legal profession), it was accepted in spring 1998 that it was not practicable to do so yet. Clinical negligence is more difficult to fund through conditional fee arrangements than ordinary personal injury litigation. Even before the prospects of success of a claim can be assessed, very expensive initial investigations are often required. Lawyers are not able to carry the cost of those heavy disbursements on a no-win no-fee basis and insufficient insurance companies currently offer adequate arrangements for these risks.

Schedule 2 to the Access to Justice Act 1999 begins:

> *The services which may not be funded as part of the Community Legal Service are as follows.*
>
>   *1.   Services consisting of the provision of help (beyond the provision of general information about the law and the legal system and the availability of legal services) in relation to —*
>
>   *(a)   allegations of negligently caused injury, death or damage to property apart from allegations relating to clinical negligence . . .*

Consequently, funding is available in principle provided the claimant satisfies the means test and can bring himself within the Funding Code Guidance for Clinical Negligence.

In order to secure, extend or maintain funding from the Legal Services Commission the claimant must satisfy certain requirements set out in the Funding Code and summarised below. Whenever you give advice to a funded claimant you must be aware of these requirements and your obligations towards the Fund and must advise accordingly.

(a) *Specialist practitioners only.* Applications for funding for clinical negligence cases can only be made by certain specialist solicitors firms. These firms are members of the Law Society and/or AVMA's specialist panels (see **Chapter 13**).

(b) *Alternative dispute resolution.* Alternatives to litigation must be considered throughout the case. Where mediation (or the NHS complaints system in cases of value under £10,000) is offered and refused by the claimant, funding may be refused or stopped unless the specialist practitioner can justify the refusal.

(c) *Investigative Help.* Where investigations are needed before the prospects of success can be determined an application can be made for 'Investigative Help'. This will only be granted where a specialist practitioner is 'satisfied on the basis of the limited information available of the real possibility that negligent acts or omissions were responsible' for the injury. Funding granted for investigations will be limited to obtaining clinical notes and records, obtaining one medical report perrelevant specialism and thereafter obtaining counsel's opinion.

(d) *Full Representation.* This will not be granted where the prospects of success are unclear, borderline or poor. Moreover, the *minimum* cost benefits of damages to costs must be as follows:

(i)   1:1 — ie, likely damages must exceed likely costs — for cases with 80% or better prospects of success;

(ii)   1.5:1 — ie, likely damages must exceed 1.5 times likely costs — for cases with 60–80% prospects of success

(iii)   2:1 — ie, damages must be at least twice likely costs — for the cases where the prospects of success are 50–60%

(e) *Part 36 offers, payments in to court, offers to mediate or to refer to an early neutral evaluation or other form of settlement.* Where the claimant declines an offer to settle or to mediate, etc which you, as legal adviser, consider to be a reasonable offer, you are obliged to inform the Legal Services Commission of the position.

14.2.2   Solicitors' negligence

The position in relation to funding for most solicitors' negligence cases is clear. It is available subject to the ordinary means and merits test set out in the Funding Code (see the *Civil Litigation Manual* and the *Opinion Writing Manual*).

However, the Access to Justice Act 1999, Sch 2, para 1, has the effect of excluding solicitors' negligence cases in certain circumstances. Paragraph 1 is set out below:

The services which may not be funded as part of the Community Legal Service are as follows.

1.   Services consisting of the provision of help (beyond the provision of general information about the law and the legal system and the availability of legal services) in relation to –

(a)   allegations of negligently caused injury, death or damage to property, apart from allegations relating to clinical negligence,

(b)   conveyancing,

(c)   boundary disputes,

(d)   the making of wills,

(e)   matters of trust law,

(f)   defamation or malicious falsehood,

(g)   matters of company or partnership law, or

(h)   other matters arising out of the carrying on of a business.

The Lord Chancellor gives this specific guidance for the application of the above to solicitors' negligence cases in the Funding Code:

The word 'property' in paragraph 1(a) is not intended to exclude intangible property, for example . . . a legal claim (which it might be argued can itself be considered a type of property) . . . . But paragraph 1(a) is not intended to exclude claims for professional negligence against a lawyer for damaging a legal claim, for example by failing to issue proceedings within the limitation period. A professional negligence claim might still be excluded by one of the other provisions of paragraph 1, for example if the original claim concerned the conduct of a case arising in the carrying on of business.

The Funding Code attempts to paraphrase this by saying that 'professional negligence claims where the subject matter of the original action was not in itself an excluded category' will generally be within the scheme.

From this it is clear that a claim against a solicitor for failing to advise properly in relation to a boundary dispute will not be eligible for funding. The position remains less than clear in relation to a claim against a solicitor who acted negligently in relation to a personal injury claim (eg, by failing to issue within the limitation period). The guidance notes appear to be contradictory on this point.

14.2.3 Other professions

From the parts of the Access to Justice Act 1999 and Funding Code set out above, it is clear that funding is available in principle in relation to professional negligence claims, provided the claimant can satisfy the normal means and merits tests. However, there will be times when Sch 2 excludes these claims. For example, a claimant who received negligently drawn up business accounts from an accountant will be precluded from applying for funding by the operation of Sch 2, para 1(h). Likewise, funding will not be available to a claimant whose architect has negligently damaged his property by the operation of Sch 2, para 1(a).

14.3 Conditional fees

All civil cases (save family) may now be the subject of an enforceable conditional fee agreement (Access to Justice Act 1999, s 27). It is the intention of the government that this will allow for a greater access to justice for more classes of people and that the availability of conditional fee arrangements will lessen the impact of the removal of legal aid funding in many areas of litigation, particularly personal injury.

14.3.1   What is a conditional fee?

A conditional fee is a fee (payable to the solicitor and/or barrister) which is wholly dependent upon the outcome of the case:

No-win   No-fee

Win   Normal fee plus success fee

Winning means a money settlement even if heavily discounted for reasons relating to liability or contributory negligence.

The success fee is limited to 100% of the normal fee (Conditional Fee Agreements Order 2000, SI 2000/823).

14.3.2   Calculating the success fee

The success fee is intended to compensate the lawyer for the risk of losing the case. In practice, it needs to compensate you for the other cases which you in fact lose. Assume three cases of equal value each with a 66% chance of success. In theory you will win two and lose one. In order to compensate you for the loss of the fee in the losing case, you will need an uplift on your fees of 50% in each winning case. For example:

Conventional Funding:			
Case 1	Won	Fee	£2,000
Case 2	Won	Fee	£2,000
Case 3	Lost	Fee	£2,000
			£6,000

Conditional Fee:			
Case 1	Won	Fee	£2,000
		Success fee	£1,000
Case 2	Won	Fee	£2,000
		Success fee	£1,000
Case 3	Lost	Fee	£ none
			£6,000

In reality this is only a starting point. There are additional costs to lawyers in conditional fee cases, such as delay in payment, which need to be taken in to account in calculating the success fee. On the other hand, cases which settle are classed as winning cases for the purpose of the conditional fee arrangement and the reality is that cases which have a reasonable chance of succeeding at trial are likely to settle (eg, in the examples above for 66% of the value of the claim).

14.3.3   Who pays the success fee?

Since April 2000, s 58A(6), Access to Justice Act 1999 has allowed for success fees to be recovered from the losing party in a case. You can expect defendants to take issue with the level of your success fee when costs are taxed at the end of a case. Consequently, it will be necessary for you to justify the percentage uplift which you have claimed. This will be dependant upon your risk analysis of the case which will be carefully scrutinised (with the benefit of hindsight) at a disputed costs hearing. You should have a good and clear note of your risk assessment and the calculation of your success fee and not rely upon your instructing solicitor to set your success fee alone. For cases concerning the reasonableness of the uplift see *Callery v Gray (No 2)* [2001] EWCA Civ 1246, [2001] 1 WLR 2142, and *Halloran v Delaney* [2002] EWCA Civ 1258, [2003] 1 WLR 28.

14.3.4 If the defendant wins, who pays its costs?

The court will make its usual costs order, unaffected by the funding arrangements of the claimant, ie, the claimant to pay the defendant's costs. This would be a financial disaster to most claimants in many cases and therefore, before a conditional fee arrangement is entered into, the claimant will normally take out a policy of insurance to cover this eventuality. This insurance is often called 'after-the-event insurance'. Regulation 29 of the Conditional Fee Agreements Regulations 2000, SI 2000/692, allows for the courts to award costs orders against the losing party to cover the cost of the insurance premium, but this is limited, see *Re Claims Direct Test Cases* [2003] EWCA Civ 136, The Times, 18 February 2003, and *Sarwar v Allam* [2001] EWCA Civ 1401, [2002] 1 WLR 125.

14.4 Conclusion

It should be clear from all the matters discussed in this chapter that the accurate assessment and quantification of risk in each case is central to every funding decision for a claimant whether it is in relation to a conditional fee, a State-funded or a privately paid-for case. Risk assessment involves:

- Analysis of the strengths and weaknesses of the case based on the law, facts and available evidence.
- An estimate of the prospects of success, expressed where possible in percentage or other clear terms.
- An estimate of the likely damages at settlement and/or after trial.
- An estimate of the likely costs to date and at the relevant date(s) of settlement or trial. (Where this is not available to you as counsel, you should ask your instructing solicitor to provide this to the client and/or the funding body.)
- A consideration of the ratio of the likely damages to the costs in the case.
- Based on that information, an assessment of the risks to the client and/or the funding bodies.

In your written opinions and in your advice to the client in conference that risk assessment needs to be made clearly and explicitly.

Alternative approaches to settling disputes

15.1 Introduction

Before any case reaches trial you should consider alternative methods of resolving the dispute. The belief that litigation should only be used as a last resort is central to the reforms of civil procedure and State funding for civil cases over the last few years. The Lord Chancellor's Department has consistently promoted the use of alternative dispute resolution (ADR). In a Consultation Paper in November 1999, ADR was described as 'simpler, cheaper, quicker, less stressful and less damaging' than litigation. The promotion of ADR provokes some strong reactions from lawyers. As one said: 'It is as if the Department of Health were to issue leaflets advocating the use of aromatherapy.' At present, ADR is much talked about and relatively little used. Parties are now obliged to consider using an alternative method of resolving their disputes before the court will give directions for the case to be pursued through conventional routes. There are arguments that cases involving professional negligence are particularly suited to ADR. Consequently, you need to understand what ADR is, what its future role will be and when to advise your client to use it.

15.2 What is meant by alternative dispute resolution?

The title covers all types of dispute resolution other than the trial process. Examples include arbitration, determination by an expert, certain complaint procedures, ombudsman procedures, early neutral evaluation, negotiation between the parties (the most used and most familiar ADR), mediation and conciliation. For a further discussion of the types of ADR available and what they involve, see the *Negotiation Manual*, **Chapter 20**.

15.3 Procedure: when must you consider it?

15.3.1 Civil procedure rules

The Civil Procedure Rules 1998 make only two express references to the use of ADR:

(a) *Part 1, the Overriding Objective*. Under r 1.4 is the list of the court's duty to actively manage cases. Under r 1.4(2)(e) the court is specifically obliged to 'encourage the parties to use an alternative dispute resolution procedure if the court considers that appropriate' and to facilitate the use of such procedure.

(b) *Part 26, Case Management.* Under r 26.4(1) a party may, when filing the completed allocation questionnaire, make a written request for the proceedings to be stayed while the parties try to settle the dispute by alternative dispute resolution or other means.

The rule goes on to provide that the court may also stay proceedings of its own initiative when no party requests it, if it considers that such a stay would be appropriate. The initial stay is for one month but can be extended.

There is important guidance as to how courts are to encourage or facilitate ADR in the Legal Services Commission Funding Code.

The court can adjourn proceedings so that ADR can be attempted. The court can refuse costs where ADR has been unreasonably rejected (see *Dunnett v Railtrack plc* [2002] EWCA Civ 303, [2002] 1 WLR 2434).

15.3.2   Pre-action protocols

The Pre-action Protocol for Personal Injury Claims makes no express reference to ADR but it does say that 'litigation should be a last resort'.

The Pre-action Protocol for the Resolution of Clinical Disputes, Part 5, is titled 'Alternative Approaches to Settling Disputes'. It reminds the reader that courts increasingly expect parties to resolve their differences through ADR and asks the parties to bear in mind the usefulness of ADR. It then sets out various possible alternative methods such as using the NHS complaints procedure, mediation, arbitration, determination by an expert and early neutral evaluation.

In small track cases the only real opportunity once litigation has begun to consider ADR is at the allocation stage. In fast and multi-track cases, however, the court uses its case management powers and so ought to consider ADR at more stages: allocation, case management conferences and pre-trial reviews.

15.3.3   Should courts be allowed to make compulsory references to ADR?

There are good arguments to suggest that the success rate of ADR is dependent upon the parties' willingness to use it and that compelling an unwilling party to a form of dispute resolution other than court proceedings would be counter-productive. Indeed, it is likely to be contrary to art 6 of the European Convention on Human Rights which contains the right to a fair and public hearing by an independent tribunal established by law. However, there is one known decision of a court making an ADR order despite resistance from one party (*Kinstreet Ltd v Balmargo Corp Ltd* (1999) LTL 3/12/99, Arden J). It is also possible for costs penalties to be made against parties who unreasonably refuse to use ADR or are obstructive during the course of it under CPR, r 44.3(4), where the court can take the conduct of parties into account.

15.4   Which cases are suitable for ADR?

The Legal Services Commission has considered the role of ADR in the Funding Code Decision Making Guidance (April 2003). ADR is considered generally in section 7 of the

Guidance and particularly in relation to clinical negligence cases in section 18.8. The Commission seeks to encourage but not to force parties to arbitrate. The Guidance states that parties should consider ADR at every stage of proceedings and should record any reasons for not pursuing it. The circumstances in which various types of ADR are particularly suitable are as follows:

(a) Any form of ADR where the costs of litigation will exceed the money at issue.

(b) Mediation or conciliation where parties wish to preserve a continuing relationship. (This might well be appropriate in cases of ongoing professional/client relationships.)

(c) Arbitration where speed is required and there is no ongoing relationship to preserve.

(d) Ombudsmen and regulator schemes can provide a cheap alternative when redress is sought against a company but only offers limited remedies.

(e) Early neutral evaluation might be appropriate where there is a dispute over a point of law or where one party has a realistic view of their chances of success. (Although the Civil Procedure Rules provide for interim applications, eg, an application to strikeout, which might apply in many such cases).

(f) A dispute which involves difficult technical evaluation might be suitable for mediation or determination by an expert. (This could be useful in clinical negligence cases).

(g) Sensitive information can be kept private under ADR unlike open court.

(h) Mediation has been seen to work in seemingly intractable multi-party cases.

15.5 Benefits of ADR

Are ADR proceedings genuinely simpler, cheaper, quicker, less stressful and less damaging than court proceedings? Consider the following:

(a) ADR proceedings are certainly less formal. This means that the preparation can be less extensive and cheaper and the situation less intimidating to a lay participant.

(b) It is often possible to find earlier and more convenient dates than when relying on court listing systems.

(c) The process can be more constructive than litigation. Parties tend to look towards a mutually satisfactory solution rather than dwelling on the faults and weaknesses of the other side.

(d) Whereas at trial one party usually wins and another loses, in ADR such as mediation, settlements can include benefits for both sides.

(e) Parties can also arrive at compromises which include elements which a court could not order, eg, apologies or an agreement to carry out further medical treatment or other services for free.

(f) Privacy: ADR is not in open court and so publicity of sensitive information can be avoided.

15.6 Disadvantages of ADR

- There is no straightforward method to appeal an ADR outcome.
- If ADR fails and litigation is continued, costs tend to be increased.
- If ADR fails and litigation is continued, you may have shown more of your hand than you would tactically have chosen to do in litigation.
- It can be misused by parties who enter into it for the wrong reasons, eg, for delaying tactics, to put pressure on the other side.
- Funding may be difficult to arrange.

15.7 Future of ADR

It has to be likely that the use of ADR will increase given the emphasis on it in the Civil Procedure Rules 1998, pre-action protocols and the Funding Code. That is certainly the intention of the Lord Chancellor's Department. However, despite attempts to encourage ADR over some years now, it is still rarely used. Each party is under a duty to *consider* whether ADR is appropriate in each case. You should take time to consider the various ADR options in the light of the value of the case, the potential costs, the issues, the relationship between the people involved, and the stage the case has reached. Once you have done this you should be in a position to advise for or against ADR. As one lawyer has said of such cases: 'They are like elephants, easy to recognise but hard to define.'

APPENDIX 1
PRACTICE DIRECTION — PROTOCOLS

GENERAL

1.1   This practice direction applies to the pre-action protocols which have been approved by the Head of Civil Justice.

1.2   The pre-action protocols which have been approved are set out in para 5.1. Other pre-action protocols may subsequently be added.

1.3   Pre-action protocols outline the steps parties should take to seek information from and to provide information to each other about a prospective legal claim.

1.4   The objectives of pre-action protocols are:

(1)   to encourage the exchange of early and full information about the prospective legal claim,

(2)   to enable parties to avoid litigation by agreeing a settlement of the claim, before the commencement of proceedings,

(3)   to support the efficient management of proceedings where litigation cannot be avoided.

COMPLIANCE WITH PROTOCOLS

2.1   The Civil Procedure Rules enable the court to take into account compliance or non-compliance with an applicable protocol when giving directions for the management of proceedings (see rr 3.1(4) and (5) and 3.9 (e)) and when making orders for costs (see r 44.3 (5)a)).

2.2   The court will expect all parties to have complied in substance with the terms of an approved protocol.

2.3   If, in the opinion of the court, non-compliance has led to the commencement of proceedings which might otherwise not have needed to be commenced, or has led to costs being incurred in the proceedings that might otherwise not have been incurred, the orders the court may make include:

(1)   an order that the party at fault pay the costs of the proceedings, or part of those costs, of the other party or parties;

(2)   an order that the party at fault pay those costs on an indemnity basis;

(3)   if the party at fault is a claimant in whose favour an order for the payment of damages or some specified sum is subsequently made, an order depriving that party of interest on such sum and in respect of such period as may be specified, and/or awarding interest at a lower rate than that at which interest would otherwise have been awarded;

(4)   if the party at fault is a defendant and an order for the payment of damages or some specified sum is subsequently made in favour of the claimant, an order awarding interest on such sum and in respect of such period as may be specified at a higher rate, not exceeding 10 per cent above base rate (cf r 36.21 (2)), than the rate at which interest would otherwise have been awarded.

2.4   The court will exercise its powers under paras 2.1 and 2.3 with the object of placing the innocent party in no worse a position than he would have been in if the protocol had been complied with.

3.1   A claimant may be found to have failed to comply with a protocol by, for example:

(a)   not having provided sufficient information to the defendant, or

(b)   not having followed the procedure required by the protocol to be followed (eg not having followed the medical expert instruction procedure set out in the Personal Injury Protocol).

3.2   A defendant may be found to have failed to comply with a protocol by, for example:

(a)   not making a preliminary response to the letter of claim within the time fixed for that purpose by the relevant protocol (21 days under the Personal Injury Protocol, 14 days under the Clinical Negligence Protocol),

(b)   not making a full response within the time fixed for that purpose by the relevant protocol (three months of the letter of claim under the Clinical Negligence Protocol, three months from the date of acknowledgment of the letter of claim under the Personal Injury Protocol),

(c)   not disclosing documents required to be disclosed by the relevant protocol.

3.3   The court is likely to treat this practice direction as indicating the normal, reasonable way of dealing with disputes. If proceedings are issued and parties have not complied with this practice direction or a specific protocol, it will be for the court to decide whether sanctions should be applied.

3.4   The court is not likely to be concerned with minor infringements of the practice direction or protocols. The court is likely to look at the effect of non-compliance on the other party when deciding whether to impose sanctions.

3.5   This practice direction does not alter the statutory time limits for starting court proceedings. A claimant is required to start proceedings within those time limits and to adhere to subsequent time limits required by the rules or ordered by the court. If proceedings are for any reason started before the parties have followed the procedures in this practice direction, the parties are encouraged to agree to apply to the court for a stay of the proceedings while they follow the practice direction.

PRE-ACTION BEHAVIOUR IN OTHER CASES

4.1   In cases not covered by any approved protocol, the court will expect the parties, in accordance with the overriding objective and the matters referred to in r 1.1(2)(a), (b) and (c), to act reasonably in exchanging information and documents relevant to the claim and generally in trying to avoid the necessity for the start of proceedings.

4.2   Parties to a potential dispute should follow a reasonable procedure, suitable to their particular circumstances, which is intended to avoid litigation. The procedure should not be regarded as a prelude to inevitable litigation. It should normally include:

(a)   the claimant writing to give details of the claim;

(b)   the defendant acknowledging the claim letter promptly;

(c)   the defendant giving within a reasonable time a detailed written response; and

(d)   the parties conducting genuine and reasonable negotiations with a view to settling the claim economically and without court proceedings.

4.3   The claimant's letter should:

(a)   give sufficient concise details to enable the recipient to understand and investigate the claim without extensive further information;

(b) enclose copies of the essential documents which the claimant relies on;

(c) ask for a prompt acknowledgment of the letter, followed by a full written response within a reasonable stated period;

(For many claims, a normal reasonable period for a full response may be one month).

(d) state whether court proceedings will be issued if the full response is not received within the stated period;

(e) identify and ask for copies of any essential documents, not in his possession, which the claimant wishes to see;

(f) state (if this is so) that the claimant wishes to enter into mediation or another alternative method of dispute resolution; and

(g) draw attention to the court's powers to impose sanctions for failure to comply with this practice direction and, if the recipient is likely to be unrepresented, enclose a copy of this practice direction.

4.4   The defendant should acknowledge the claimant's letter in writing within 21 days of receiving it. The acknowledgment should state when the defendant will give a full written response. If the time for this is longer than the period stated by the claimant, the defendant should give reasons why a longer period is needed.

4.5   The defendant's full written response should as appropriate:

(a) accept the claim in whole or in part and make proposals for settlement; or

(b) state that the claim is not accepted.

If the claim is accepted in part only, the response should make clear which part is accepted and which part is not accepted.

4.6   If the defendant does not accept the claim or part of it, the response should:

(a) give detailed reasons why the claim is not accepted, identifying which of the claimant's contentions are accepted and which are in dispute;

(b) enclose copies of the essential documents which the defendant relies on;

(c) enclose copies of documents asked for by the claimant, or explain why they are not enclosed;

(d) identify and ask for copies of any further essential documents, not in his possession, which the defendant wishes to see; and

(The claimant should provide these within a reasonably short time or explain in writing why he is not doing so).

(e) state whether the defendant is prepared to enter into mediation or another alternative method of dispute resolution.

4.7   If the claim remains in dispute, the parties should promptly engage in appropriate negotiations with a view to settling the dispute and avoiding litigation.

4.8   Documents disclosed by either party in accordance with this practice direction may not be used for any purpose other than resolving the dispute, unless the other party agrees.

4.9   The resolution of some claims, but by no means all, may need help from an expert. If an expert is needed, the parties should wherever possible and to save expense engage an agreed expert.

4.10   Parties should be aware that, if the matter proceeds to litigation, the court may not allow the use of an expert's report, and that the cost of it is not always recoverable.

INFORMATION ABOUT FUNDING ARRANGEMENTS

4A.1   Where a person enters into a funding arrangement within the meaning of r 43.2 (1)(k) he should inform other potential parties to the claim that he has done so.

4A.2   Paragraph 4A. 1 applies to all proceedings whether proceedings to which a pre-action protocol applies or otherwise.

(Rule 44.3B (1)(c) provides that a party may not recover any additional liability for any period in the proceedings during which he failed to provide information about a funding arrangement in accordance with a rule, practice direction or court order)

COMMENCEMENT

5.1   The following table sets out the protocols currently in force, the date they came into force and their date of publication:

Protocol	Coming into force	Publication
Personal Injury	26 April 1999	January 1999
Clinical Negligence	26 April 1999	January 1999
Construction and Engineering Disputes	2 October 2000	September 2000
Defamation	2 October 2000	September 2000
Professional Negligence	16 July 2001	May 2001
Judicial Review	4 March 2002	3 December 2001

5.2   The court will take compliance or non-compliance with a relevant protocol into account where the claim was started after the coming into force of that protocol but will not do so where the claim was started before that date.

5.3   Parties in a claim started after a relevant protocol came into force, who have, by work done before that date, achieved the objectives sought to be achieved by certain requirements of that protocol, need not take any further steps to comply with those requirements. They will not be considered to have not complied with the protocol for the purposes of para 2 and 3.

5.4   Parties in a claim started after a relevant protocol came into force, who have not been able to comply with any particular requirements of that protocol because the period of time between the publication date and the date of coming into force was too short, will not be considered to have not complied with the protocol for the purposes of paras 2 and 3.

APPENDIX 2
PRE-ACTION PROTOCOL FOR PERSONAL INJURY CLAIMS

CONTENTS

1 INTRODUCTION

1.1 Lord Woolf in his final Access to Justice Report of July 1996 recommended the development of pre-action protocols:

> To build on and increase the benefits of early but well informed settlement which genuinely satisfy both parties to dispute.

1.2 The aims of pre-action protocols are:
- more pre-action contact between the parties
- better and earlier exchange of information
- better pre-action investigation by both sides
- to put the parties in a position where they may be able to settle cases fairly and early without litigation
- to enable proceedings to run to the court's timetable and efficiently, if litigation does become necessary.

1.3 The concept of protocols is relevant to a range of initiatives for good litigation and pre-litigation practice, especially:
- predictability in the time needed for steps pre-proceedings
- standardisation of relevant information, including documents to be disclosed.

1.4 The courts will be able to treat the standards set in protocols as the normal reasonable approach to pre-action conduct. If proceedings are issued, it will be for the court to decide whether non-compliance with a protocol should merit adverse consequences. Guidance on the court's likely approach will be given from time to time in practice directions.

1.5 If the court has to consider the question of compliance after proceedings have begun, it will not be concerned with minor infringements, eg failure by a short period to provide relevant information. One minor breach will not exempt the 'innocent' party from following the protocol. The court will look at the effect of non-compliance on the other party when deciding whether to impose sanctions.

2   NOTES OF GUIDANCE

2.1   The protocol has been kept deliberately simple to promote ease of use and general acceptability. The notes of guidance which follow relate particularly to issues which arose during the piloting of the protocol.

SCOPE OF THE PROTOCOL

2.2   This protocol is intended to apply to all claims which include a claim for personal injury) except industrial disease claims (and to the entirety of those claims: not only to the personal injury element of a claim which also includes, for instance, property damage.

2.3   This protocol is primarily designed for those road traffic, tripping and slipping and accident at work cases which include an element of personal injury with a value of less than £15,000 which are likely to be allocated to the fast track. This is because time will be of the essence, after proceedings are issued, especially for the defendant, if a case is to be ready for trial within 30 weeks of allocation. Also, proportionality of work and costs to the value of what is in dispute is particularly important in lower value claims. For some claims within the value 'scope' of the fast track some flexibility in the timescale of the protocol may be necessary; see also paragraph 3.8.

2.4   However, the 'cards on the table' approach advocated by the protocol is equally appropriate to some higher value claims. The spirit, if not the letter of the protocol, should still be followed for multi-track type claims. In accordance with the sense of the civil justice reforms, the court will expect to see the spirit of reasonable pre-action behaviour applied in all cases, regardless of the existence of a specific protocol. In particular with regard to personal injury cases worth more than £15,000, with a view to avoiding the necessity of proceedings parties are expected to comply with the protocol as far as possible eg in respect of letters before action, exchanging information and documents agreeing experts.

2.5   The timetable and the arrangements for disclosing documents and obtaining expert evidence may need to be varied to suit the circumstances of the case. Where one or both parties consider the detail of the protocol is not appropriate to the case, and proceedings are subsequently issued, the court will expect an explanation as to why the protocol has not been followed, or has been varied.

EARLY NOTIFICATION

2.6   The claimant's legal representative may wish to notify the defendant and/or his insurer as soon as they know a claim is likely to be made, but before they are able to send a detailed letter of claim, particularly for instance, when the defendant has no or limited knowledge of the incident giving rise to the claim or where the claimant is incurring significant expenditure as a result of the accident which he hopes the defendant might pay for, in whole or in part. If the claimant's representative chooses to do this, it will not start the timetable for responding.

THE LETTER OF CLAIM

2.7   The specimen letter of claim at Annex A will usually be sent to the individual defendant. In practice, he/she may have no personal financial interest in the financial outcome of the claim/dispute because he/she is insured. Court imposed sanctions for non-compliance with the protocol may be ineffective against an insured. This is why the protocol emphasises the importance of passing the letter of claim to the insurer and the possibility that the insurance cover might be affected. If an insurer receives the letter of claim only after some delay by the insured, it would not be unreasonable for the insurer to ask the claimant for additional time to respond.

REASONS FOR EARLY ISSUE

2.8   The protocol recommends that a defendant be given three months to investigate and respond to a claim before proceedings are issued. This may not always be possible, particularly where a claimant only consults a solicitor close to the end of any relevant limitation period. In these circumstances, the claimant's solicitor should give as much notice of the intention to issue proceedings as is practicable and the parties should consider whether the court might be invited to extend time for service of the claimant's supporting documents and for service of any defence, or alternatively, to stay the proceedings while the recommended steps in the protocol are followed.

STATUS OF LETTERS OF CLAIM AND RESPONSE

2.9   Letters of claim and response are not intended to have the same status as a statement of case in proceedings. Matters may come to light as a result of investigation after the letter of claim has been sent, or after the defendant has responded, particularly if disclosure of documents takes place outside the recommended three-month period. These circumstances could mean that the 'pleaded' case of one or both parties is presented slightly differently than in the letter of claim and response. It would not be consistent with the spirit of the protocol for a party to 'take a point' on this in the proceedings, provided that there was no obvious intention by the party who changed their position to mislead the other party.

DISCLOSURE OF DOCUMENTS

2.10   The aim of the early disclosure of documents by the defendant is not to encourage 'fishing expeditions' by the claimant, but to promote an early exchange of relevant information to help in clarifying or resolving issues in dispute. The claimant's solicitor can assist by identifying in the letter of claim or in a subsequent letter the particular categories of documents which they consider are relevant.

EXPERTS

2.11   The protocol encourages joint selection of, and access to, experts. Most frequently this will apply to the medical expert, but on occasions also to liability experts, eg engineers. The protocol promotes the practice of the claimant obtaining a medical report, disclosing it to the defendant who then asks questions and/or agrees it and does not obtain his own report. The protocol provides for nomination of the expert by the claimant in personal injury claims because of the early stage of the proceedings and the particular nature of such claims. If proceedings have to be issued, a medical report must be attached to these proceedings. However, if necessary after proceedings have commenced and with the permission of the court, the parties may obtain further expert reports. It would be for the court to decide whether the costs of more than one expert's report should be recoverable.

2.12   Some solicitors choose to obtain medical reports through medical agencies, rather than directly from a specific doctor or hospital. The defendant's prior consent to the action should be sought and, if the defendant so requests, the agency should be asked to provide in advance the names of the doctor(s) whom they are considering instructing.

NEGOTIATIONS/SETTLEMENT

2.13   Parties and their legal representatives are encouraged to enter into discussions and/or negotiations prior to starting proceedings. The protocol does not specify when or how this might be done but parties should bear in mind that the courts increasingly take the view that litigation should be a last resort, and that claims should not be issued prematurely when a settlement is in reasonable prospect.

STOCKTAKE

2.14   Where a claim is not resolved when the protocol has been followed, the parties might wish to carry out a 'stocktake' of the issues in dispute, and the evidence that the court is likely to need to decide those issues, before proceedings are started. Where the defendant is insured and the pre-action steps have been conducted by the insurer, the insurer would normally be expected to nominate solicitors to act in the proceedings and the claimant's solicitor is recommended to invite the insurer to nominate solicitors to act in the proceedings and do so 7–14 days before the intended issue date.

3   THE PROTOCOL

LETTER OF CLAIM

3.1   The claimant shall send to the proposed defendant two copies of a letter of claim, immediately sufficient information is available to substantiate a realistic claim and before issues of quantum are addressed in detail. One copy of the letter is for the defendants, the second for passing on to his insurers.

3.2   The letter shall contain a **clear summary of the facts** on which the claim is based together with an indication of the **nature of any injuries** suffered and of **any financial loss incurred**. In cases of road traffic accidents, the letter should provide the name and address of the hospital where treatment has been obtained and the claimant's hospital reference number.

3.3   Solicitors are recommended to use a **standard format** for such a letter — an example is at Annex A: this can be amended to suit the particular case.

3.4   The letter should ask for **details of the insurer** and that a copy should be sent by the proposed defendant to the insurer where appropriate. If the insurer is known, a copy shall be sent directly to the insurer. Details of the claimant's National Insurance number and date of birth should be supplied to the defendant's insurer once the defendant has responded to the letter of claim and confirmed the identity of the insurer. This information should not be supplied in the letter of claim.

3.5   **Sufficient information** should be given in order to enable the defendant's insurer/solicitor to commence investigations and at least put a broad valuation on the 'risk'.

3.6   The **defendant should reply within 21 calendar days** of the date of posting of the letter identifying the insurer (if any). If there has been no reply by the defendant or insurer within 21 days, the claimant will be entitled to issue proceedings.

3.7   The **defendant**('s insurers) will have a **maximum of three months** from the date of acknowledgment of the claim **to investigate**. No later than the end of that period the defendant (insurer) shall reply, stating whether liability is denied and, if so, giving reasons for their denial of liability.

3.8   Where the accident occurred outside England and Wales and/or where the defendant is outside the jurisdiction, the time periods of 21 days and three months should normally be extended up to 42 days and six months.

3.9   Where **liability is admitted**, the presumption is that the defendant will be bound by this admission for all claims with a total value of up to £15,000.

DOCUMENTS

3.10   If the **defendant denies liability**, he should enclose with the letter of reply, **documents** in his possession which are **material to the issues** between the parties, and which would be likely to be ordered to be disclosed by the court, either on an application for pre-action disclosure, or on disclosure during proceedings.

3.11   Attached at Annex B are **specimen**, but non-exhaustive, **lists** of documents likely to be material in different types of claim. Where the claimant's investigation of the case is well advanced, the letter of claim could indicate which classes of documents are considered relevant for early disclosure. Alternatively these could be identified at a later stage.

3.12   Where the defendant admits primary liability, but alleges contributory negligence by the claimant, the defendant should give reasons supporting those allegations and disclose those documents from Annex B which are relevant to the issues in dispute. The claimant should respond to the allegations of contributory negligence before proceedings are issued.

SPECIAL DAMAGES

3.13   The claimant will send to the defendant as soon as practicable a schedule of special damages with supporting documents, particularly where the defendant has admitted liability.

EXPERTS

3.14   Before any party instructs an expert he should give the other party a list of the **name**(s) of **one or more experts** in the relevant speciality whom he considers are suitable to instruct.

3.15   Where a medical expert is to be instructed the claimant's solicitor will organise access to relevant medical records — see specimen letter of instruction at Annex C.

3.16   **Within 14 days** the other party may indicate **an objection** to one or more of the named experts. The first party should then instruct a mutually acceptable expert. It must be emphasised that if the claimant nominates an expert in the original letter of claim, the defendant has 14 days to object to one or more of the named experts after expiration of the period of 21 days within which he has to reply to the letter of claim, as set out in paragraph 3.6.

3.17   If the second party objects to all the listed experts, the parties may then instruct **experts of their own choice**. It would be for the court to decide subsequently, if proceedings are issued, whether either party had acted unreasonably.

3.18   If the **second party does not object to an expert nominated**, he shall not be entitled to rely on his own expert evidence within that particular speciality unless:

    (a) the first party agrees,

    (b) the court so directs, or

    (c) the first party's expert report has been amended and the first party is not prepared to disclose the original report.

3.19   **Either party may send to an agreed expert written questions** on the report, relevant to the issues, via the first party's solicitors. The expert should send answers to the questions separately and directly to each party.

3.20   The cost of a report from an agreed expert will usually be paid by the instructing first party: the costs of the expert replying to questions will usually be borne by the party which asks the questions.

3.21   Where the defendant admits liability in whole or in part, before proceedings are issued, any medical report obtained by agreement under this protocol should be disclosed to the other party. The claimant should delay issuing proceedings for 21 days from disclosure of the report, to enable the parties to consider whether the claim is capable of settlement. The Civil Procedure Rules Part 36 permit claimants and defendants to make offers to settle pre-proceedings. Parties should always consider before issuing if it is appropriate to make a Part 36 offer. If such an offer is made, the party making the offer must always supply sufficient evidence and/or information to enable the offer to be properly considered.

ANNEX A LETTER OF CLAIM

To

Defendant

Dear Sirs

Re: **Claimant's full name**
                Claimant's full address
                Claimant's Clock or Works Number
                Claimant's Employer *(name and address)*

We are instructed by the above named to claim damages in connection with ***an accident at work/road traffic accident/tripping accident*** on day of *(year)* at *(place of accident which must be sufficiently detailed to establish location)*

Please confirm the identity of your insurers. Please note that the insurers will need to see this letter as soon as possible and it may affect your insurance cover and/or the conduct of any subsequent legal proceedings if you do not send this letter to them.

The circumstances of the accident are:—
(brief outline)

The reason why we are alleging fault is:
(simple explanation eg defective machine, broken ground)

A description of our clients' injuries is as follows:—
(brief outline)

(In cases of road traffic accidents)
Our client *(state hospital reference number)* received treatment for the injuries at *(name and address of hospital)*.

He is employed as *(occupation)* and has had the following time off work *(dates of absence)*. His approximate weekly income is *(insert if known)*.

If you are our client's employers, please provide us with the usual earnings details which will enable us to calculate his financial loss.

We are obtaining a police report and will let you have a copy of the same upon your undertaking to meet half the fee.

We have also sent a letter of claim to *(name and address)* and a copy of that letter is attached. We understand their insurers are *(name, address and claims number if known)*.

At this stage of our enquiries we would expect the documents contained in parts (**insert appropriate parts of standard disclosure list**) to be relevant to this action.

A copy of this letter is attached for you to send to your insurers. Finally we expect an acknowledgment of this letter within 21 days by yourselves or your insurers.

Yours faithfully

ANNEX B STANDARD DISCLOSURE LISTS FAST TRACK DISCLOSURE

ROAD TRAFFIC ACCIDENT CASES

SECTION A

In all cases where liability is at issue—

(i)   Documents identifying nature, extent and location of damage to defendant's vehicle where there is any dispute about point of impact.

(ii)   MOT certificate where relevant.

(iii)   Maintenance records where vehicle defect is alleged or it is alleged by defendant that there was an unforeseen defect which caused or contributed to the accident.

SECTION B

Accident involving commercial vehicle as potential defendant—

(i)   Tachograph charts or entry from individual control book.

(ii)   Maintenance and repair records required for operators' licence where vehicle defect is alleged or it is alleged by defendants that there was an unforeseen defect which caused or contributed to the accident.

SECTION C

Cases against local authorities where highway design defect is alleged—

(i)   Documents produced to comply with of the Road Traffic Act 1988, s 39, in respect of the duty designed to promote road safety to include studies into road accidents in the relevant area and documents relating to measures recommended to prevent accidents in the relevant area.

HIGHWAY TRIPPING CLAIMS

Documents from highway authority for a period of 12 months prior to the accident—

(i)   Records of inspection for the relevant stretch of highway.

(ii)   Maintenance records including records of independent contractors working in relevant area.

(iii)   Records of the minutes of highway authority meetings where maintenance or repair policy has been discussed or decided.

(iv)   Records of complaints about the state of highways.

(v)   Records of other accidents which have occurred on the relevant stretch of highway.

WORKPLACE CLAIMS

(i)   Accident book entry.

(ii)   First aider report.

(iii)   Surgery record.

(iv)   Foreman/supervisor accident report.

(v)   Safety representatives accident report.

(vi)   RIDDOR report to HSE.

(vii)   Other communications between defendants and HSE.

(viii)   Minutes of Health and Safety Committee meeting(s) where accident/matter considered.

(ix)   Report to DSS.

(x)   Documents listed above relative to any previous accident/matter identified by the claimant and relied upon as proof of negligence.

(xi)   Earnings information where defendant is employer.

Documents produced to comply with requirements of the Management of Health and Safety at Work Regulations 1992 —

(i)   Pre-accident Risk Assessment required by Regulation 3.

(ii)   Post-accident Reassessment required by Regulation 3.

(iii)   Accident Investigation Report prepared in implementing the requirements of Regulations 4, 6 and 9.

(iv)   Health Surveillance Records in appropriate cases required by Regulation 5.

(v)   Information provided to employees under Regulation 8.

(vi)   Documents relating to the employees health and safety training required by Regulation 11.

WORKPLACE CLAIMS — DISCLOSURE WHERE SPECIFIC REGULATIONS APPLY

SECTION A — WORKPLACE (HEALTH, SAFETY AND WELFARE) REGULATIONS 1992 (SI 1992/3004)

(i)   Repair and maintenance records required by reg 5.

(ii)   Housekeeping records to comply with the requirements of reg 9.

(iii)   Hazard warning signs or notices to comply with reg 17 (traffic routes).

SECTION B — PROVISION AND USE OF WORK EQUIPMENT REGULATIONS 1992 (SI 1992/2932)

(i)   Manufacturers' specifications and instructions in respect of relevant work equipment establishing its suitability to comply with reg 5.

(ii)   Maintenance log/maintenance records required to comply with reg 6.

(iii)   Documents providing information and instructions to employees to comply with reg 8.

(iv)   Documents provided to the employee in respect of training for use to comply with reg 9.

(v)   Any notice, sign or document relied upon as a defence to alleged breaches of regs 14 to 18 dealing with controls and control systems.

(vi)   Instruction/training documents issued to comply with the requirements of reg 22 in so far as it deals with maintenance operations where the machinery is not shut down.

(vii)   Copies of markings required to comply with reg 23.

(viii)   Copies of warnings required to comply with reg 24.

SECTION C — PERSONAL PROTECTIVE EQUIPMENT AT WORK REGULATIONS 1992 (SI 1992/2966)

(i)   Documents relating to the assessment of the personal protective equipment to comply with reg 6.

(ii)   Documents relating to the maintenance and replacement of personal protective equipment to comply with reg 7.

(iii)   Record of maintenance procedures for personal protective equipment to comply with reg 7.

(iv)   Records of tests and examinations of personal protective equipment to comply with reg 7.

(v)   Documents providing information, instruction and training in relation to the personal protective equipment to comply with reg 9.

(vi)   Instructions for use of personal protective equipment to include the manufacturers' instructions to comply with reg 10.

SECTION D — MANUAL HANDLING OPERATIONS REGULATIONS 1992 (SI 1992/2793)

(i)   Manual handling risk assessment carried out to comply with the requirements of reg 4(1)(b)(i).

(ii)   Reassessment carried out post-accident to comply with requirements of reg 4(1)(b)(i).

(iii)   Documents showing the information provided to the employee to give general indications related to the load and precise indications on the weight of the load and the heaviest side of the load if the centre of gravity was not positioned centrally to comply with reg 4(1)(b)(iii).

(iv)   Documents relating to training in respect of manual handling operations and training records.

SECTION E — HEALTH AND SAFETY (DISPLAY SCREEN EQUIPMENT) REGULATIONS 1992 (SI 1992/2792)

(i)   Analysis of work stations to assess and reduce risks carried out to comply with the requirements of reg 2.

(ii)   Reassessment of analysis of work stations to assess and reduce risks following development of symptoms by the claimant.

(iii)   Documents detailing the provision of training including training records to comply with the requirements of reg 6.

(iv)   Documents providing information to employees to comply with the requirements of reg 7.

SECTION F — CONTROL OF SUBSTANCES HAZARDOUS TO HEALTH REGULATIONS 1988 (SI 1988/1657)

(i)   Risk assessment carried out to comply with the requirements of reg 6.

(ii)   Reviewed risk assessment carried out to comply with the requirements of reg 6.

(iii)   Copy labels from containers used for storage handling and disposal of carcinogenics to comply with the requirements of reg 7(2A)(h).

(iv)   Warning signs identifying designation of areas and installations which may be contaminated by carcinogenics to comply with the requirements of reg 7(2A)(h).

(v)   Documents relating to the assessment of the personal protective equipment to comply with reg 7(3A).

(vi)   Documents relating to the maintenance and replacement of personal protective equipment to comply with reg 7(3A).

(vii)   Record of maintenance procedures for personal protective equipment to comply with reg 7(3A).

(viii)   Records of tests and examinations of personal protective equipment to comply with reg 7(3A).

(ix)   Documents providing information, instruction and training in relation to the personal protective equipment to comply with reg 7(3A).

(x)   Instructions for use of personal protective equipment to include the manufacturers' instructions to comply with reg 7(3A).

(xi) Air monitoring records for substances assigned a maximum exposure limit or occupational exposure standard to comply with the requirements of reg 7.

(xii) Maintenance examination and test of control measures records to comply with reg 9.

(xiii) Monitoring records to comply with the requirements of reg 10.

(xiv) Health surveillance records to comply with the requirements of reg 11.

(xv) Documents detailing information, instruction and training including training records for employees to comply with the requirements of reg 12.

(xvi) Labels and health and safety data sheets supplied to the employers to comply with the CHIP regs.

SECTION G — CONSTRUCTION (DESIGN AND MANAGEMENT) REGULATIONS 1994 (SI 1994/3140)

(i) Notification of a project form (HSE F10) to comply with the requirements of reg 7.

(ii) Health and safety plan to comply with requirements of reg 15.

(iii) Health and safety file to comply with the requirements of regs 12 and 14.

(iv) Information and training records provided to comply with the requirements of reg 17.

(v) Records of advice from and views of persons at work to comply with the requirements of reg 18.

SECTION H — PRESSURE SYSTEMS AND TRANSPORTABLE GAS CONTAINERS REGULATIONS 1989 (SI 1989/2169)

(i) Information and specimen markings provided to comply with the requirements of reg 5.

(ii) Written statements specifying the safe operating limits of a system to comply with the requirements of reg 7.

(iii) Copy of the written scheme of examination required to comply with the requirements of reg 8.

(iv) Examination records required to comply with the requirements of reg 9.

(v) Instructions provided for the use of operator to comply with reg 11.

(vi) Records kept to comply with the requirements of reg 13.

(vii) Records kept to comply with the requirements of reg 22.

SECTION I — LIFTING PLANT AND EQUIPMENT (RECORDS OF TEST AND EXAMINATION ETC.) REGULATIONS 1992 (SI 1992/195)

(i) Record kept to comply with the requirements of reg 6.

SECTION J — THE NOISE AT WORK REGULATIONS 1989 (SI 1989/1790)

(i) Any risk assessment records required to comply with the requirements of regs 4 and 5.

(ii) Manufacturers' literature in respect of all ear protection made available to claimant to comply with the requirements of reg 8.

(iii) All documents provided to the employee for the provision of information to comply with reg 11.

SECTION K — CONSTRUCTION (HEAD PROTECTION) REGULATIONS 1989 (SI 1989/2209)

(i) Pre-accident assessment of head protection required to comply with reg 3(4).

(ii)   Post-accident reassessment required to comply with reg 3(5).

SECTION L — CONSTRUCTION (GENERAL PROVISIONS) REGULATIONS 1961 (SI 1961/1580)

(i)   Report prepared following inspections and examinations of excavations etc. to comply with the requirements of reg 9.

(ii)   Report prepared following inspections and examinations of work in coffer-dams and caissons to comply with the requirements of regs 17 and 18.

N.B. Further standard discovery lists will be required prior to full implementation.

ANNEX C   LETTER OF INSTRUCTION TO MEDICAL EXPERT

Dear Sir,

Re: *(Name and Address)*

D.O.B. —

Telephone No. —

Date of Accident —

We are acting for the above named in connection with injuries received in an accident which occurred on the above date. The main injuries appear to have been *(main injuries)*.

We should be obliged if you would examine our Client and let us have a full and detailed report dealing with any relevant pre-accident medical history, the injuries sustained, treatment received and present condition, dealing in particular with the capacity for work and giving a prognosis.

It is central to our assessment of the extent of our Client's injuries to establish the extent and duration of any continuing disability. Accordingly, in the prognosis section we would ask you to specifically comment on any areas of continuing complaint or disability or impact on daily living. If there is such continuing disability you should comment upon the level of suffering or inconvenience caused and, if you are able, give your view as to when or if the complaint or disability is likely to resolve.

Please send our Client an appointment direct for this purpose. Should you be able to offer a cancellation appointment please contact our Client direct. We confirm we will be responsible for your reasonable fees.

We are obtaining the notes and records from our Client's GP and Hospitals attended and will forward them to you when they are to hand/or please request the GP and Hospital records direct and advise that any invoice for the provision of these records should be forwarded to us.

In order to comply with Court Rules we would be grateful if you would insert above your signature a statement that the contents are true to the best of your knowledge and belief.

In order to avoid further correspondence we can confirm that on the evidence we h there is no reason to suspect we may be pursuing a claim against the hospital or it

We look forward to receiving your report within _____ weeks. If be able to prepare your report within this period please telephone us upo instructions.

When acknowledging these instructions it would assist if you c the likely time scale for the provision of your report and als

Yours faithfully

APPENDIX 3
PRE-ACTION PROTOCOL FOR THE RESOLUTION OF CLINICAL DISPUTES

Clinical Disputes Forum

CONTENTS

EXECUTIVE SUMMARY

1.   The Clinical Disputes Forum is a multi-disciplinary body which was formed in 1997, as a result of Lord Woolf's 'Access to Justice' inquiry. One of the aims of the Forum is to find less adversaria͏l   cost-effective ways of resolving disputes about health-care an͏ ͏   ames and addresses of the Chairman and Secretary of

's first major initiative. It has been drawn up carefully,
ith most of the key stakeholders in the medico-legal

vhen something has 'gone wrong' with a patient's
ed with that treatment and/or the outcome. This
rements for clinical governance within health-care;
this more open culture might be achieved when

ps for patients and healthcare providers, and
te arises. This should facilitate and speed up
increase the prospects that disputes can be

by a working party of the Clinical Disputes
ncellor's Department, the Department of

Health and NHS Executive, the Law Society, the Legal Aid Board and many other key organisations.

1   WHY THIS PROTOCOL?

MISTRUST IN HEALTHCARE DISPUTES

1.1   The number of complaints and claims against hospitals, GPs, dentists and private healthcare providers is growing as patients become more prepared to question the treatment they are given, to seek explanations of what happened, and to seek appropriate redress. Patients may require further treatment, an apology, assurances about future action, or compensation. These trends are unlikely to change. The Patients' Charter encourages patients to have high expectations, and a revised NHS Complaints Procedure was implemented in 1996. The civil justice reforms and new Rules of Court should make litigation quicker, more user friendly and less expensive.

1.2   It is clearly in the interests of patients, healthcare professionals and providers that patients' concerns, complaints and claims arising from their treatment are resolved as quickly, efficiently and professionally as possible. A climate of mistrust and lack of openness can seriously damage the patient/clinician relationship, unnecessarily prolong disputes (especially litigation), and reduce the resources available for treating patients. It may also cause additional work for, and lower the morale of, healthcare professionals.

1.3   At present there is often mistrust by both sides. This can mean that patients fail to raise their concerns with the healthcare provider as early as possible. Sometimes patients may pursue a complaint or claim which has little merit, due to a lack of sufficient information and understanding. It can also mean that patients become reluctant, once advice has been taken on a potential claim, to disclose sufficient information to enable the provider to investigate that claim efficiently and, where appropriate, resolve it.

1.4   On the side of the healthcare provider this mistrust can be shown in a reluctance to be honest with patients, a failure to provide prompt clear explanations, especially of adverse outcomes (whether or not there may have been negligence) and a tendency to 'close ranks' once a claim is made.

WHAT NEEDS TO CHANGE

1.5   If that mistrust is to be removed, and a more cooperative culture is to develop—

- healthcare professionals and providers need to adopt a constructive approach to complaints and claims. They should accept that concerned patients are entitled to an explanation and an apology, if warranted, and to appropriate redress in the event of negligence. An overly defensive approach is not in the long-term interest of their main goal: patient care;
- patients should recognise that unintended and/or unfortunate consequences of medical treatment can only be rectified if they are brought to the attention of the healthcare provider as soon as possible.

1.6   A protocol which sets out 'ground rules' for the handling of disputes at their early stages should, if it is to be subscribed to, and followed—

- encourage greater openness between the parties;
- encourage parties to find the most appropriate way of resolving the particular dispute;
- reduce delay and costs;
- reduce the need for litigation.

WHY THIS PROTOCOL NOW?

1.7   Lord Woolf in his Access to Justice Report in July 1996, concluded that major causes of costs and delay in medical negligence litigation occur at the pre-action stage. He recommended that patients and their advisers, and healthcare providers, should work more closely together to try to resolve disputes cooperatively, rather than proceed to litigation. He specifically recommended a pre-action protocol for medical negligence cases.

1.8   A fuller summary of Lord Woolf's recommendations is at Annex D.

WHERE THE PROTOCOL FITS IN

1.9   Protocols serve the needs of litigation and pre-litigation practice, especially—
- predictability in the time needed for steps pre-proceedings;
- standardisation of relevant information, including records and documents to be disclosed.

1.10   Building upon Lord Woolf's recommendations, the Lord Chancellor's Department is now promoting the adoption of protocols in specific areas, including medical negligence.

1.11   It is recognised that contexts differ significantly. For example: patients tend to have an ongoing relationship with a GP, more so than with a hospital; clinical staff in the National Health Service are often employees, while those in the private sector may be contractors; providing records quickly may be relatively easy for GPs and dentists, but can be a complicated procedure in a large multi-department hospital. The protocol which follows is intended to be sufficiently broadly based, and flexible, to apply to all aspects of the health service: primary and secondary; public and private sectors.

ENFORCEMENT OF THE PROTOCOL AND SANCTIONS

1.12   The civil justice reforms will be implemented in April 1999. One new set of Court Rules and procedures is replacing the existing rules for both the High Court and county courts. This and the personal injury protocol are being published with the Rules, practice directions and key court forms. The courts will be able to treat the standards set in protocols as the normal reasonable approach to pre-action conduct.

1.13   If proceedings are issued it will be for the court to decide whether non-compliance with a protocol should merit sanctions. Guidance on the court's likely approach will be given from time to time in practice directions.

1.14   If the court has to consider the question of compliance after proceedings have begun it will not be concerned with minor infringements, eg failure by a short period to provide relevant information. One minor breach will not entitle the 'innocent' party to abandon following the protocol. The court will look at the effect of non-compliance on the other party when deciding whether to impose sanctions.

2   THE AIMS OF THE PROTOCOL

2.1   The **general** aims of the protocol are—
- to maintain/restore the patient/healthcare provider relationship;
- to resolve as many disputes as possible without litigation.

2.2   The **specific** objectives are—

OPENNESS

- to encourage early communication of the perceived problem between patients and healthcare providers;
- to encourage patients to voice any concerns or dissatisfaction with their treatment as soon as practicable;

- to encourage healthcare providers to develop systems of early reporting and investigation for serious adverse treatment outcomes and to provide full and prompt explanations to dissatisfied patients;
- to ensure that sufficient information is disclosed by both parties to enable each to understand the other's perspective and case, and to encourage early resolution.

TIMELINESS

- to provide an early opportunity for healthcare providers to identify cases where an investigation is required and to carry out that investigation promptly;
- to encourage primary and private healthcare providers to involve their defence organisations or insurers at an early stage;
- to ensure that all relevant medical records are provided to patients or their appointed representatives on request, to a realistic timetable by any healthcare provider;
- to ensure that relevant records which are not in healthcare providers' possession are made available to them by patients and their advisers at an appropriate stage;
- where a resolution is not achievable to lay the ground to enable litigation to proceed on a reasonable timetable, at a reasonable and proportionate cost and to limit the matters in contention;
- to discourage the prolonged pursuit of unmeritorious claims and the prolonged defence of meritorious claims.

AWARENESS OF OPTIONS

- to ensure that patients and healthcare providers are made aware of the available options to pursue and resolve disputes and what each might involve.

2.3   This protocol does not attempt to be prescriptive about a number of related clinical governance issues which will have a bearing on healthcare providers' ability to meet the standards within the protocol. Good clinical governance requires the following to be considered—

(a)   **Clinical risk management**: the protocol does not provide any detailed guidance to healthcare providers on clinical risk management or the adoption of risk management systems and procedures. This must be a matter for the NHS Executive, the National Health Service Litigation Authority, individual trusts and providers, including GPs, dentists and the private sector. However, effective coordinated, focused clinical risk management strategies and procedures can help in managing risk and in the early identification and investigation of adverse outcomes.

(b)   **Adverse outcome reporting**: the protocol does not provide any detailed guidance on which adverse outcomes should trigger an investigation. However, health-care providers should have in place procedures for such investigations, including recording of statements of key witnesses. These procedures should also cover when and how to inform patients that an adverse outcome has occurred.

(c)   **The professional's duty to report**: the protocol does not recommend changes to the codes of conduct of professionals in healthcare, or attempt to impose a specific duty on those professionals to report known adverse outcomes or untoward incidents. Lord Woolf in his final report suggested that the professional bodies might consider this. The General Medical Council is preparing guidance to doctors about their duty to report adverse incidents and to cooperate with inquiries.

3   THE PROTOCOL

3.1   This protocol is not a comprehensive code governing all the steps in clinical disputes. Rather it attempts to set out **a code of good practice** which parties should follow when litigation might be a possibility.

3.2   The **commitments** section of the protocol summarises the guiding principles which healthcare providers and patients and their advisers are invited to endorse when dealing with patient dissatisfaction with treatment and its outcome, and with potential complaints and claims.

3.3   The **steps** section sets out in a more prescriptive form, a recommended sequence of actions to be followed if litigation is a prospect.

GOOD PRACTICE COMMITMENTS

3.4   **Healthcare providers** should—

(i)   ensure that **key staff**, including claims and litigation managers, are appropriately trained and have some knowledge of healthcare law, and of complaints procedures and civil litigation practice and procedure;

(ii)   develop an approach to **clinical governance** that ensures that clinical practice is delivered to commonly accepted standards and that this is routinely monitored through a system of clinical audit and clinical risk management (particularly adverse outcome investigation);

(iii)   set up **adverse outcome reporting systems** in all specialties to record and investigate unexpected serious adverse outcomes as soon as possible. Such systems can enable evidence to be gathered quickly, which makes it easier to provide an accurate explanation of what happened and to defend or settle any subsequent claims;

(iv)   use the results of **adverse incidents and complaints positively** as a guide to how to improve services to patients in the future;

(v)   ensure **that patients receive clear and comprehensible information** in an accessible form about how to raise their concerns or complaints;

(vi)   establish **efficient and effective systems of recording and storing patient records**, notes, diagnostic reports and X-rays, and to retain these in accordance with Department of Health guidance (currently for a minimum of eight years in the case of adults, and all obstetric and paediatric notes for children until they reach the age of 25);

(vii)   **advise patients** of a serious adverse outcome and provide on request to the patient or the patient's representative an oral or written explanation of what happened, information on further steps open to the patient, including where appropriate an offer of future treatment to rectify the problem, an apology, changes in procedure which will benefit patients and/or compensation.

3.5   **Patients and their advisers** should—

(i)   **report any concerns and dissatisfaction** to the healthcare provider as soon as is reasonable to enable that provider to offer clinical advice where possible, to advise the patient if anything has gone wrong and take appropriate action;

(ii)   consider the **full range of options** available following an adverse outcome with which a patient is dissatisfied, including a request for an explanation, a meeting, a complaint, and other appropriate dispute resolution methods (including mediation) and negotiation, not only litigation;

(iii)   **inform the healthcare provider when the patient is satisfied** that the matter has been concluded: legal advisers should notify the provider when they are no longer acting for the patient, particularly if proceedings have not started.

PROTOCOL STEPS

3.6   The steps of this protocol which follow have been kept deliberately simple. An illustration of the likely sequence of events in a number of healthcare situations is at Annex A.

OBTAINING THE HEALTH RECORDS

3.7   Any request for records by the **patient** or their adviser should—

- **provide sufficient information** to alert the healthcare provider where an adverse outcome has been serious or had serious consequences;

- be as **specific as possible** about the records which are required.

3.8   Requests for copies of the patient's clinical records should be made using the Law Society and Department of Health approved **standard forms** (enclosed at Annex B), adapted as necessary.

3.9   The copy records should be provided **within 40 days** of the request and for a cost not exceeding the charges permissible under the Access to Health Records Act 1990 (currently a maximum of £10 plus photocopying and postage).

3.10   In the rare circumstances that the healthcare provider is in difficulty in complying with the request within 40 days, the **problem should be explained** quickly and details given of what is being done to resolve it.

3.11   It will not be practicable for healthcare providers to investigate in detail each case when records are requested. But healthcare providers should **adopt a policy on which cases will be investigated** (see paragraph 3.5 on clinical governance and adverse outcome reporting).

3.12   If the healthcare provider fails to provide the health records within 40 days, the patient or their adviser can then apply to the court for an **order for pre-action disclosure**. The new Civil Procedure Rules should make pre-action applications to the court easier. The court will also have the power to impose costs sanctions for unreasonable delay in providing records.

3.13   If either the patient or the healthcare provider considers **additional health records are required from a third party**, in the first instance these should be requested by or through the patient. Third party healthcare providers are expected to cooperate. The Civil Procedure Rules will enable patients and healthcare providers to apply to the court for pre-action disclosure by third parties.

LETTER OF CLAIM

3.14   Annex C1 to this protocol provides **a template for the recommended contents of a letter of claim:** the level of detail will need to be varied to suit the particular circumstances.

3.15   If, following the receipt and analysis of the records, and the receipt of any further advice (including from experts if necessary — see Section 4), the patient/adviser decides that there are grounds for a claim, they should then send, as soon as practicable, to the healthcare provider/potential defendant, a **letter of claim**.

3.16   This letter should contain a **clear summary of the facts** on which the claim is based, including the alleged adverse outcome, and the **main allegations of negligence**. It should also describe the **patient's injuries**, and present condition and prognosis. The **financial loss** incurred by the plaintiff should be outlined with an indication of the heads of damage to be claimed and the scale of the loss, unless this is impracticable.

3.17   In more complex cases a **chronology** of the relevant events should be provided, particularly if the patient has been treated by a number of different healthcare providers.

3.18   The letter of claim **should refer to any relevant documents**, including health records, and if possible enclose copies of any of those which will not already be in the potential defendant's possession, eg any relevant general practitioner records if the plaintiff's claim is against a hospital.

3.19   **Sufficient information** must be given to enable the healthcare provider defendant to **commence investigations** and to put an initial valuation on the claim.

3.20   Letters of claim are **not** intended to have the same formal status as a **pleading**, nor should any sanctions necessarily apply if the letter of claim and any subsequent statement of claim in the proceedings differ.

3.21   **Proceedings should not be issued until after three months from the letter of claim**, unless there is a limitation problem and/or the patient's position needs to be protected by early issue.

3.22   The patient or their adviser may want to make an **offer to settle** the claim at this early stage by putting forward an amount of compensation which would be satisfactory (possibly including any costs incurred to date). If an offer to settle is made, generally this should be supported by a medical report which deals with the injuries, condition and prognosis, and by a schedule of loss and supporting documentation. The level of detail necessary will depend on the value of the claim. Medical reports may not be necessary where there is no significant continuing injury, and a detailed schedule may not be necessary in a low value case. The Civil Procedure Rules are expected to set out the legal and procedural requirements for making offers to settle.

THE RESPONSE

3.23   Attached at Annex C2 is a template for the suggested contents of the **letter of response**.

3.24   The healthcare provider should **acknowledge** the letter of claim **within 14 days of receipt** and should identify who will be dealing with the matter.

3.25   The healthcare provider should, **within three months** of the letter of claim, provide a **reasoned answer**—

- if the **claim is admitted** the healthcare provider should say so in clear terms;
- if only **part of the claim is admitted** the healthcare provider should make clear which issues of breach of duty and/or causation are admitted and which are denied and why;
- if it is intended that any **admissions will be binding**;
- if the claim is denied, this should include specific comments on the allegations of negligence, and if a synopsis or chronology of relevant events has been provided and is disputed, the healthcare provider's version of those events;
- where additional documents are relied upon, eg an internal protocol, copies should be provided.

3.26   If the patient has made an offer to settle, the healthcare provider should **respond to that offer** in the response letter, preferably with reasons. The provider may make its own offer to settle at this stage, either as a counter-offer to the patient's, or of its own accord, but should accompany any offer by any supporting medical evidence, and/or by any other evidence in relation to the value of the claim which is in the health-care provider's possession.

3.27   If the parties reach agreement on liability, but time is needed to resolve the value of the claim, they should aim to agree a reasonable period.

4   EXPERTS

4.1   In clinical negligence disputes **expert opinions** may be needed—

- on breach of duty and causation;
- on the patient's condition and prognosis;
- to assist in valuing aspects of the claim.

4.2   The civil justice reforms and the new **Civil Procedure Rules** will encourage economy in the use of experts and a **less adversarial expert culture**. It is recognised that in clinical negligence disputes, the parties and their advisers will require flexibility in their approach to expert evidence. Decisions on whether experts might be instructed jointly, and on whether reports might be disclosed sequentially or by exchange, should rest with the parties and their advisers. Sharing expert evidence may be appropriate on issues relating to the value of the claim. However, this protocol does not attempt to be prescriptive on issues in relation to expert evidence.

4.3   Obtaining expert evidence will often be an expensive step and may take time, especially in specialised areas of medicine where there are limited numbers of suitable experts. Patients and healthcare providers, and their advisers, will therefore need to consider carefully how best to obtain any necessary expert help quickly and cost-effectively. Assistance with locating a suitable expert is available from a number of sources.

5   ALTERNATIVE APPROACHES TO SETTLING DISPUTES

5.1   It would not be practicable for this protocol to address in any detail how a patient or their adviser, or healthcare provider, might decide which method to adopt to resolve the particular problem. But the courts increasingly expect parties to try to settle their differences by agreement before issuing proceedings.

5.2   Most disputes are resolved by **discussion and negotiation**. Parties should bear in mind that carefully planned face-to-face meetings may be particularly helpful in exploring further treatment for the patient, in reaching understandings about what happened, and on both parties' positions, in narrowing the issues in dispute and, if the timing is right, in helping to settle the whole matter.

5.3   Summarised below are some other alternatives for resolving disputes—

- The revised NHS Complaints Procedure, which was implemented in April 1996, is designed to provide patients with an explanation of what happened and an apology if appropriate. It is not designed to provide compensation for cases of negligence. However, patients might choose to use the procedure if their only, or main, goal is to obtain an explanation, or to obtain more information to help them decide what other action might be appropriate.

- Mediation may be appropriate in some cases: this is a form of facilitated negotiation assisted by an independent neutral party. It is expected that the new Civil Procedure Rules will give the court the power to stay proceedings for one month for settlement discussions or mediation.

- Other methods of resolving disputes include arbitration, determination by an expert, and early neutral evaluation by a medical or legal expert. The Legal Services Commission has produced a booklet on Alternatives to Court (CLS Information Leaflet No. 23) (London: Legal Services Commission, 2001), which lists a number of organisations that provide alternative dispute resolution services.

ANNEX A   ILLUSTRATIVE FLOWCHART

Patient (P)   Healthcare Provider (HCP)

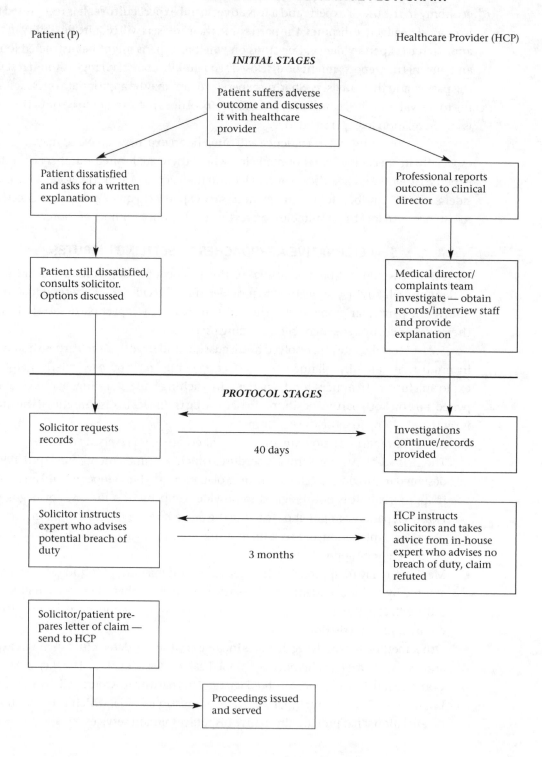

INITIAL STAGES

Patient suffers adverse outcome and discusses it with healthcare provider

Patient dissatisfied and asks for a written explanation

Professional reports outcome to clinical director

Patient still dissatisfied, consults solicitor. Options discussed

Medical director/ complaints team investigate — obtain records/interview staff and provide explanation

PROTOCOL STAGES

Solicitor requests records

40 days

Investigations continue/records provided

Solicitor instructs expert who advises potential breach of duty

3 months

HCP instructs solicitors and takes advice from in-house expert who advises no breach of duty, claim refuted

Solicitor/patient pre-pares letter of claim — send to HCP

Proceedings issued and served

ANNEX B

MEDICAL NEGLIGENCE AND PERSONAL INJURY CLAIMS

A PROTOCOL FOR OBTAINING HOSPITAL MEDICAL RECORDS APPLICATION ON BEHALF OF A PATIENT FOR HOSPITAL MEDICAL RECORDS FOR USE WHEN COURT PROCEEDINGS ARE CONTEMPLATED

PURPOSE OF THE FORMS

This application form and response forms have been prepared by a working party of the Law Society's Civil Litigation Committee and approved by the Department of Health for use in NHS and Trust hospitals.

The purpose of the forms is to standardise and streamline the disclosure of medical records to a patient's solicitors, who are investigating pursuing a personal injury claim against a third party, or a medical negligence claim against the hospital to which the application is addressed and/or other hospitals or general practitioners.

USE OF THE FORMS

Use of the forms is entirely voluntary and does not prejudice any party's right under the Access to Health Records Act 1990, the Data Protection Act 1984, or ss 33 and 34 of the Supreme Court Act 1981. However, it is Department of Health policy that patients be permitted to see what has been written about them, and that healthcare providers should make arrangements to allow patients to see all their records, not only those covered by the Access to Health Records Act 1990. The aim of the forms is to save time and costs for all concerned for the benefit of the patient and the hospital and in the interests of justice. Use of the forms should make it unnecessary in most cases for there to be exchanges of letters or other enquiries. If there is any unusual matter not covered by the form, the patient's solicitor may write a separate letter at the outset.

CHARGES FOR RECORDS

The Access to Health Records Act 1990 prescribes a maximum fee of £10. Photocopying and postage costs can be charged in addition. No other charges may be made.

The NHS Executive guidance makes it clear to healthcare providers that 'it is a perfectly proper use' of the 1990 Act to request records in that framework for the purpose of potential or actual litigation, whether against a third party or against the hospital or trust.

The 1990 Act does not permit differential rates of charges to be levied if the application is made by the patient, or by a solicitor on his or her behalf, or whether the response to the application is made by the healthcare provider directly (the medical records manager or a claims manager) or by a solicitor.

The NHS Executive guidance recommends that the same practice should be followed with regard to charges when the records are provided under a voluntary agreement as under the 1990 Act, except that in those circumstances the £10 access fee will not be appropriate.

The NHS Executive also advises—

- that the cost of photocopying may include 'the cost of staff time in making copies' and the costs of running the copier (but not costs of locating and sifting records);

- that the common practice of setting a standard rate for an application or charging an administration fee is not acceptable because there will be cases when this fails to comply with the 1990 Act.

RECORDS: WHAT MIGHT BE INCLUDED

X-rays and test results form part of the patient's records. Additional charges for copying X-rays are permissible. If there are large numbers of X-rays, the records officer should check with the patient/solicitor before arranging copying.

Reports on an 'adverse incident' and reports on the patient made for risk management and audit purposes may form part of the records and be disclosable: the exception will be any specific record or report made solely or mainly in connection with an actual or potential claim.

RECORDS: QUALITY STANDARDS

When copying records healthcare providers should ensure—

1.   All documents are legible, and complete, if necessary by photocopying at less than 100% size.

2.   Documents larger than A4 in the original, eg ITU charts, should be reproduced in A3, or reduced to A4 where this retains readability.

3.   Documents are only copied on one side of paper, unless the original is two sided.

4.   Documents should not be unnecessarily shuffled or bound and holes should not be made in the copied papers.

ENQUIRIES/FURTHER INFORMATION

Any enquiries about the forms should be made initially to the solicitors making the request. Comments on the use and content of the forms should be made to the Secretary, Civil Litigation Committee, The Law Society, 113 Chancery Lane, London WC2A 1PL, telephone (020) 7320 5739, or to the NHS Management Executive, Quarry House, Quarry Hill, Leeds LS2 7UE.

The Law Society

May 1998

APPLICATION ON BEHALF OF A PATIENT FOR HOSPITAL MEDICAL RECORDS FOR USE WHEN COURT PROCEEDINGS ARE CONTEMPLATED

This should be completed as fully as possible

Insert Hospital Name and Address

| TO: Medical Records Officer |
| Hospital |

1(a)	Full name of patient (including previous surnames)	
(b)	Address now	
(c)	Address at start of treatment	
(d)	Date of birth (and death, if applicable)	
(e)	Hospital ref. no if available	
(f)	N.I. number, if available	
2	This application is made because the patient is considering	
	(a) a claim against your hospital as detailed in para. 7 overleaf	YES/NO
	(b) pursuing an action against someone else	YES/NO
3	Department(s) where treatment was received	
4	Name(s) of consultant(s) at your hospital in charge of the treatment	
5	Whether treatment at your hospital was private or NHS, wholly or in part	
6	A description of the treatment received, with approximate dates	
7	If the answer to Q2(a) is 'Yes' details of	
	(a) the likely nature of the claim	
	(b) grounds for the claim	
	(c) approximate dates of the events involved	
8	If the answer to Q2(b) is 'Yes' insert	
	(a) the names of the proposed defendants	
	(b) whether legal proceedings yet begun	YES/NO
	(c) if appropriate, details of the claim and action number	

9	We confirm we will pay reasonable copying charges	
10	We request prior details of	
	(a) photocopying and administration charges for medical records	YES/NO
	(b) number of and cost of copying X-ray and scan films	YES/NO
11	Any other relevant information, particular requirements, or any particular documents *not* required (eg copies of computerised records)	
	Signature of Solicitor	
	Name	
	Address	
	Ref.	
	Telephone Number	
	Fax number	

Please print name beneath each signature.
Signature by child over 12 but under
18 years also requires signature by parent

Signature of patient

_____

Signature of parent or
next friend if appropriate

_____

Signature of personal representative
where patient has died

FIRST RESPONSE TO APPLICATION FOR HOSPITAL RECORDS

	NAME OF PATIENT Our ref Your ref	
1	Date of receipt of patient's application	
2	We intend that copy medical records will be dispatched within 6 weeks of that date	YES/NO
3	We require prepayment of photocopying charges	YES/NO
4	If estimate of photocopying charges requested or prepayment required the amount will be	£ / notified to you
5	The cost of X-ray and scan films will be	£ / notified to you
6	If there is any problem, we shall write to you within those 6 weeks	YES/NO
7	Any other information	
	Please address further correspondence to	
	Signed	
	Direct telephone number	
	Direct fax number	
	Dated	

SECOND RESPONSE ENCLOSING PATIENT'S HOSPITAL MEDICAL RECORDS

Address   Our Ref.

Your Ref.

	NAME OF PATIENT:	
1	We confirm that the enclosed copy medical records are all those within the control of the hospital, relevant to the application which you have made to the best of our knowledge and belief, subject to paras 2–5 below	YES/NO
2	Details of any other documents which have not yet been located	
3	Date by when it is expected that these will be supplied	
4	Details of any records which we are not producing	
5	The reasons for not doing so	
6	An invoice for copying and administration charges is attached	YES/NO
	Signed	
	Date	

ANNEX C   TEMPLATES FOR LETTERS OF CLAIM AND RESPONSE

C1 LETTER OF CLAIM

ESSENTIAL CONTENTS

1.   **Client's name, address, date of birth, etc.**
2.   **Dates of allegedly negligent treatment**
3.   **Events giving rise to the claim:**
- an outline of what happened, including details of other relevant treatments to the client by other healthcare providers.
4.   **Allegation of negligence and causal link with injuries:**
- an outline of the allegations or a more detailed list in a complex case;
- an outline of the causal link between allegations and the injuries complained of.
5.   **The Client's injuries, condition and future prognosis**
6.   **Request for clinical records (if not previously provided)**
- use the Law Society form if appropriate or adapt;
- specify the records required;
- if other records are held by other providers, and may be relevant, say so;
- state what investigations have been carried out to date, eg information from client and witnesses, any complaint and the outcome, if any clinical records have been seen or experts advice obtained.
7.   **The likely value of the claim**
- an outline of the main heads of damage, or, in straightforward cases, the details of loss.

OPTIONAL INFORMATION

What investigations have been carried out

An offer to settle without supporting evidence

Suggestions for obtaining expert evidence

Suggestions for meetings, negotiations, discussion or mediation

POSSIBLE ENCLOSURES

Chronology

Clinical records request form and client's authorisation

Expert report(s)

Schedules of loss and supporting evidence

C2 LETTER OF RESPONSE

ESSENTIAL CONTENTS

1. Provide **requested records** and invoice for copying:
- explain if records are incomplete or extensive records are held and ask for further instructions;
- request additional records from third parties.
2. **Comments on events and/or chronology:**
- if events are disputed or the healthcare provider has further information or documents on which they wish to rely, these should be provided, eg internal protocol;
- details of any further information needed from the patient or a third party should be provided.
3. **If breach of duty and causation are accepted:**
- suggestions might be made for resolving the claim and/or requests for further information;
- a response should be made to any offer to settle.
4. **If breach of duty and/or causation are denied:**
- a bare denial will not be sufficient. If the healthcare provider has other explanations for what happened, these should be given at least in outline;
- suggestions might be made for the next steps, eg further investigations, obtaining expert evidence, meetings/ negotiations or mediation, or an invitation to issue proceedings.

OPTIONAL MATTERS

An offer to settle if the patient has not made one, or a counter offer to the patient's with supporting evidence

POSSIBLE ENCLOSURES:

Clinical records

Annotated chronology

Expert reports

ANNEX D   LORD WOOLF'S RECOMMENDATIONS

1.   Lord Woolf in his Access to Justice Report in July 1996, following a detailed review of the problems of medical negligence claims, identified that one of the major sources of **costs and delay is at the pre-litigation** stage because—

(a)   Inadequate incident reporting and record keeping in hospitals, and mobility of staff, make it difficult to establish facts, often several years after the event.

(b)   Claimants must incur the cost of an expert in order to establish whether they have a viable claim.

(c)   There is often a long delay before a claim is made.

(d)   Defendants do not have sufficient resources to carry out a full investigation of every incident, and do not consider it worthwhile to start an investigation as soon as they receive a request for records, because many cases do not proceed beyond that stage.

(e)   Patients often give the defendant little or no notice of a firm intention to pursue a claim. Consequently, many incidents are not investigated by the defendants until after proceedings have started.

(f)   Doctors and other clinical staff are traditionally reluctant to admit negligence or apologise to, or negotiate with, claimants for fear of damage to their professional reputations or career prospects.

2.   Lord Woolf acknowledged that under the present arrangements **healthcare providers,** faced with possible medical negligence claims, have a number of **practical problems** to contend with—

(a)   Difficulties of finding patients' records and tracing former staff, which can be exacerbated by late notification and by the health care provider's own failure to identify adverse incidents.

(b)   The healthcare provider may have only treated the patient for a limited time or for a specific complaint: the patient's previous history may be relevant but the records may be in the possession of one of several other healthcare providers.

(c)   The large number of potential claims which do not proceed beyond the stage of a request for medical records, or an explanation; and that it is difficult for health-care providers to investigate fully every case whenever a patient asks to see the records.

ANNEX E   HOW TO CONTACT THE FORUM

THE CLINICAL DISPUTES FORUM

Chairman
    Dr Alastair Scotland
    Medical Director and Chief Officer
    National Clinical Assessment Authority
    9th Floor, Market Towers
    London
    SW8 5NQ   Telephone: (020) 7273 0850
Secretary
    Sarah Leigh
    c/o Margaret Dangoor
    3 Clydesdale Gardens
    Richmond
    Surrey
    TW10 5EG   Telephone: (020) 8408 1012

APPENDIX 4
PRE-ACTION PROTOCOL FOR CONSTRUCTION AND ENGINEERING DISPUTES

CONTENTS

1 INTRODUCTION

1.1   This pre-action protocol applies to all construction and engineering disputes (including professional negligence claims against architects, engineers and quantity surveyors).

EXCEPTIONS

1.2   A claimant shall not be required to comply with this protocol before commencing proceedings to the extent that the proposed proceedings (i) are for the enforcement of the decision of an adjudicator to whom a dispute has been referred pursuant to s 108 of the Housing Grants, Construction and Regeneration Act 1996 ('the 1996 Act'), (ii) include a claim for interim injunctive relief, (iii) will be the subject of a claim for summary judgment pursuant to Part 24 of the Civil Procedure Rules, or (iv) relate to the same or substantially the same issues as have been the subject of recent adjudication under the 1996 Act, or some other formal alternative dispute resolution procedure.

OBJECTIVES

1.3   The objectives of this protocol are as set out in PD Protocols, namely:

(i)   to encourage the exchange of early and full information about the prospective legal claim;

(ii)   to enable parties to avoid litigation by agreeing a settlement of the claim before commencement of proceedings; and

(iii)   to support the efficient management of proceedings where litigation cannot be avoided.

COMPLIANCE

1.4   If proceedings are commenced, the court will be able to treat the standards set in this protocol as the normal reasonable approach to pre-action conduct. If the court has to consider the question of compliance after proceedings have begun, it will be concerned with substantial compliance and not minor departures, eg failure by a short period to provide relevant information. Minor departures will not exempt the 'innocent' party from following the protocol. The court will look at the effect of non-compliance on the other party when deciding whether to impose sanctions. For sanctions generally, see PD Protocols, para 2 'Compliance with Protocols'.

2   OVERVIEW OF PROTOCOL

GENERAL AIM

2   The general aim of this protocol is to ensure that before court proceedings commence:

    (i)   the claimant and the defendant have provided sufficient information for each party to know the nature of the other's case;

    (ii)   each party has had an opportunity to consider the other's case, and to accept or reject all or any part of the case made against him at the earliest possible stage;

    (iii)   there is more pre-action contact between the parties;

    (iv)   better and earlier exchange of information occurs;

    (v)   there is better pre-action investigation by the parties;

    (vi)   the parties have met formally on at least one occasion with a view to

        •   defining and agreeing the issues between them; and

        •   exploring possible ways by which the claim may be resolved;

    (vii)   the parties are in a position where they may be able to settle cases early and fairly without recourse to litigation; and

    (viii)   proceedings will be conducted efficiently if litigation does become necessary.

3   THE LETTER OF CLAIM

3.1   Prior to commencing proceedings, the claimant or his solicitor shall send to each proposed defendant (if appropriate to his registered address) a copy of a letter of claim which shall contain the following information:

    (i)   the claimant's full name and address;

    (ii)   the full name and address of each proposed defendant;

    (iii)   a clear summary of the facts on which each claim is based;

    (iv)   the basis on which each claim is made, identifying the principal contractual terms and statutory provisions relied on;

    (v)   the nature of the relief claimed: if damages are claimed, a breakdown showing how the damages have been quantified; if a sum is claimed pursuant to a contract, how it has been calculated; if an extension of time is claimed, the period claimed;

    (vi)   where a claim has been made previously and rejected by a defendant, and the claimant is able to identify the reason(s) for such rejection, the claimant's grounds of belief as to why the claim was wrongly rejected;

    (vii)   the names of any experts already instructed by the claimant on whose evidence he intends to rely, identifying the issues to which that evidence will be directed.

4   DEFENDANT'S RESPONSE

THE DEFENDANT'S ACKNOWLEDGMENT

4.1   Within 14 calendar days of receipt of the letter of claim, the defendant should acknowledge its receipt in writing and may give the name and address of his insurer (if any). If there has been no acknowledgment by or on behalf of the defendant within 14 days, the claimant will be entitled to commence proceedings without further compliance with this protocol.

OBJECTIONS TO THE COURT'S JURISDICTION OR THE NAMED DEFENDANT

4.2.1 If the defendant intends to take any objection to all or any part of the claimant's claim on the grounds that (i) the court lacks jurisdiction, (ii) the matter should be referred to arbitration, or (iii) the defendant named in the letter of claim is the wrong defendant, that objection should be raised by the defendant within 28 days after receipt of the letter of claim. The letter of objection shall specify the parts of the claim to which the objection relates, setting out the grounds relied on, and, where appropriate, shall identify the correct defendant (if known). Any failure to take such objection shall not prejudice the defendant's rights to do so in any subsequent proceedings, but the court may take such failure into account when considering the question of costs.

4.2.2 Where such notice of objection is given, the defendant is not required to send a letter of response in accordance with para 4.3.1 in relation to the claim or those parts of it to which the objection relates (as the case may be).

4.2.3 If at any stage before the claimant commences proceedings, the defendant withdraws his objection, then para 4.3 and the remaining part of this protocol will apply to the claim or those parts of it to which the objection related as if the letter of claim had been received on the date on which notice of withdrawal of the objection had been given.

THE DEFENDANT'S RESPONSE

4.3.1 Within 28 days from the date of receipt of the letter of claim, or such other period as the parties may reasonably agree (up to a maximum of four months), the defendant shall send a letter of response to the claimant which shall contain the following information:

    (i) the facts set out in the letter of claim which are agreed or not agreed, and if not agreed, the basis of the disagreement;

    (ii) which claims are accepted and which are rejected, and if rejected, the basis of the rejection;

    (iii) if a claim is accepted in whole or in part, whether the damages, sums or extensions of time claimed are accepted or rejected, and if rejected, the basis of the rejection;

    (iv) if contributory negligence is alleged against the claimant, a summary of the facts relied on;

    (v) whether the defendant intends to make a counterclaim, and if so, giving the information which is required to be given in a letter of claim by para 3(iii) to (vi) above;

    (v) the names of any experts already instructed on whose evidence it is intended to rely, identifying the issues to which that evidence will be directed.

4.3.2 If no response is received by the claimant within the period of 28 days (or such other period as has been agreed between the parties), the claimant shall be entitled to commence proceedings without further compliance with this protocol.

CLAIMANT'S RESPONSE TO COUNTERCLAIM

4.4 The claimant shall provide a response to any counterclaim within the equivalent period allowed to the defendant to respond to the letter of claim under para 4.3.1 above.

5 PRE-ACTION MEETING

5.1 As soon as possible after receipt by the claimant of the defendant's letter of response, or (if the claimant intends to respond to the counterclaim) after receipt by the defendant of the claimant's letter of response to the counterclaim, the parties should normally meet.

5.2   The aim of the meeting is for the parties to agree what are the main issues in the case, to identify the root cause of disagreement in respect of each issue, and to consider (i) whether, and if so how, the issues might be resolved without recourse to litigation, and (ii) if litigation is unavoidable, what steps should be taken to ensure that it is conducted in accordance with the overriding objective as defined in r 1.1 of the Civil Practice Rules.

5.3   In some circumstances, it may be necessary to convene more than one meeting. It is not intended by this protocol to prescribe in detail the manner in which the meetings should be conducted. But the court will normally expect that those attending will include:

(i)   where the party is an individual, that individual, and where the party is a corporate body, a representative of that body who has authority to settle or recommend settlement of the dispute;

(ii)   a legal representative of each party (if one has been instructed);

(iii)   where the involvement of insurers has been disclosed, a representative of the insurer (who may be its legal representative); and

(iv)   where a claim is made or defended on behalf of some other party (such as, for example, a claim made by a main contractor pursuant to a contractual obligation to pass on subcontractor claims), the party on whose behalf the claim is made or defended and/or his legal representatives.

5.4   In respect of each agreed issue or the dispute as a whole, the parties should consider whether some form of alternative dispute resolution procedure would be more suitable than litigation, and if so, endeavour to agree which form to adopt.

5.5   If the parties are unable to agree on a means of resolving the dispute other than by litigation they should use their best endeavours to agree:

(i)   whether, if there is any area where expert evidence is likely to be required, a joint expert may be appointed, and if so, who that should be; and (so far as is practicable)

(ii)   the extent of disclosure of documents with a view to saving costs; and

(iii)   the conduct of the litigation with the aim of minimising cost and delay.

5.6   Any party who attended any pre-action meeting shall be at liberty to disclose to the court:

(i)   that the meeting took place, when and who attended;

(ii)   the identity of any party who refused to attend, and the grounds for such refusal;

(iii)   if the meeting did not take place, why not; and

(iv)   any agreements concluded between the parties.

5.7   Except as provided in para 5.6, everything said at a pre-action meeting shall be treated as 'without prejudice'.

6   LIMITATION OF ACTION

6.1   If by reason of complying with any part of this protocol a claimant's claim may be time-barred under any provision of the Limitation Act 1980, or any other legislation which imposes a time limit for bringing an action, the claimant may commence proceedings without complying with this protocol. In such circumstances, a claimant who commences proceedings without complying with all, or any part, of this protocol must apply to the court on notice for directions as to the timetable and form of procedure to be adopted, at the same time as he requests the court to issue proceedings. The court will consider whether to order a stay of the whole or part of the proceedings pending compliance with this protocol.

APPENDIX 5
PROFESSIONAL NEGLIGENCE PRE-ACTION PROTOCOL

This protocol merges the two protocols previously produced by the Solicitors Indemnity Fund (SIF) and Claims against Professionals (CAP).

CONTENTS

A	Introduction
B	Overview of protocol
C	Guidance notes

A INTRODUCTION

A1   This protocol is designed to apply when a claimant wishes to claim against a professional (other than construction professionals and healthcare providers) as a result of that professional's alleged negligence or equivalent breach of contract or breach of fiduciary duty. Although these claims will be the usual situation in which the protocol will be used, there may be other claims for which the protocol could be appropriate. For a more detailed explanation of the scope of the protocol see Guidance Note C2.

A2   The aim of this protocol is to establish a framework in which there is an early exchange of information so that the claim can be fully investigated and, if possible, resolved without the need for litigation. This includes:

   (a)   ensuring that the parties are on an equal footing;
   (b)   saving expense;
   (c)   dealing with the dispute in ways which are proportionate:
       (i)   to the amount of money involved;
       (ii)   to the importance of the case;
       (iii) to the complexity of the issues;
       (iv)   to the financial position of each party;
   (d)   ensuring that it is dealt with expeditiously and fairly.

A3   This protocol is not intended to replace other forms of pre-action dispute resolution (such as internal complaints procedures, the Surveyors and Valuers Arbitration Scheme, etc.). Where such procedures are available, parties are encouraged to consider whether they should be used. If, however, these other procedures are used and fail to resolve the dispute, the protocol should be used before litigation is started, adapting it where appropriate. See also Guidance Note C3.

A4   The courts will be able to treat the standards set in this protocol as the normal reasonable approach. If litigation is started, it will be for the court to decide whether sanctions should be imposed as a result of substantial non-compliance with a protocol. Guidance on the courts' likely approach is given in PD Protocols. The court is likely to disregard minor departures from this protocol and so should the parties as between themselves.

A5   Both in operating the timetable and in requesting and providing information during the protocol period, the parties are expected to act reasonably, in line with the court's expectations of them. See also Guidance Note C1.2.

B   THE PROTOCOL

B1   PRELIMINARY NOTICE
(See also Guidance Note C3.1)

B1.1   As soon as the claimant decides there is a reasonable chance that he will bring a claim against a professional, the claimant is encouraged to notify the professional in writing.

B1.2   This letter should contain the following information:

(a)   the identity of the claimant and any other parties;

(b)   a brief outline of the claimant's grievance against the professional;

(c)   if possible, a general indication of the financial value of the potential Claim.

B1.3   This letter should be addressed to the professional and should ask the professional to inform his professional indemnity insurers, if any, immediately.

B1.4   The professional should acknowledge receipt of the claimant's letter within 21 days of receiving it. Other than this acknowledgment, the protocol places no obligation upon either party to take any further action.

B2   LETTER OF CLAIM

B2.1   As soon as the claimant decides there are grounds for a claim against the professional, the claimant should write a detailed letter of claim to the professional.

B2.2   The letter of claim will normally be an open letter (as opposed to being 'without prejudice') and should include the following:

(a)   The identity of any other parties involved in the dispute or a related dispute.

(b)   A clear chronological summary (including key dates) of the facts on which the claim is based. Key documents should be identified, copied and enclosed.

(c)   The allegations against the professional. What has he done wrong? What has he failed to do?

(d)   An explanation of how the alleged error has caused the loss claimed.

(e)   An estimate of the financial loss suffered by the claimant and how it is calculated. Supporting documents should be identified, copied and enclosed. If details of the financial loss cannot be supplied, the claimant should explain why and should state when he will be in a position to provide the details. This information should be sent to the professional as soon as reasonably possible.

If the claimant is seeking some form of non-financial redress, this should be made clear.

(f)   Confirmation whether or not an expert has been appointed. If so, providing the identity and discipline of the expert, together with the date upon which the expert was appointed.

(g)   A request that a copy of the letter of claim be forwarded immediately to the professional's insurers, if any.

B2.3   The letter of claim is not intended to have the same formal status as a statement of case. If, however, the letter of claim differs materially from the statement of case in subsequent proceedings, the court may decide, in its discretion, to impose sanctions.

B2.4 If the claimant has sent other letters of claim (or equivalent) to any other party in relation to this dispute or related dispute, those letters should be copied to the professional. (If the claimant is claiming against someone else to whom this protocol does not apply, please see Guidance Note C4.)

B3   THE LETTER OF ACKNOWLEDGMENT

B3.1 The professional should acknowledge receipt of the letter of claim within 21 days of receiving it.

B4   INVESTIGATIONS

B4.1 The professional will have three months from the date of the letter of acknowledgment to investigate.

B4.2 If the professional is in difficulty in complying with the three-month time period, the problem should be explained to the claimant as soon as possible. The professional should explain what is being done to resolve the problem and when the professional expects to complete the investigations. The claimant should agree to any reasonable request for an extension of the three-month period.

B4.3 The parties should supply promptly, at this stage and throughout, whatever relevant information or documentation is reasonably requested. (Please see Guidance Note C5.)
(If the professional intends to claim against someone who is not currently a party to the dispute, please see Guidance Note C4.)

B5   LETTER OF RESPONSE AND LETTER OF SETTLEMENT

B5.1 As soon as the professional has completed his investigations, the professional should send to the claimant:

    (a)   a letter of response; or

    (b)   a letter of settlement; or

    (c)   both.

The letters of response and settlement can be contained within a single letter.

The letter of response

B5.2 The letter of response will normally be an open letter (as opposed to being 'without prejudice') and should be a reasoned answer to the claimant's allegations:

    (a)   If the claim is admitted the professional should say so in clear terms.

    (b)   If only part of the claim is admitted the professional should make clear which parts of the claim are admitted and which are denied.

    (c)   If the claim is denied in whole or in part, the letter of response should include specific comments on the allegations against the professional and, if the claimant's version of events is disputed, the professional should provide his version of events.

    (d)   If the professional is unable to admit or deny the claim, the professional should identify any further information which is required.

    (e)   If the professional disputes the estimate of the claimant's financial loss, the letter of response should set out the professional's estimate. If an estimate cannot be provided, the professional should explain why and should state when he will be in a position to provide an estimate. This information should be sent to the claimant as soon as reasonably possible.

    (f)   Where additional documents are relied upon, copies should be provided.

B5.3 The letter of response is not intended to have the same formal status as a defence. If, however, the letter of response differs materially from the defence in subsequent proceedings, the court may decide, in its discretion, to impose sanctions.

The letter of settlement

B5.4 The letter of settlement will normally be a without prejudice letter and should be sent if the professional intends to make proposals for settlement. It should:

(a) Set out the professional's views to date on the claim identifying those issues which the professional believes are likely to remain in dispute and those which are not. (The letter of settlement does not need to include this information if the professional has sent a letter of response.)

(b) Make a settlement proposal or identify any further information which is required before the professional can formulate its proposals.

(c) Where additional documents are relied upon, copies should be provided.

Effect of letter of response and/or letter of settlement

B5.5 If the letter of response denies the claim in its entirety and there is no letter of settlement, it is open to the claimant to commence proceedings.

B5.6 In any other circumstance, the professional and the claimant should commence negotiations with the aim of concluding those negotiations within six months of the date of the letter of acknowledgment (not from the date of the letter of response).

B5.7 If the claim cannot be resolved within this period:

(a) The parties should agree within 14 days of the end of the period whether the period should be extended and, if so, by how long.

(b) The parties should seek to identify those issues which are still in dispute and those which can be agreed.

(c) If an extension of time is not agreed it will then be open to the claimant to commence proceedings.

B6   ALTERNATIVE DISPUTE RESOLUTION

B6.1 The parties can agree at any stage to take the dispute (or any part of the dispute) to mediation or some other form of alternative dispute resolution (ADR).

B6.2 In addition, any party at any stage can refer the dispute (or any part of the dispute) to an ADR agency for mediation or some other form of ADR.

B6.3 When approached by a party or an ADR agency with a proposal that ADR be used, the other party or parties should respond within 14 days stating that:

(a) they agree to the proposal; or

(b) they agree that ADR will be or may be appropriate, but they believe it has been suggested prematurely. They should state when they anticipate it would or may become appropriate; or

(c) they agree that ADR is appropriate, but not the form of ADR proposed (if any). They should state the form of ADR which they believe to be appropriate; or

(d) they do not accept that any form of ADR is appropriate. They should state their reasons.

This letter should be copied to the other party or parties and can be disclosed to the court on the issue of costs.

B6.4 It is expressly recognised that no party can or should be forced to mediate or enter into any other form of ADR.

B7   EXPERTS

(The following provisions apply where the claim raises an issue of professional expertise whose resolution requires expert evidence.)

B7.1 If the claimant has obtained expert evidence prior to sending the letter of claim, the professional will have equal right to obtain expert evidence prior to sending the letter of response/letter of settlement.

B7.2 If the claimant has not obtained expert evidence prior to sending the letter of claim, the parties are encouraged to appoint a joint expert. If they agree to do so, they should seek to agree the identity of the expert and the terms of the expert's appointment.

B7.3 If agreement about a joint expert cannot be reached, all parties are free to appoint their own experts.

(For further details on experts see Guidance Note C6.)

B8   PROCEEDINGS

B8.1 Unless it is necessary (for example, to obtain protection against the expiry of a relevant limitation period) the claimant should not start court proceedings until:

(a) the letter of response denies the claim in its entirety and there is no letter of settlement (see para B5.5 above); or

(b) the end of the negotiation period (see paras B5.6 and B5.7 above). (For further discussion of statutory time limits for the commencement of litigation, please see Guidance Note C7.)

B8.2 Where possible 14 days' written notice should be given to the professional before proceedings are started, indicating the court within which the claimant is intending to commence litigation.

B8.3 Proceedings should be served on the professional, unless the professional's solicitor has notified the claimant in writing that he is authorised to accept service on behalf of the professional.

C   GUIDANCE NOTES

C1   INTRODUCTION

C1.1 The protocol has been kept simple to promote ease of use and general acceptability. The guidance notes which follow relate particularly to issues on which further guidance may be required.

C1.2 The Woolf reforms envisages that parties will act reasonably in the pre-action period. Accordingly, in the event that the protocol and the guidelines do not specifically address a problem, the parties should comply with the spirit of the protocol by acting reasonably.

C2   SCOPE OF PROTOCOL

C2.1 The protocol is specifically designated for claims of negligence against professionals. This will include claims in which the allegation against a professional is that they have breached a contractual term to take reasonable skill and care. The protocol is also appropriate for claims of breach of fiduciary duty against professionals.

C2.2 The protocol is not intended to apply to claims:

(a) against architects, engineers and quantity surveyors — parties should use the Construction and Engineering Disputes (CED) protocol;

(b) against healthcare providers — parties should use the Pre-action Protocol for the Resolution of Clinical Disputes;

(c) concerning defamation — parties should use the Pre-action Protocol for Defamation.

C2.3 'Professional' is deliberately left undefined in the protocol. If it becomes an issue as to whether a defendant is or is not a professional, parties are reminded of the overriding need to act reasonably (see paras A4 and C1.2 above). Rather than argue about the definition of 'professional', therefore, the parties are invited to use this protocol, adapting it where appropriate.

C2.4 The protocol may not be suitable for disputes with professionals concerning intellectual property claims, etc. Until specific protocols are created for those claims, however, parties are invited to use this protocol, adapting it where necessary.

C2.5 Allegations of professional negligence are sometimes made in response to an attempt by the professional to recover outstanding fees. Where possible these allegations should be raised before litigation has commenced, in which case the parties should comply with the protocol before either party commences litigation. If litigation has already commenced it will be a matter for the court whether sanctions should be imposed against either party. In any event, the parties are encouraged to consider applying to the court for a stay to allow the protocol to be followed.

C3   INTERACTION WITH OTHER PRE-ACTION METHODS OF DISPUTE RESOLUTION

C3.1 There are a growing number of methods by which disputes can be resolved without the need for litigation, eg, internal complaints procedures, the Surveyors and Valuers Arbitration Scheme, and so on. The preliminary notice procedure of the protocol (see para B1) is designed to enable both parties to take stock at an early stage and to decide before work starts on preparing a letter of claim whether the grievance should be referred to one of these other dispute resolution procedures. (For the avoidance of doubt, however, there is no obligation on either party under the protocol to take any action at this stage other than giving the acknowledgment provided for in para B1.4).

C3.2 Accordingly, parties are free to use (and are encouraged to use) any of the available pre-action procedures in an attempt to resolve their dispute. If appropriate, the parties can agree to suspend the protocol timetable whilst the other method of dispute resolution is used.

C3.3 If these methods fail to resolve the dispute, however, the protocol should be used before litigation is commenced. Because there has already been an attempt to resolve the dispute, it may be appropriate to adjust the protocol's requirements. In particular, unless the parties agree otherwise, there is unlikely to be any benefit in duplicating a stage which has in effect already been undertaken. However, if the protocol adds anything to the earlier method of dispute resolution, it should be used, adapting it where appropriate. Once again, the parties are expected to act reasonably.

C4   MULTI-PARTY DISPUTES

C4.1 Paragraph B2.2(a) of the protocol requires a claimant to identify any other parties involved in the dispute or a related dispute. This is intended to ensure that all relevant parties are identified as soon as possible.

C4.2 If the dispute involves more than two parties, there are a number of potential problems. It is possible that different protocols will apply to different defendants. It is possible that defendants will claim against each other. It is possible that other parties will be drawn into the dispute. It is possible that the protocol timetable against one party will not be synchronised with the protocol timetable against a different party. How will these problems be resolved?

C4.3 As stated in para C1.2 above, the parties are expected to act reasonably. What is 'reasonable' will, of course, depend upon the specific facts of each case. Accordingly, it would be inappropriate for the protocol to set down generalised rules. Whenever a problem arises, the parties are encouraged to discuss how it can be overcome. In doing so, parties are reminded of the protocol's aims which include the aim to resolve the dispute without the need for litigation (para A2 above).

C5   INVESTIGATIONS

C5.1 Paragraph B4.3 is intended to encourage the early exchange of relevant information, so that issues in the dispute can be clarified or resolved. It should not be used as a 'fishing expedition' by either party. No party is obliged under para B4.3 to disclose any document which a court could not order them to disclose in the pre-action period.

C5.2 This protocol does not alter the parties' duties to disclose documents under any professional regulation or under general law.

C6   EXPERTS

C6.1 Expert evidence is not always needed, although the use and role of experts in professional negligence claims is often crucial. However, the way in which expert evidence is used in, say, an insurance brokers' negligence case, is not necessarily the same as in, say, an accountants' case. Similarly, the approach to be adopted in a £10,000 case does not necessarily compare with the approach in a £10 million case. The protocol therefore is designed to be flexible and does not dictate a standard approach. On the contrary it envisages that the parties will bear the responsibility for agreeing how best to use experts.

C6.2 If a joint expert is used, therefore, the parties are left to decide issues such as: the payment of the expert, whether joint or separate instructions are used, how and to whom the expert is to report, how questions may be addressed to the expert and how the expert should respond, whether an agreed statement of facts is required, and so on.

C6.3 If separate experts are used, the parties are left to decide issues such as: whether the experts' reports should be exchanged, whether there should be an experts' meeting, and so on.

C6.4 Even if a joint expert is appointed, it is possible that parties will still want to instruct their own experts. The protocol does not prohibit this.

C7   PROCEEDINGS

C7.1 This protocol does not alter the statutory time limits for starting court proceedings. A claimant is required to start proceedings within those time limits.

C7.2 If proceedings are for any reason started before the parties have followed the procedures in this protocol, the parties are encouraged to agree to apply to the court for a stay whilst the protocol is followed.

APPENDIX 6
THE LAW AND YOU: CODE OF GUIDANCE ON EXPERT EVIDENCE

A guide for experts and those instructing them for the purpose of court
proceedings
Expert Witness Institute

PREAMBLE

In framing this Code, the Working Party has taken account of the Civil Procedure Rules (CPR) and the practice directions as they exist on 1 December 2001, together with any case law on their interpretation. The Code of Guidance is designed to help experts and those instructing them in all cases where the CPR apply. It is intended to facilitate better communication and dealings both between the expert and the instructing party and between the parties; as such it is drawn in general terms so as to provide guidance for every court of law in the civil jurisdiction and in every type of civil litigation. (Part 35)

Part 35 of the CPR applies in every case where an expert is instructed to give or prepare evidence for the purpose of court proceedings. Part 35 is of limited application in the small claims court where, with some exceptions, its provisions do not apply. Assistance from an expert may be needed at various stages of a dispute and for different purposes. The expert always owes a duty to exercise reasonable skill and care to the person instructing him or her, and to comply with any relevant professional code of ethics. (CPR, rr 27.2(1)(e) and 35.2)

However, when the expert is instructed to give or prepare evidence for the purpose of court proceedings, rather than to give advice before they have started, Part 35 applies. Under r 35.3(1) the expert owes a duty to help the court on matters within his expertise, and this duty overrides any obligation to the person from whom the expert has received instructions or by whom the expert is paid. The extent to which the Rules may require the expert to disclose to the court, and to other parties to court proceedings, matters which would otherwise be confidential to the client and privileged from disclosure is dealt with in paras 3 and 4 below. (CPR, r 35.3(1) and (2))

I EXPERTS

1. An expert witness is under an overriding duty to help the court to deal with the case 'justly'. That is the overriding obligation of the court under CPR, r 1.1(1), and it is further defined in r 1.1(2) as follows:

Dealing with a case justly includes, so far as is practicable —
    (a)   ensuring that the parties are on an equal footing;
    (b)   saving expense;
    (c)   dealing with the case in ways which are proportionate —
        (i)   to the amount of money involved;
        (ii)   to the importance of the case;
        (iii) to the complexity of the issues; and

(iv)   to the financial position of each party;

(d)   ensuring that it is dealt with expeditiously and fairly; and

(e)   allotting to it an appropriate share of the court's resources, while taking into account the need to allot resources to other cases.

(CPR, r 1.1(2))

2.   Some courts have published their own guides which supplement the CPR for proceedings in those courts. These contain provisions affecting expert evidence and an expert witness should be familiar with them when they are relevant to his evidence. (CPR, Part 49)

3.   Any advice given by an expert before court proceedings are started is likely to be confidential to the client and privileged from disclosure to other parties. But where the expert is asked to give or prepare evidence for the purpose of court proceedings, so that Part 35 applies, s/he is required to state the substance of the instructions s/he has received. The court has the power to order the expert to disclose what his or her instructions were. (CPR, r 35.10(3) and (4))

4.   Although the point has yet to be definitively decided, the power to order disclosure may in certain circumstances extend to instructions or advice that were privileged when they were given. (PD 3)

5.   The expert should also be aware that any failure by him to comply with the Rules or court orders or any excessive delay for which the expert is responsible may result in the party who instructed him being penalised in costs and even in extreme cases being debarred from placing the expert's evidence before the court.

APPOINTMENT

6.   Those intending to instruct an expert to give or prepare evidence for the purpose of court proceedings should consider whether evidence from that expert is appropriate, taking account of the principles set out in Parts 1 and 35 of the CPR, and in particular whether:

(a)   the evidence is relevant to a matter which is in dispute between the parties. An expert witness may be able to:

(i)   give relevant opinion evidence;

(ii)   help to establish relevant facts;

(iii)   identify the issues which require decision by the court; and

(iv)   explore areas where agreement may be possible;

(b)   the expert has expertise relevant to the issue on which an opinion is sought;

(c)   the expert has the experience, expertise and training appropriate to the value, complexity and importance of the case;

(d)   the objects referred to under (a) can be achieved by the appointment of a single joint expert;

(e)   the expert will be able to:

(i)   produce a report;

(ii)   deal with questions for or by other experts; and

(iii)   have discussions with other experts all within a reasonable time and at a cost proportionate to the matters in issue; and

(f) the expert will be available to attend the trial, if his attendance is required.

(CPR, rr 1.1(2) and 35.1)

7.   Those instructing experts should also bear in mind:

(a)   that no party can call an expert or put in evidence an expert's report without the court's permission; and

(b)   that the court may limit the amount of the expert's fees and expenses that the party who wishes to rely on the expert may recover from any other party. (CPR, r 35.4(1) and (4))

TERMS OF APPOINTMENT

8.   Terms of appointment should be agreed at the outset and should include:

(a)   the basis of the expert's charges (either daily or hourly rates and an estimate of the time likely to be required, or a fee for the services);

(b)   any travelling expenses and other disbursements;

(c)   rates for attendance at court and provisions for payment on late notice of cancellation of a court hearing;

(d)   time for delivery of report;

(e)   time for making payment; and

(f)   whether fees are to be paid by a third party.

When necessary, arrangements should be made for dealing with questions to experts and discussions between experts, including any directions given by the court, and provision should be made for the cost of this work.

PAYMENT

9.   Payments contingent upon the nature of the expert evidence given in legal proceedings, or upon the outcome of a case, must not be offered or accepted. To do so would contravene the expert's overriding duty to the court. (CPR, r 35.3)

DEFERMENT OF PAYMENT

10.   Agreement to delay payment of an expert's fee until after the conclusion of the case is permissible as long as the amount of the fee does not depend on the outcome of the case.

INSTRUCTIONS

11.   Those instructing experts should ensure that they give clear instructions, including the following:

(a)   basic information, such as names, addresses, telephone numbers, dates of birth and dates of incidents;

(b)   the nature and extent of expertise which is called for;

(c)   the purpose of requesting the advice or report, a description of the matter to be investigated, the principal known issues and the identity of all parties;

(d)   the statement(s) of case (if any), those documents which form part of standard disclosure and witness statements which are relevant to the advice or report;

(e)   where proceedings have not been started, whether proceedings are being contemplated and, if so, whether the expert is asked only for advice; and

(f)   where proceedings have been started, the date of any hearing and in which court and to which track they have been allocated.

12.   Experts who do not receive clear instructions should request clarification and indicate that they are not prepared to act unless and until such clear instructions are received.

13.   Experts must neither express an opinion outside the scope of their field of expertise, nor accept any instructions to do so. Experts must not accept instructions if they are not satisfied they can comply with any orders that have been made. Where an expert has already been instructed, the expert should notify those instructing him/her

immediately if the expert considers s/he may not be able to comply with an order. (CPR, r 35.3(1) and (2))

THE EXPERT'S REPORT

14. In preparing their reports, experts:

(a) should maintain professional objectivity and impartiality at all times;

(b) in addressing questions of fact and opinion, should keep the two separate and discrete; and

(c) where there are facts in dispute:

(i) should not express a view in favour of one or other disputed sets of facts, unless, because of their particular learning and experience, they perceive one set of facts as being improbable or less probable, in which case they may express that view, and should give reasons; and

(ii) should express separate opinions on every set of facts in dispute. (CPR, r 35.3)

INFORMATION

15. All experts' reports should contain the following information:

(a) the expert's academic and professional qualifications;

(b) a statement of the source of instructions and the purpose of the advice or report;

(c) a chronology of the relevant events;

(d) a statement of the methodology used, in particular what laboratory or other tests (if any) were employed, by whom and under whose supervision;

(e) details of the documents or any other evidence upon which any aspects of the advice or report is based;

(f) relevant extracts of literature or any other material which might assist the court in deciding the case; and

(g) a summary of conclusions reached. (CPR, r 35.10; PD 35, para 2.2*)

CONTENT OF REPORT

16. In providing a report experts:

(a) must address it to the court and not to any of the parties;

(b) must include a statement setting out the substance of all instructions (whether written or oral). The statement should summarise the facts and instructions given to the expert which are material to the opinions expressed in the report or upon which those opinions are based;

(c) where there is a range of opinion in the matters dealt with in the report, give:

(i) a summary of the range of opinion; and

(ii) the reasons for his own opinion.

(d) must express any qualification of, or reservation to, their opinion;

(e) if such opinion was not formed independently, should make clear the source of the opinion;

(f) must declare that the report has been prepared in accordance with this Code and the requirements of the Civil Procedure Rules; and

(g) must include a statement of truth, as required by PD 35, para 2.3.* (CPR, r 35.10; r 35.10(2); PD 35, paras 2.1,* 2.2(3),* 2.2(6),* 2.2(9),* 2.3* and 2.4*) [See note 1 at end of Code.]

AMENDMENT

17.   Experts:

(a)   must not be asked to, and must not, amend, expand or alter any part of the report in a manner which distorts the expert's true opinion; but

(b)   may be invited to amend or expand a report to ensure accuracy and internal consistency, completeness, relevance to the issues and clarity.

18.   Before disclosure of any report, the expert should be given the opportunity to review, and if necessary, update the contents of the report.

PROCEDURE

19.   Experts should:

(a)   be kept informed regularly about any deadlines for the preparation of their advice or reports;

(b)   be advised promptly about any timetable for the proceedings set by the court, or any changes thereto;

(c)   be provided without delay with further or updated instructions where the progress of case requires this; and

(d)   be provided with any order or notice making any provision in relation to expert evidence.

20.   Following completion of the report, experts should be:

(a)   advised as soon as reasonably practicable of the following:

(i)   whether, and if so when, the report will be disclosed to the other party; and

(ii)   if so disclosed, the date of disclosure;

(b)   given the opportunity to consider and comment upon other reports which deal with the same issues; and

(c)   kept informed of the progress of the action, including any amendments to the statements of case relevant to the expert's opinion.

21.   Experts should communicate promptly with those instructing them any change of opinion and the reasons therefor.

22.   The court has power to direct a party to provide information to which it has access and which is not reasonably available to the other party. If the expert requires further information for the purposes of his report which s/he thinks may fall within this category, s/he should notify those instructing him accordingly. (CPR, r 35.9; PD 35, para 3*) CPR 35.14

23.   Experts may file with the court a written request for directions to assist them in carrying out their function as experts, and they may do so without giving notice to any party. (CPR, r 35.14) [See note 2.]

QUESTIONS FOR EXPERTS

24.   A party may put written questions to another party's expert about that expert's report:

(a)   for the purpose of clarifying the report in accordance with CPR, r 35.6; and

(b)   within the time limits prescribed within r 35.6(2) and PD 35, para 5.1;* or

(c)   otherwise as the court may direct or the parties agree. Any such questions should be answered within 28 days unless the court directs otherwise. The expert's reply shall be treated as part of the expert's report. If experts have any queries or concerns in respect of questions put by a party they should in the first instance seek clarification from those instructing them. Where a party puts a written question to an expert instructed by another party in accordance with r 35.6(2) and the expert does not answer the question, the court may order that the party who instructed the expert may not rely on the evidence of that expert or that the party may not recover the expert's fees and expenses from any other party.

(CPR, r 35.6; r 35.6(3) and (4); PD 35, para 5*)

CONFERENCES AND DISCUSSIONS

25.   The parties and their lawyers should seek to reach agreement about, and consider taking steps to clarify, the issues by way of:

(a)   conference or discussion with experts; and/or

(b)   discussion between experts for opposing parties in order to narrow the issues and identify:

(i)   the extent of the agreement between experts;

(ii)   the points of disagreement and the reasons for disagreement;

(iii)   action, if any, which may be taken to resolve the outstanding points of disagreement; and

(iv)   any issues not raised in the agenda for discussion and the extent to which these issues may be agreed.

(CPR, r 35.12)

26.   The parties, their lawyers and experts should cooperate to produce concise agendas for any discussion between experts, which should, so far as possible:

(a)   be circulated 28 days before the date fixed for the discussion;

(b)   be agreed seven days before the date fixed for the discussion;

(c)   consist of questions which are clearly stated and apply, where necessary, the correct legal test;

(d)   consist of questions which, by their nature, are closed, that is to say, capable of being answered 'yes' or 'no'; and

(e)   include questions which enable the experts to state the reasons for their agreement or disagreement.

27.   The discussion may take place face to face or by any other appropriate means proportionate to the circumstances of the case and the court track. Lawyers will not normally be present at such discussions. If lawyers do attend they should not normally intervene save to answer questions put to them by the experts or to advise them on the law.

28.   If there has been a discussion, a statement of the areas of and the reasons for agreement and disagreement should be prepared and agreed. This should be done at the meeting or, in the event of discussion at a distance, promptly between the experts, usually before the discussion is concluded. This statement may have to be produced to the court, but shall not be binding on the parties. A copy of the statement should be provided to the parties. The content of the discussion between the experts may not be referred to in court unless the parties expressly agree. The parties should consider making such an agreement and record it or any failure to agree in the statement. (CPR, r 35.12(4) and (5))

29.   Those instructing experts must not give, and experts must not accept, instructions not to reach agreement at such discussions on areas within the competence of experts.

ATTENDANCE AT TRIAL

30.   The parties should consider whether the use of available audio-visual facilities might avoid unnecessary attendance at court by the experts without compromising a party's presentation of its case.

31.   Those instructing experts should inform them promptly whether attendance at trial will be required, and if so inform them of the date and venue fixed for the hearing of

the case. In applying to fix dates for the trial, those instructing experts should, as far as possible, take account of the availability of experts.

32.   Experts must take all steps to ensure availability to attend court but should be alerted to the fact that a solicitor may need to serve a witness summons in the event of difficulties.

33.   If a party wishes its expert to attend a hearing in a fast-track claim, the burden is on that party to persuade the court that the case is so exceptional that the overriding objective requires such attendance. (CPR, r 35.5(2))

II   SINGLE JOINT EXPERTS

(CPR, rr 35.7; 35.7(1) and (2); 35.8 and 35.8(3)(a))

34.   The court has the power to direct the appointment of a single joint expert selected by the parties. The court may also select the expert to be appointed, if the parties cannot agree who it should be, and may give directions regarding the amount and payment of the expert's fees.

35.   The spirit as well as the letter of rr 35.7 and 35.8 call upon the parties to consider from the outset of the proceedings whether appointment of a single joint expert is appropriate (para 6(d) above). The courts encourage such appointments particularly in cases where the sums involved are not large and the issues are not complex.

36.   The appointment of a single joint expert does not prevent a party from instructing his own expert to advise him.

37.   A party may propose the appointment as single joint expert of an expert who has already advised him in the case, but this may mean disclosing to the other party any privileged or confidential information the expert has received and any advice s/he has given.

38.   Parties should bear in mind that a single joint expert may be appointed to deal with some but not all of the issues requiring expert evidence, with a view to promoting agreement on those issues and of narrowing the scope of expert evidence. In a case involving a number of disciplines, a single joint expert in the dominant discipline may be appointed to coordinate a single report. (PD 35, para 6*)

39.   The parties may send separate instructions to a single joint expert, but if they do, they must provide a copy to the other party. Wherever possible the instructions should be agreed, and they should be in writing. Instructions should comply strictly with the provisions relating to parties' experts. In the event of any meeting with the single joint expert an opportunity must be offered to the other parties and their legal representatives to attend the meeting. (CPR, r 35.8(1) and (2))

40.   The single joint expert owes the same duties of professional competence as does an expert instructed by one of the parties, and the same overriding obligation to the court. The conduct of the single joint expert should be determined by the principles of fairness and transparency. The expert should not communicate with or meet either party independently of the others. The expert's report should comply strictly with the provisions relating to those of parties' experts set out under paras 14 to 16 above, and the expert may be questioned and must provide answers in the same manner as set out in para 24 above. (CPR, r 35.3)

41.   If the single joint expert is unable to prepare a report within the terms of reference of both parties the expert should, as a first step, seek the help of the parties to resolve the conflict. If this is unsuccessful, the single joint expert may seek directions from the court.

42.   The single joint expert may also seek further information and directions from the court as set out in paras 22 and 23 above.

[* These references have been updated.

Note 1. This list of contents is based on an earlier version of PD 35. The current version of PD 35 is differently worded (see **11.3.11.3**).

Note 2. This is no longer true. Unless the court orders otherwise, an expert must provide a copy of any proposed request for directions: (a) to his or her instructing party at least seven days before filing the request; and (b) to all other parties at least four days before filing.]

INDEX